Compulsion in Religion

Compulsion in Religion

*Saddam Hussein, Islam, and
the Roots of Insurgencies in Iraq*

SAMUEL HELFONT

OXFORD
UNIVERSITY PRESS

OXFORD

UNIVERSITY PRESS

Oxford University Press is a department of the University of Oxford. It furthers
the University's objective of excellence in research, scholarship, and education
by publishing worldwide. Oxford is a registered trade mark of Oxford University
Press in the UK and certain other countries.

Published in the United States of America by Oxford University Press
198 Madison Avenue, New York, NY 10016, United States of America.

Library of Congress Cataloging-in-Publication Data
Names: Helfont, Samuel, author.
Title: Compulsion in religion : Saddam Hussein, Islam, and the roots of
insurgencies in Iraq / Samuel Helfont.
Description: New York, NY : Oxford University Press, 2018. |
Includes bibliographical references and index.
Identifiers: LCCN 2017041408 (print) | LCCN 2017049303 (ebook) |
ISBN 9780190843328 (Updf) | ISBN 9780190843335 (Epub) |
ISBN 9780190843311(hardcover : alk. paper)
Subjects: LCSH: Islam and state—Iraq—History. | Islam and politics—Iraq—History. |
Iraq—Politics and government—1958- | Hussein, Saddam, 1937–2006. |
Hizb al-Ba'th al-Arabi al-Ishtiraki (Iraq)
Classification: LCC BP173.6 (ebook) | LCC BP173.6 .H45 2018 (print) |
DDC 322/.10956709049—dc23
LC record available at https://lccn.loc.gov/2017041408

For Tally-le

CONTENTS

PART IV **The Invasion of Iraq and the Emergence
of Religious Insurgencies**

PREFACE AND ACKNOWLEDGMENTS

The origins of this book can be traced to the invasion of Iraq in spring of 2003. I was 22 years old at the time and I found myself aboard an amphibious warfare ship, the USS Duluth, in the northern reaches of the Persian Gulf. I was a member of a small intelligence collection team from the now defunct Naval Security Group, which was the Navy's command at the National Security Agency (NSA). We worked out of a small container— no bigger than a minivan—that was welded onto the deck of the ship and loaded with our equipment. In addition to providing intelligence, we broadcasted a radio station into Iraq as part of a psychological operations (PSYOPS) mission. Prior to the invasion, we began playing a mix of Arab and American music along with US propaganda and instructions for Iraqis. American aircraft dropped flyers into southern Iraq encouraging people to tune in. From what I understand, our station was quite popular.

The USS Duluth offloaded a contingent of Marines who made their way through Kuwait and then fought into Iraq. With the Marines ashore, the ship became a staging platform for Navy SEALs and Polish Special Forces. They seized Iraq's oil infrastructure including its Gulf Oil Terminals, which were used to pump oil onto tankers too large for Iraq's shallow ports. When the SEALs and Poles arrived on the main terminal, they found around two dozen Iraqi soldiers standing under a towering portrait of Saddam. They were brought aboard the Duluth and became some of the conflict's first prisoners of war.

The Duluth's primary mission during the initial months of the war was to secure these oil terminals. They were located in perilous geopolitical waters. Iran and Iraq had fought bitterly over them during the 1980s; and when we arrived, I saw that they were still riddled with blast marks and mangled metal. Even in 2003, the Iranians had not completely relinquished their claims to the area. Members of Iran's Islamic Revolutionary Guard Corps Navy would periodically approach us in small boats, attempting to press their case. Our proximity to the shore also made us targets for various Iraqi insurgents. After I returned to the United States, a waterborne suicide attack killed several American service members on the main terminal.

This location gave me a front row seat to the first days of the invasion. We were sandwiched between the Iraqi coast on one side and nearly 100 warships on the other. During the initial days of the war, these ships unleashed a barrage of missiles and strike aircraft—the so-called "shock and awe." I remember feeling ill at ease watching dozens of missiles flying overhead and listening to the rumble of artillery ashore. Sometimes I had disconcerting thoughts about the consequences of each explosion. How many people were just obliterated? Who were they? What were they like? What was their history, and how had it come to this?

Over the years, I have continued to think about those events and to contemplate my small part in them. In hindsight, the entire ordeal seems a surreal spectacle. I have frequently been troubled by questions surrounding what we were doing there and how it had gone so wrong. There is no way to answer those questions definitively. However, I hope this book illuminates an important part of Iraqi history and, in doing so, helps to explain why the American occupation sputtered into tragedy.

Many people and institutions have assisted my journey from those strange days in 2003 to the completion of this book. The manuscript grew out of a PhD dissertation that I wrote in the Department of Near Eastern Studies at Princeton University. I could not have asked for a more supportive and intellectually stimulating environment in which to spend six years of graduate school. My advisor, Bernard Haykel, provided a steady stream of meticulous advice. Qasim Zaman and Cyrus Schayegh also guided me through the process. Michael Reynolds introduced me to the sources that I used in this project and encouraged me to explore them. James LaRegina was an outstanding resource for all administrative needs. Michael Cook and Mark Cohen were excellent Directors of Graduate Studies. Wolfgang Danspeckgruber helped to broaden my view of religion and politics beyond the Middle East. Aaron Rock-Singer, Jacob Olidort, Simon and Maria Fuchs, Lindsay Stephenson, Zach Foster, David Weil, Eric Lob, Deniz Kilincoglu, Sivil Cakir, Kate Manbachi, Dror Weil, Christian Sahner, Kevin Bell, Oded Zinger, Nadav Samin, and Lev Weitz were amazing colleagues and a constant source of good advice. The Department of Near Eastern Studies and the Graduate School at Princeton provided me with ample freedom and resources to pursue my studies.

I have spent the two years since I left Princeton at the University of Pennsylvania, where I owe a great debt to Walter McDougall, Frank Plantan, Tomoharu Nishino, Anna Viden, Isa Camyar, Sara McGuire, Mark Castillo, and all my students. At the Foreign Policy Research Institute where I am also a fellow, I would like to thank the late Harvey Sicherman, Alan Luxenberg, Mike Noonan, Megan Hannan, Maia Otarashvili, Eli S. Gilman, Dom Tierney, and Barak Mendelsohn for all their feedback over the years. I would also like to thank the staff at the unfortunately now defunct Conflict Records Research Center at the National Defense University for agreeing to vet and release a number of important documents that I used in this project. I also need to thank the staffs at the Hoover Institution Archives at Stanford University—especially Haidar Raad Hadi—as well as the Near East Section at the Library of Congress, the Rare Books and Special Collections Department at Princeton University, and the Moshe Dayan Center at Tel Aviv University. Their professionalism and commitment to making historical material available are an incredible resource for all scholars.

Anne Dellinger and Angela Chnapko at Oxford University Press have been fantastic and very supportive. The anonymous reviews that I received were very helpful. Outside these institutions, Brandon Freedman, Alda Benjamin, Aaron Faust, Dina Khoury, Joseph Sassoon, David Patel, and Michael Brill have all helped me to dissect and make sense of the sources that I used for this project. Cornell Overfield has been a fantastic research assistant, intern, and editor for the later stages of this project. I am certain that I will be embarrassed to learn that some people who had a great impact on this book have been left off this list. I must ask their forgiveness in advance.

In addition to my academic colleagues, I would like to especially thank David and Avivit Aharony for all their assistance as well as my parents Rand and Beth. Though they are too young to understand, I would like to thank my sons Edden and Nadav. Edden was born during the course of my studies at Princeton and Nadav while I was at Penn. They inspire me every day.

In the spirit of saving the most important acknowledgment for last, my wife Tally has managed to provide both the confidence that I needed to finish this project as well the humility I needed to keep my feet firmly on the ground. She has been the sounding board for all my ideas and the proofreader of every text that I have produced. Often I feel that she understands my arguments better than I do. This book is as much hers as it is mine, and I will never be able to thank her adequately for her patience, perseverance, and unquestioning love throughout the process of writing it.

Compulsion in Religion

Introduction

Religion and Authoritarianism in Saddam's Iraq

*T*here is no compulsion in religion. So states the famous Qur'anic verse.[1] There are two basic interpretations of these words. The first, and more prominent, is that the verse prohibits imposing religion by force. The second interpretation suggests that the verse is not a divine injunction but simply a statement of fact—that it is impossible to compel others in matters of religion.[2] With regard to these two views, Saddam Hussein ignored the former and disproved the latter. It is impossible for any regime to completely eradicate dissent, especially in matters of faith. Nevertheless, over the course of a quarter century as president, Saddam, who ruled Iraq from 1979 to 2003, worked diligently and to some extent successfully to impose the Ba'th Party's Arab nationalist interpretation of religion on a critical mass of Iraqi society. The process by which he accomplished this task had profound implications for the history of Ba'thist Iraq and the religious insurgencies that emerged in the country following the American-led invasion in 2003.

That the fall of Saddam's regime led to insurgencies in Iraq is not a new idea. But because these insurgencies were led mostly by self-described religious parties, one needs to study the manner that Saddam's regime-controlled religion and religious actors to understand how and why they emerged. The former regime's internal archives provide the full details of the regime's policies the first time.[3] Thus, this book combines an analysis of previously available material—including newspapers, conference proceedings, oral histories, and some hitherto unused Arabic publications—with insights gained from those archival records. In bringing together archival and published sources, the book attempts to offer the most comprehensive explanation so far of the Ba'thist regime's policies toward religion and how Ba'thists related to Iraq's religious landscape. In light of this new information, it then reinterprets the rise of religious insurgencies in post-2003 Iraq.

Although this book uses publicly available sources, one must acknowledge that these sources have often led to misinterpretations about Saddam's religious policies, especially in the 1990s. Many outside analysts saw the prominence of regime-sponsored religion in the 1990s as indicating that Saddam's Ba'thist regime had shifted from an Arab nationalist ideology toward political Islam, or that Saddam had cynically adopted Islamism to penetrate Iraqi society.[4] Indeed, it is tempting to view Saddam's increased instrumentalization[5] of religion as evidence of an ideological transformation that paralleled the broader, regional turn toward political Islam in the final decades in the 20th century. However, the regime's internal documents clearly dispel this theory. Saddam's interpretation of Islam remained fairly consistent throughout his rule; and his regime's policies on religion during the 1990s were a culmination of earlier plans, rather than a break with the past.

Thus, whereas a number of observers have argued that Saddam abandoned his Arab nationalist roots in favor of Islamism,[6] the Iraqi archival records reveal that Saddam's increasing instrumentalization of Islam should not be attributed to an ideological shift. Instead, as this book suggests, it resulted from the integration of Iraq's religious landscape into the Ba'thist regime's authoritarian system. This process was part of a larger project of authoritarian consolidation that the regime termed "Ba'thification" (*tab'ith*).[7] The Ba'thists preferred not to destroy independent or even hostile social institutions; rather, through the process of Ba'thification, they hollowed them out and then filled them with indoctrinated loyalists. The regime could thus integrate those once independent institutions into its authoritarian structures and appropriate their legitimacy.

The regime's records describe explicitly how this strategy of Ba'thification was developed to control social institutions dedicated to workers, women, students, and others. Although religious institutions were not specifically mentioned in the Party's doctrine on Ba'thification, the regime's goals with regard to religious institutions were quite similar to its goals for other social institutions. However, Saddam's policies toward religion differed to some extent from his policies toward other social institutions because, like all regimes, his regime's history and ideology predisposed its supporters to be more adept at operating in particular social spheres. Whereas Saddam intended for his regime to dominate all aspects of Iraqi society, the history and ideology of the Ba'thist regime meant that it lacked trusted supporters who could penetrate the religious landscape effectively early in Saddam's rule. Nevertheless, like other authoritarian regimes, the Ba'thists remained flexible and adaptive. In that regard, access to Iraq's internal records allows for a case study that details in an unpresented fashion how an authoritarian regime in the Middle East was able to plan, overcome some initial setbacks, learn, and eventually build the institutions and bureaucracies required to control Iraqi religion.

Using the process of Ba'thification to instill Ba'thist ideas and operatives in Iraq's religious landscape afforded Saddam a perception of control[8] over Islamic discourse in Iraq and consequently the necessary level of confidence to introduce his Ba'thist ideas on religion into the public sphere. Perhaps even more important, the integration of Iraq's religious landscape into the regime's authoritarian[9] system provided the Ba'thists the means to transmit their views on religion to the Iraqi people. By the end of Saddam's presidency, his regime had developed a critical mass of Iraqi religious leaders who could speak authoritatively about Islam and who were willing to promote a version of the religion that legitimized Ba'thist rule. As a result, the regime was able to incorporate its views on religion into its public policies in a way that had been impossible previously. In that sense, the increase in regime-sponsored religion in Iraq was, at its heart, a story about the Ba'thist regime's increasing penetration into Iraq's religious landscape as well as the resistance to this process by formerly independent religious leaders.

Focusing on Ba'thification helps to contextualize Saddam's religious policies in a new way. It roots discussions about Ba'thist views on religion within the authoritarian structures were necessary for this aspect of the regime's ideology to operate in Iraq. This contextualization of Saddam's religious policies helps to clarify how and why religious insurgencies emerged in the country following his regime's demise. Throughout the final decade of Saddam's rule, his regime vigorously promoted religion in Iraq. However, it did so in a controlled environment. The regime considered its authoritarian structures to be necessary to instrumentalize Islamic symbols and rhetoric without empowering potentially hostile elements within Iraq's religious landscape. The Ba'thists rooted out Islamists or followers of other religious tendencies that challenged the unity or security of the state. This strategy made sense considering that the ability to organize has proven one of the most important factors in social scientific explanations for internal rebellions against ruling regimes.[10]

Following the American-led invasion of Iraq in 2003, religion remained prominent in Iraqi public life, but the system that Saddam had put in place to contain it was destroyed. Sunni and Shi'i extremists who had been suppressed and silenced were suddenly free to operate in the open. They thrived in an atmosphere where religion had been actively promoted and formed militant organizations that have torn the country apart.

EXPLORING RELIGION AND STATE UNDER
THE AUTHORITARIAN RULE

Saddam was not the first dictator to instrumentalize religion. Rulers of all stripes have done so for centuries. As Machiavelli counseled his prince, "it is well to seem pious, faithful, humane, religious, and sincere, and also to be so." But, as Machiavelli continued, when necessary, a ruler must "be able to change to the opposite qualities."[11] Similarly, authoritarian regimes in the 20th century have tended to view religion as one of numerous social institutions that they could manipulate and control. Saddam's strategies and policies toward religion should be contextualized as part of this broader historical trend among non-democratic regimes in the 20th century.

While religion was certainly part of the social fabric that 20th century authoritarian regimes wished to control, it offered unique challenges and opportunities. On one hand, religion has been extremely useful to authoritarian leaders; on the other hand, it has often been incredibly dangerous. Rulers of modern authoritarian states have been forced to negotiate this duality very carefully. To reap the potential benefits of religion while attempting to minimize the threats it can pose, non-democratic rulers in the 20th century tended to favor a strategy of co-opting, coercing, and creating religious leaders who were loyal to their regimes. Rulers then used these pro-regime religious leaders to penetrate existing religious institutions as well as create new ones. In doing so, authoritarian leaders attempted to control religious actors and institutions in a manner that allowed their regimes to instrumentalize them politically while mitigating the potential risks that religion could pose as a competing source of authority.

The benefits of religion for authoritarian rulers are fairly straightforward. Political scientists and psychologists have long established a correlation between religiosity and obedience to authority figures. Put simply, "religious individuals tend to be authoritarians and authoritarians tend to be religious."[12] Many 20th century authoritarian leaders seem to have understood this dynamic instinctively. Nazis in Germany and Fascists in Italy both actively instrumentalized religion to further entrench their regimes. In doing so, they portrayed themselves as the defenders of traditional values against the evil innovations of "the enemy" (whomever that happened to be). As Mussolini argued, "In the Fascist State religion is looked upon as one of the deepest manifestations of the spirit; it is therefore not only respected, but defended and protected."[13]

It does not follow, however, that Nazis and Fascists had an amicable relationship with traditional Christian clergy in their countries. In fact, the opposite was true. They disliked any institutions that had the potential to remain independent of their all-powerful states.[14] Despite this queasiness with regard to the traditional religious establishments in their states, Nazis and Fascists recognized the power of religion and saw it as beneficial. This held true even for more radical Nazis who frowned on Christianity altogether. Hannah Arendt quotes one such anti-Christian Nazi official who nevertheless attempted to appropriate religion: "The more accurately we recognize and observe the laws of nature and life . . . so much the more do we conform to the will of the Almighty. The more insight we have into the will of the Almighty, the greater will be our successes."[15] Although his theology was decidedly non-Christian, the Nazi official leaned on the persuasive power of religion. In many ways, this was an effective strategy. Some religious leaders under these regimes were prone toward obedience. In Nazi Germany, a cardinal once informed Hitler that the Church was "aware of its sacred duty to deepen in the hearts of the faithful that respect and obedience towards the constituted authorities which was a religious virtue, and to lead all segments of the people to make sacrifices and to participate in the promotion of the common good."[16] Moreover, this propensity for obedience continued even after it became clear that the Nazis wished to crush the Church and had begun to openly, and violently, attack Christian institutions. As John S. Conway asserts in his study of Church and state in Nazi Germany, "Church leaders, clinging to the desperate hope that such events were merely isolated incidents and not part of a deliberate policy, ruled that it was the Church's duty to obey the nation's rulers and not protest."[17]

This phenomenon continued well after the fall of the Nazis and Fascists. It also extended far beyond the borders of Europe. In Latin America, authoritarian governments on both the left and right have instrumentalized the Catholic Church. Leftists invoked liberation theology, and right-wing dictators developed close relationships with more traditional Church institutions.[18] East Asian regimes have made similar use of religion. In Vietnam, for instance, the communist regime has highlighted similarities between "Ho Chi Minh Thought" and Confucianism, arguing that "nationalism builds on Confucianism."[19]

Thus, it is quite clear that religion can be very useful to authoritarian leaders. Yet the relationship between religion and authoritarianism is not as simple as it may first appear. Elites often consider religious education to be a good means of social pacification. However, in promoting religious education, authoritarian rulers have sometimes introduced religion into the political sphere and thus made it a legitimate form of political contestation. Religious actors were then able to use it to undermine authoritarian rule. For example, when Hosni Mubarak promoted Islamic education in Egypt, he hoped to quell descent, but he unintentionally empowered the Muslim Brotherhood.[20]

One could take this argument further. Not only have the results of instrumentalizing religion been unpredictable, religion seems to have a unique ability to resist authoritarianism. In Iraq, the regime's intelligence reports bemoaned that some extremely pious Iraqis did not fear the regime's coercive techniques or long prison sentences. In fact, these pious Iraqis viewed their exposure to the regime's violence as a necessary sacrifice and accepted it as their inevitable fate.[21] Elsewhere during the latter half of the 20th century, Middle Eastern autocrats crushed almost all opposition. The only form of resistance they were unable to neutralize was Islamism. It was no coincidence that when the Iranian Shah was finally deposed, an Islamic regime replaced him. Similar examples can be drawn from the fallout of the Arab Spring in 2011.

There are, of course, many well-known parallels to this phenomenon outside the Islamic world as well. In Poland, for example, the Catholic Church was one of the only institutions capable of challenging communist rule. Even in a regime as brutal as Nazi Germany, Hitler was never able to fully eliminate the Catholic or the Protestant Churches' independence. The regime regularly encountered clergy who would pepper their sermons with sayings such as "they can take my head but not my convictions."[22] As Hitler admitted when discussing his evolving view on how to deal with the Church, "Early in 1933, I took the view: dynamite. Later I realized that one can't break the Church over one's knee."[23] As such, in their classic work, *Totalitarian Dictatorship and Autocracy*, Carl Friedrich and Zbigniew Brzezinski classify religion (the Church in their study) as one of the "islands of separateness" from the otherwise all-encompassing state.[24] They argue that in places like Nazi Germany, "no other organization" except for the Churches (both Catholic and Protestant) were able "to resist . . . a totalitarian system for twelve full years."[25]

Even in authoritarian regimes with an explicitly anti-religious ideology, such as the Soviet Union, the state had difficulty eliminating religion and the religious establishment. When the Bolsheviks took power in 1917, they attempted to eradicate religion and other forms of "superstition" from Russian life. To implement this on the popular level, they even created the League of the Militant Atheists (originally named "The League of the Godless"), which had the full power of the state at its disposal.[26] However, even the Soviet state—with its powerful security forces and ambitions to impose an atheist ideology—could not always bend religious leaders into doing the state's bidding or eliminate religion's central place in society.

For example, in his classic *Gulag Archipelago*, Aleksandr Solzhenitsyn discussed the Russian Patriarch Tikhon's testimony at the Moscow Church Trial of 1922. The presiding judge asked the Patriarch, "Do you consider the state's laws obligatory or not?" The Patriarch replied, "Yes, I recognize them as long as they do not contradict the rules of piety." In other words, the Patriarch answered to divine authority rather than state authority.[27] As a result of such resistance, the communists were forced to reconsider their militant approach toward the Russian Orthodox Church. In November 1927, as Merle Fainsod shows, a Communist Party resolution acknowledged that "the church and sects were still very powerful, that they had been putting forward their own candidates in soviet and cooperative elections in the villages, and that they were even collecting funds among believers for the construction of new churches." Later investigations showed that even Party members continued to attend church and baptize their children. In the Soviet district of Smolensk, some higher ranking Party officials were scandalized to learn that someone no less than the local secretary of the League of Militant Atheists had baptized his children and kept Christian icons in his home. By 1930, the Communist Party was forced to roll back some of its direct attacks on religion.[28]

The Soviets began to promote their own religious leadership, known appropriately as "red priests," who they organized into what they termed the "Living Church."[29] Decades later, Friedrich and Brzezinski continued to argue that "opposition to the Soviet antireligious policies . . . existed and still persists." Even under Stalin's iron fist, they recount, numerous underground theological societies and church groups endured. Tellingly, although the life of an Orthodox Priest in the Soviet Union was filled with unimaginable danger and uncertainty, the number of applicants for the seminaries consistently outnumbered the positions available.[30]

A similar phenomenon occurred in China under an equally oppressive and atheistic regime. Although the Chinese Communist Party wished to eliminate what it termed peasant "superstition," Vincent Goossaert and David A. Palmer show that "Party leaders stressed the need to avoid needlessly alienating peasants by attacking their gods." For example, although Mao likened "divine authority" to a "thick rope" that bound peasants to the feudal system, he was wary of confronting it directly. His early experiences had led him to believe that religion was too powerful a force to assault head-on. Instead, he hoped that social and economic advancement would cause religion to gradually disappear. Thus, he argued, "It is the peasants who made the idols, and when the time comes they will cast the idols aside with their own hands; there is no need for anyone else to do it for them prematurely."[31] As in the Soviet Union, religion did not simply disappear, and the Maoists were eventually forced to come to terms with it. By mid-century, the Chinese Communist Party began to institutionalize religion, relegating their hope of its disappearance to a long-term strategy meant for the distant future. Like the Soviet "red priests," the Chinese communists did so by developing a cadre of sympathetic religious leaders. Collectively, they became known as the "religious sector," and they were legitimized in place of other, less cooperative religious leaders.[32]

Thus, the Soviet Union and the Chinese Communist Party eventually had to come to terms with religion, but they did not do so by adopting the traditional religious discourse of their respective countries. Instead, they responded to challenges that religion posed by co-opting, coercing, and creating religious leaders who could penetrate their respective religious landscapes and then attempt to bring the institutions of their countries into line with the ruling regimes' desires. In other words, they attempted to graft their own ideology onto their religious landscapes. Thus, the Soviets created a "Living Church" and the Chinese a "religious sector."

These institutions molded religion into something more ideologically acceptable to their regimes. Hence, an Archbishop in the Living Church once declared, "The atheists do divine work and the commune is the ideal of Christianity."[33] In Nazi Germany a similar phenomenon took place. In addition to cracking down on the traditional Catholic and Protestant Churches in Germany, the Nazis promoted the "German Christians." This organization transformed traditional Christianity into something more acceptable to Nazis. For example, the German Christians regarded Jewish conversion to Christianity as "a grave danger." They explained: "Through its [Jewish conversion's] doors alien blood is imported into the body of our nation." In contradiction to traditional Christian teachings, they forbade it.[34]

One could argue that a process of give and take was inherent in the interaction between these authoritarian regimes and religion. These regimes both influenced religion and were influenced by it. To some extent, that is correct, and this book will demonstrate that Iraqi religious leaders were not always docile objects of the regime's policy. Nevertheless, to describe the phenomenon in such neutral terms does not do justice to the asymmetrical nature of the relationship between authoritarian states and the religious landscape. Clearly, for atheistic regimes such as the Soviet Union or Maoist China, any concession to religion was an alteration of their original ideology; but these were minor when compared with the wholesale transformations that these regimes imposed on their respective religious landscapes. The creation of a "Living Church" in the Soviet Union or the "religious sector" in communist China were not minor twists on traditional religion: they were the complete transformation of it. These institutions molded religion into something ideologically acceptable to their regimes, not the other way around.

As these examples demonstrate, the relationship between religion and authoritarianism is dual natured. For an authoritarian leader, religion is at once a tremendous asset and a dire threat.

AUTHORITARIAN RELIGION AND THE RISE
OF RELIGIOUS INSURGENCIES IN IRAQ

Saddam's religious policies were comparable to those of other 20th-century dictators in Europe, Asia, and Latin America. Similar to their authoritarian counterparts around the globe, the Iraqi Ba'thists were well aware of both the opportunities and threats that religion posed. Iraqi Ba'thists spoke of religion being both "dangerous and great,"[35] and they readily discussed "the dual-nature of religious expression" (*izdwajiyyat al-ta'bir 'an al-din*), as in the following: "Indeed the dual-nature of religious expression and the sensitivity in dealing with it in Arab society, especially lately, has caused the problem of religion to be one of the most dangerous problems present in modern Arab society."[36] In other words, Saddam and his Ba'thist followers understood the dichotomy discussed previously. Although religion had certain benefits, the regime would need to proceed cautiously. Only after gaining control of religious discourse and the authoritative institutions that produced it in the country would the Ba'thists full-heartedly instrumentalize Islam.

In navigating the dual nature of religion's relationship to the authoritarian state, Saddam attempted to appropriate religion without empowering a difficult-to-contain religious opposition. To do so, he first needed to control religious leaders. Ba'thism includes clear teachings on the positive role of religion, and therefore Ba'thist leaders maintained a natural propensity to instrumentalize it. Although there existed a gap between Ba'thist ideology and traditional interpretations of religion in Iraq, it was much narrower than what the communists faced in Russia or China. It would be an overstatement to insist that the Iraqi Ba'thists were not at all affected by religious sentiments in their country and the region—especially the rising tide of political Islam. However, these sentiments had only a minor influence on the substance of the Ba'thists' interpretation of religion in Iraq.

In that sense, the relationship between Saddam's regime and Iraq's religious landscape was even more asymmetric than others. But even regimes with deeply ingrained religious ideologies cannot simply dictate their views to their societies. These regimes need to put a system in place to propagate their ideas. For example, following the September 11th attacks in the United States, Saudi Arabia came under considerable international pressure to reform its religious education program; but to accomplish this, the Saudi regime had to do more than simply declare a new religious outlook. As the Saudi official who led the reform efforts explained, "When you close the door, the teacher can always put the book aside and talk." In other words, no matter what the textbook stated, or the official policy dictated, a religious teacher's piety may lead him or her to act in a manner not conducive to the official ideology. Thus, to truly change a policy toward religion, the state needed not only to make ideological adjustments but also to have the right people implementing the policy on the ground. The Saudi official continued: "With thirty thousand schools and a half a million teachers, it is very hard to change the system quickly." And as he correctly acknowledged, "that is true everywhere, not just in Saudi."[37]

Similarly, the Ba'thists needed to create a cadre of trusted religious leaders to instrumentalize religion. Although Ba'thism included a reverence for Islam as an Arab religion, Saddam did not initially control Iraq's religious landscape. In the 1970s, he feared that promoting religion in Iraq would empower Iraqi religious leaders who were hostile toward his regime. In the months prior to becoming president in 1979, he formed a strategy to map, penetrate, and eventually control Iraq's religious landscape. The resulting policies were accelerated due to a budding religious insurgency in southern Iraq, and then, a year later in 1980, in response to the beginning of the Iran-Iraq War. The regime began co-opting religious leaders it felt it could win over and eliminating others it deemed problematic. Throughout the 1980s, the regime also established religious institutions designed to produce religious leaders who held an ideologically acceptable interpretation of Islam as an Arab religion and who were loyal to Saddam.

The cadre of religious leaders that these institutions produced became the foundation on which Saddam instituted his religious policies during the last decade of his rule. In addition to preaching an interpretation of Islam that bolstered the Ba'thist regime's legitimacy, these trusted religious leaders cooperated closely with the regime's domestic intelligence services as they created the security architecture necessary for monitoring religious activity in the country. The regime viewed this capacity building as essential for its strategy to instrumentalize religion because it denied its potential adversaries the opportunity to use religious institutions as a place to organize opposition or rebellion against the regime.[38]

Ultimately, in 2003, the American led invasion destroyed the authoritarian structures that these religious actors populated and thus unhinged the forces that they were designed to contain. Freed of the constraints provided by Saddam's authoritarianism, religious insurgencies emerged.

Looking Forward

This book addresses Saddam's religious policies and the emergence of religious insurgencies in four chronologically organized parts. These parts then break down into thematic chapters. Part I includes chapters 1–5 and covers the first decade of Saddam's presidency, 1979–1989. It focuses on the regime's penetration of Iraq's religious landscape. The regime needed to do so to gain some level of control over Islamic discourse before it could attempt to instrumentalize religion in its policies and thus contain the threat of religious insurgencies. Chapter 1 discusses Saddam's rise to power, his views on Islam, and his regime's attempt to map the religious landscape of the country. Chapter 2 discusses the regime's strategy of institutionalizing and bureaucratizing the religious landscape. It also shows how this strategy, especially in the context of the Iran-Iraq War, allowed the Ba'thists to co-opt and coerce Iraqi religious leaders. Chapter 3 covers strategies that the regime employed to penetrate Shi'i religious institutions in Iraq as well as the question of the regime's view of sectarianism. Chapter 4 demonstrates how the regime was able to suppress the Islamic opposition among both Sunnis and Shi'is in Iraq. Finally, chapter 5 discusses the limits to the regime's policies of co-optation and coercion as well as subtle resistance to these policies by Iraqi religious leaders. The chapter then outlines the Ba'thists' attempts to overcome these limitations, especially with regard to sectarianism, by creating new institutions like Saddam University for Islamic Studies.

Part II of the book contains chapters 6–7. It covers the Gulf Crisis of 1990–1991 and its aftermath. Chapter 6 shows that the regime's instrumentalization of religion during the conflict stemmed from the authoritarian structures that it had put in place over the previous decade. Chapter 7 outlines how the aftermath of the Gulf Crisis continued to shape Iraq's religious landscape and set the stage for the regime's policies during the last decade of Saddam's rule.

Part III includes chapters 8–11. It discusses Saddam's Faith Campaign, 1993–2003. The scope of the book changes slightly during this period because the Kurds managed to form a semi-autonomous zone in northern Iraq. This Kurdish region was largely outside of the regime's control during the Faith Campaign; and for the most part, it did not produce indigenous religious insurgencies following 2003. Therefore, the book focuses primary on Arab regions of Iraq from 1991 onward. The chapters in Part III anchor the regime's policies during the Faith Campaign within its authoritarian structures. Chapter 8 calls for a reassessment of state-society relations in 1990s Iraq based on the regime's internal records. It then outlines the regime's religious policies in that context. Chapter 9 covers the regime's relationship with the Shi'is during this period and demonstrates that the Ba'thists had a much closer working relationship with Shi'i religious leaders and institutions than has previously been acknowledged. Chapter 10 provides an overview of the regime's mechanisms for controlling Iraq's religious landscape during the 1990s. It describes the regime's reorganization of its security services and state bureaucracies, which it designed to incorporate and work with co-opted religious leaders. Chapter 11 shows how the regime put its authoritarian system to work in instrumentalizing Islam.

Part IV of the book includes chapters 12 and 13. It discusses the legacies of Saddam's religious policies during and after the American-led invasion in 2003. Chapter 12 describes how the nature of Saddam's policies contributed to American misperceptions about the relationship between religion and state in Iraq. These misperception spawned ill-conceived war plans that shattered both Iraq's authoritarian system and the social institutions on which a new Iraq was supposed to be built. Chapter 13 covers the rise of religious insurgencies in post-2003 Iraq. It demonstrates how groups and individuals, which had been contained by Saddam's authoritarian system, launched destructive religious insurgencies.

Finally, the Conclusion reflects on religious insurgencies in Iraq and what they tell us about the manner in which Saddam ruled, as well as the prospects for a unified, stable Iraq in the future.

PART I

The Penetration of Iraq's Religious Landscape 1979–1989

Saddam Takes Control

S addam did not take control of Iraq in a vacuum. He inherited an existing relationship between his regime and the Iraqi religious landscape. The regime's history of repression could not be wished away, nor could the regional political contexts in which he would need to operate. But Saddam also inherited a fairly rich Ba'thist intellectual heritage, which had a good deal to say about religion, and Islam in particular. This heritage offered what he considered to be powerful tools to face the challenges that lay before him. This chapter will discuss this background and how Saddam attempted to use it to his advantage as he assumed the presidency of Iraq in 1979. It will then discuss the initial steps he took to consolidate his power and contain uprisings within Iraq's religious landscape.

SADDAM'S RISE TO POWER

On March 12, 1979, Saddam convened and then chaired an Extraordinary Meeting of Iraq's High National Security Council.[1] The meeting was "extraordinary" in more ways than one. In addition to falling outside the regular schedule of the High National Security Council meetings, it also set a framework for dramatically transforming religion and politics in Iraq.

The meeting occurred at a crucial point in Saddam's career. He faced a litany of crises. An Islamic revolution was brewing in neighboring Iran that threatened to engulf Iraq's Shi'i majority and inflame Sunni Islamists. Elsewhere, rumors of a plan to neuter Saddam's growing grip on power were ubiquitous. Saddam was not yet the president of Iraq, and some factions within his ruling Ba'th Party were hoping to prevent his seemingly inevitable accession by uniting Iraq with neighboring Syria. In doing so, they hoped Syria's president, Hafez al-Assad, could check Saddam's ambitions.

Saddam possessed a natural talent for sniffing out both real and imagined conspiracies. The resulting purges and executions have become well-known symbols of his regime. Saddam's actions in 1979 were perhaps the pinnacle of this trend. He was aware that some of his counterparts in the Ba'thist regime wished to undermine him. But after a decade of acting as Iraq's behind-the-scenes strongman, he was finally going to take the reins of power and eliminate these rivals. He declared himself president three months later in July 1979.

Saddam's bloody rise to power has been well documented.[2] There were, however, critical aspects of it that eluded outside observers. To entrench himself firmly in the presidency, he needed not only to eliminate rivals within the regime but also to establish control over spheres of Iraqi society that could threaten his rule. The religious sphere was particularly dangerous in that regard. The Iraqi Ba'thists opposed the rising tide of Islamism both in Iraq and regionally, and they feared it was gaining traction among Iraqi youth. Ayatollah Ruhollah Khomeini's return to Iran a month earlier, in February 1979, threatened to inflame religious opposition in Iraq as well. A low-grade insurgency seemed to be developing among Iraqi Shi'is that echoed recent Iranian experiences, and many Sunni Islamists were sympathetic to their cause. To head off this potential threat, Saddam needed to find a way to manage Islamic discourse in Iraq before it turned completely against his Ba'thist regime. The most straightforward means of protecting Iraqi youth from this trend and thus

containing the threat of insurgency was to control Iraq's religious landscape. Channeling Mao Zedong, Iraqi counterinsurgency policy from the
early years of Saddam's presidency argued that insurgents "live among the
masses like fish in water, and when the two are separated, great harm is
done to the insurgents."[3] In other words, the Iraqi regime wished to defeat the threat of an Islamist revolution by denying potential insurgents
a religious-political context in which they could operate. This meant that
the regime needed to ensure that Iraq's religious landscape, and through
it, popular understandings of Islam, was hostile to Islamists. It was with
this purpose in mind that Saddam called to order the Extraordinary High
National Security Council in March 1979.

The goal of the meeting was clear-cut. Saddam hoped to implement an
important, yet thus far unacknowledged plan to protect Iraqi youth by
bringing Iraq's religious life under his direct control. As will be discussed
later religion had played an important role in Ba'thist ideology since the
Party's founding. The Iraqi Ba'thists had attempted to highlight this fact in
earlier periods. When they briefly came to power in 1963, they repealed the
Personal Status Law of 1959 because it was not in accordance with Islamic
law.[4] Then, when they seized power for good in the 1968, the constitution
that they created included numerous references to Islam. The preamble
mentioned reliance on God, and the very first article cited "the spirit of
Islam" as a source of the Iraqi Republic's legitimacy. Numerous references to
religion—including a reference to "Islamic law"—can be found throughout
the document. However, Iraq's religious opposition used the Ba'thist claim
to religious legitimacy to undermine the new regime. Authoritative religious scholars, who proved to be outside the regime's control, attacked
Ba'thism as un-Islamic. After clashing with these religious leaders, the
Ba'thists made a tactical retreat on matters of religion and attempted to remove Islam from discussions about political legitimacy. In the 1970 version
of the Iraqi constitution, the only reference to the religion was the decla-
ration that "Islam is the state religion." There were no references to Islamic
law and no attempts to tie the regime's legitimacy to Islam.[5]

Throughout the late 1960s and 1970s, the Ba'thists constantly clashed
with religious leaders in Iraq. The resulting atrocities outraged Islamic

activists throughout the Muslim world. For example, after learning that the Iraqi regime had tortured Ayatollah Muhsin al-Hakim and killed the renowned Sunni scholar 'Abd al-Aziz al-Badri in 1969, the famous Pakistani Islamist Abul Ala Mawdudi decried, "Muslims of Pakistan are shocked to learn the fate of the ulama in Iraq."[6] The regime's repressive policies continued throughout the 1970s. It arrested, deported, and killed thousands of Shi'i religious activists.[7] Sunni Islamists fared almost as badly. In 1971, most of the Sunni Muslim Brotherhood's leadership was arrested or was forced into exile.[8] Because of these continuing clashes in the 1970s, the Iraqi Ba'thists remained wary about promoting Islam in the public sphere. They feared that doing so would lead Iraqis to seek counsel from, and thus empower, religious leaders, including Islamists, who were outside of the regime's control.[9] This tendency to suppress religion was enhanced even further because a period of rapprochement between the Iraqi Ba'thists and the Soviets in the 1970s. In exchange for Soviet support in the international arena, Moscow pressured the Ba'thists to grant more political space to Iraqi communists, who opposed any role for religion in public discourse.

By the late 1970s, the issue of religion and politics became a constant nuisance for the Ba'thists, and Saddam wanted to resolve it—or at least establish a strategy for doing so—before he became president. Although the March 1979 meeting was originally designed to protect Iraqi youth from the influence of reactionary religious movements, in practice, Saddam used the occasion to take direct control of the regime's religious policies. He decreed that he would personally manage the regime's interactions with Iraqi religious leaders. He would henceforth "give oral instructions directly to those [regime elements] concerned with coercing (*zajj*) men of religion." Yet, Saddam also expressed a desire to move away from a strategy that relied solely on violence and limited the Ba'thists' ability to instrumentalize their views on religion. He was convinced that religion, if interpreted in accordance with his desires, was not inherently threatening to the Ba'thist regime. If religion could be controlled, it had the potential to be extremely useful. Thus, Saddam's desire to begin co-opting religious leaders systematically derived not only from a fear of anti-regime religious discourse and violence but also from what he considered to be a significant opportunity to instill support for Ba'thism in Iraqi society. As such, he hoped to "direct [regime officials in their] attempts to persuade [men of religion]" to adopt an interpretation of Islam that was in line with Ba'thist thought. Saddam was certain that such an interpretation would bolster rather than undermine his rule.[10]

The March 1979 meeting also began a systematic infiltration of Iraqi mosques by specially designated Ba'thists. The first recommendation of the meeting pointed to "the necessity for good Party elements to be present in the mosques and *husayniyyat*."[11] The *husayniyyat* are prayer halls used by Shi'is, especially during religious commemorations of Shi'i Imams. Therefore, the regime treated them similar to mosques. Saddam instructed his Ba'thist supporters "to get to know the men of religion and worshipers and to build contacts with them for the sake of benefiting the Party and the revolution." Moreover—and this is very important—when meeting with religious leaders, Party members were to emphasize the official ideology of the Ba'th Party on religious matters, especially with respect to "the importance it puts on religion, men of religion, and holy places."[12] In other words, Saddam was confident that Ba'thism included a sound approach to religion. The difficulty the Ba'thists faced—at least in Saddam's mind—was that their Party's view of religion was widely misunderstood. According to this logic, the Ba'thists did not need to change their ideology or their view of religion; rather, they needed to educate and indoctrinate others about what they believed. This may sound strange for a regime that was known for its oppression of religious leaders. However, when Saddam convened the High National Security Council in March 1979, he could draw on a rich Ba'thist heritage that emphasized the importance of belief in God and maintained a reverence for Islam. Two years earlier, in 1977, Saddam had clarified his view on the importance of religion in a speech titled "A View on Religion and Heritage." In what would become a definitive statement on religion in Saddam's Iraq, he made clear that "our Party does not take a neutral stance between faith and atheism;[13] it is always on the side of faith."[14]

Such a statement was clearly rooted in Ba'thist thought. Contrary to popular portrayals of it as a militantly secular or even anti-religious ideology, Ba'thism had always included a non-traditional, yet extremely positive interpretation of Islam as an Arab religion. In that regard, the Iraqi Ba'thists were inspired by, and continued to support, a version of Ba'thist Islam that had been articulated—ironically—by a secular Christian intellectual, Michel Aflaq (1910–1989). Understanding Aflaq's views on Islam is critical for understanding the political history of Ba'thist Iraq. They provide the lens through which Saddam and his regime saw rival political movements, especially Islamists and communists. Aflaq's ideas about Islam also provide the foundation from which the Iraqi Ba'th Party's religious policies would grow and evolve.

BA'THIST ISLAM

Originally from Syria, Aflaq was educated at the Sorbonne in Paris. In the 1940s and 1950s, he emerged as a leading intellectual of Arab nationalism. His articulation of Ba'thism combined Pan-Arab nationalism, socialism, and anti-imperialism. These concepts were embodied in the Ba'th Party's official slogan: "Unity, Freedom, Socialism." However, Aflaq's writings and speeches during the Ba'th Party's formative period also outlined the relationship between Ba'thism and Islam.

As an Arab nationalist intellectual, Aflaq was a product of his time. His thought should be contextualized as such. The divide between Arab nationalism and political Islam that has come to characterize the intellectual history of the Arab world in the 20th century was often very blurry—especially in the early decades of the century. As C. Ernest Dawn suggests, Arab nationalists and Islamists share an intellectual genealogy that traces back to thinkers such as Jamal al-Din al-Afghani (d. 1897), Muhammad 'Abduh (1849–1905), and Rashid Rida (1865–1935).[15]

These intellectuals conceptualized Islam not only as a belief system but also as a means for political and social modernization. In doing so, they argued that Muslims had gone astray and that contemporary understandings of Islam did not represent the true religion of Muhammad or his companions. The earliest Muslims, they claimed, practiced an Islam that was much more dynamic. They insisted that modern Muslims should return to the age of their noble ancestors (the *salaf*). As such, some have referred to this reformist thought as salafism.[16] However, what constituted Islam as practiced by the *salaf* has often been contested. When al-Afghani and 'Abduh looked back to the age of Muhammad, they saw a dynamic Islam capable of modernization. Others would interpret the age differently. Rida shared 'Abduh's outlook, but he also saw an Islam that was decidedly Arab. Muhammad, after all, was an Arab; the Qur'an was written in Arabic; and the first Muslims were overwhelmingly Arab tribesmen. Rida's thought led in two separate directions. One of his followers, Hassan al-Banna (1906–1949), formed the Muslim Brotherhood in Egypt and became the father of modern Islamism.[17] However, Rida's emphasis on Islam as an Arab religion led other intellectuals to stress Arabism as a central feature of true Islam. This focus on Arab identity merged with, and reinforced, other intellectual movements in the region—notably by Arabs responding to Turkish nationalism and Christians who wished to transcend religious differences—to become one of the main intellectual genealogies of Arab nationalism.[18]

Followers of these two intellectual streams—Arab nationalism and Islamism—would clash later in the 20th century over the centrality of Arabism in Islam and the place of Islamic law in society. Both sides tended to recognize the importance of Islam and Arabism. However, in general, the Islamists interpreted Islam as a universalistic religion and wished to make Islamic law the foundation of the state's legal system. Arab nationalists, while respecting Islam, tended to see it as an Arab religion and did not want to make Islamic law the foundation of modern legal systems.

Interestingly, Christian Arab nationalists also tied Arab nationalism to Islam and particularly to early Islamic history.[19] For example, in 1949, Qustantin Zuraiq, the Christian rector of the Syrian University in Damascus, argued that far from being universalistic, Islam was the religion of the Arabs. Like 'Abduh and al-Afghani, he too rooted his analysis in the earliest days of Islamic history. He claimed that "in the first age," when Islam "was still in full effervescence," the original Muslims treated

"Arab Christians quite differently from the way they treated non-Arab Christians." Thus Islam, properly understood, remained a religion for all Arabs—inclusive of Christians. He made this even more explicit when he asserted that "every Arab, no matter his sect or community . . . should attempt to study Islam and understand its reality; he should also sanctify the memory of the great Prophet to whom Islam was revealed."[20]

Some took this idea even further. One Arab Christian intellectual, Khalil Iskandar Qubrisi, called for his fellow Arab Christians to convert to Islam because it was the true religion of the Arabs. He argued that Western imperialists had highjacked modern Christianity to the extent that it no longer resembled the original religion of antiquity in which they believed.[21]

Aflaq never went as far as Qubrisi, but his thought on Islam was representative of this trend among these other Christian Arab nationalists. He argued that "the Christian religion in Europe, in most of its official representation, is on the side of corruption and oppression."[22] And he asserted that Islam was a more appropriate religion for the Arabs. He explained that one of "the [most dangerous of] European concepts that has attacked the Arab mind" was the "separation of nationalism (*qawmiyya*) and religion." He averred that this may have made sense in Europe and in European history, but it was illogical for Arabs: "Indeed the Arabs are distinct from other nations in that their national awakening is akin (*iqtaraba*) to a religious message." Accordingly, Aflaq insisted that Islam was more suitable for Arabs and that it perfectly expressed the Arab outlook, which did not separate nationalism from religion.[23] There is even some (questionable) evidence that Aflaq converted to Islam later in life. The Iraqi archives have preserved a strange note that Michel Aflaq's son, Iyyad, sent to Saddam Hussein in 1995—several years after Michel had died. Iyyad claimed to have found the note in his father's Qur'an. It read, "If an accident were to occur to me, then I will die under the religion of Islam and I bear witness that there is no God but God and Muhammad is His Messenger." It was dated 1980 and signed "Ahmad Michel Aflaq," suggesting that he also took an Islamic name.[24] Thereafter, the Iraqi Ba'thists referred to him as Ahmad Michel Aflaq.[25]

Whether or not he converted, Aflaq clearly had a deep love for Islam. He articulated his ideas on the subject in three important but often overlooked essays: "In Memory of the Arab Prophet" (*Dhikra al-Rasul al-ʿArabi*), published in 1943; "Our View of Religion" (*Nazratuna lil-Din*), published in 1956; and "The Issue of Religion in the Arab Baʿth" (*Qadiyyat al-Din fi al-Baʿth al-ʿArabi*), also published in 1956. The Islam that emerged from these essays was a divine monotheism for the Arabs. It was a nationalized form of religion that was subordinate to a politicized ethnic identity rather than a universalistic religion that transcended ethnicities. As such, Aflaq insisted, "The life of the Prophet is an example of the Arab spirit in its most perfect form." And he declared, "Islam, therefore, was an Arab movement, and its meaning was to renew Arabism and to complete it. The language in which it came down [to Muhammad] was Arabic, its view and understanding were of the Arab mind [etc.]." In that sense, "The Muslim of [the Prophet's] time was nothing other than the Arab." At one climactic point, he drove the point home, emphatically declaring that "Muhammad was every Arab, and every Arab today is Muhammad."[26] This assertion exemplifies the essence of Aflaq's thought on Islam. All Arabs—even Christians—were necessarily the embodiment of Muhammad's mission. As Sylvia Haim has pointed out, "For Aflaq, Islam *is* Arab nationalism, and any other kind of Islam is either degenerate or an imposition of Western imperialism."[27] Accordingly, Aflaq dismissed other, universalistic, non-Arab-centric versions of Islam as inauthentic. He denounced adherents of such a universalistic Islamic identity as "reactionaries" who adhered to the outdated idea that religion was more important than nationalism.

Aflaq's ideas departed significantly from conventional interpretations and practices of Islam. His Islam did not rest on the scriptural or legal base of the Islamic tradition. He argued that "we may not be seen praying with those praying, or fasting with those who fast, but we believe in God."[28] Instead, Aflaq insisted that Islam needed to be revived "spiritually, not in its form or letter."[29] The "spirit" of Islam was, of course, Arab nationalism. However, although Aflaq reinterpreted Islam in accordance with his Arab nationalist sensibilities, he did not disassociate it from its religious content or divine nature. He referred to Muhammad's preaching as "a heavenly message." He described Muhammad and his followers as "the believers" (*al-mu'minun*) and his opponents as "the polytheists" (*al-mushrikun*). The Arab conquests were a "religious duty" for the sake of God.[30] Moreover, he described atheism as "evil," explaining, "We consider atheism to be a false position in life, a deceitful, detrimental, and void position."[31]

In making such arguments, Aflaq distinguished Ba'thism from its two main rivals—Marxism and Islamism. He alleged that the Marxists' complete dismissal of religion revealed the "simplistic" and "superficial" nature of their ideology. Yet, by subordinating Islam to Arab nationalism, Aflaq also distinguished Ba'thism from Islamist "reactionaries" who considered Islamic identity to be superior to Arab nationalism. Accordingly, Aflaq maintained that the Ba'thists needed to fight against the Islamists' reactionary religion, "but at the same time, to know the truth of religion and the truth of the human soul."[32]

As with other elements of Ba'thist ideology, Saddam's views were heavily influenced, but not identical to Aflaq's original statements. Thus, Aaron Faust aptly terms Saddam's ideology "Husseini Ba'thism."[33] As a Muslim, Saddam appears to have been much more comfortable with traditional Islamic rituals such as prayer and mosque attendance than Aflaq, and he was more open to instrumentalizing Islamic legal concepts. He was also a Sunni, which clearly influenced his ideas about Islam. Nevertheless, as will be detailed in the following chapters, Aflaq's ideas formed the basis of Ba'thist conceptions of religion in Iraq. Saddam clearly felt that if Islam was interpreted in accordance with Aflaq's thought, it could be a powerful force in support of his regime. Consequently, Saddam's speeches, both in public and in private, not only embodied the spirit of Aflaq's teachings on Islam, but they often quoted Aflaq directly.[34] Likewise, throughout the entirety of Saddam's presidency, his regime's official reports on religion—both public and private—quoted Aflaq and reflect his ideas, as did official slogans used for religious festivals.[35] In short, Aflaq's Ba'thist interpretation of Islam, with some slight variations, was the official religion of Saddam's Iraq. It remained so until the regime's downfall in 2003.

Instilling such heterodox ideas in Iraq's religious landscape was not an easy task. It required years of persistently coercing, co-opting, and creating religious leaders who would adhere to Ba'thist interpretations of religion. Such a process inevitably engendered resistance from traditional religious leaders. At times this resistance would be overt and violent; at other times it would be subtle. In the 1979 meeting of the High National Security Council, Saddam laid the foundation for the regime's strategy and for the inevitable conflicts that would ensue between the state and the Iraqi religious landscape. To manage these conflicts, Saddam painstakingly constructed an intricate network of security architecture and authoritarian structures that were capable of managing Iraqi religious life. The destruction of these institutions in 2003 ultimately unleashed the forces that they were designed to contain.

FIRST STEP: MAP THE RELIGIOUS LANDSCAPE

Before Saddam could superimpose Ba'thist interpretations of Islam onto Iraq's religious landscape, he needed first to understand who Iraq's religious leaders were, what they believed, and most importantly, whether they could be trusted. This was true, not only for religious scholars and sermon-givers in mosques; the regime was also concerned about Iraqis who held deep religious convictions but worked in other sectors of society. Previously, Iraqi Ba'thists had little contact with any religious activists, except when they caused problems. Thus, the first step in controlling Iraq's religious landscape was to map it. In addition to taking direct control over religious issues at the 1979 High National Security Council meeting, Saddam ordered regime officials to conduct "an inventory of the men of religion and their previous backgrounds," taking special note of "their family and social status." A similar "inventory" was ordered for "those who have religious preferences in the ranks of the students in university and secondary school and likewise of the farmers and workers."[36] These instructions were sent to every region of Iraq and were applied among Arabs, Kurds, Sunnis, and Shi'is with no regard for their sect or ethnicity.

On one hand, Saddam's plan allowed the regime to carry out its previous repressive policies more effectively. By mapping the religious landscape,

Saddam hoped to identify those who held "extremist" views. Then, to mitigate the threat, he instructed the Ba'th Party and the security services to "spread doubts between these elements [of religious extremists] in order to create mistrust between them" and to "separate or weaken the ties between them." [37]

On the other hand, this plan also represented a new approach to issues of religion and politics for the regime. Instead of simply repressing problematic religious elements, Saddam hoped to identify potentially useful religious actors who could help to instill Ba'thist interpretations of Islam in Iraqi society and thereby legitimate his rule. However, because the Ba'thists had limited experience working with religious actors, they had few clear allies and thus little foundation on which to begin carrying out the plan. Saddam decided first to identify individuals who could best assist his efforts. He ordered regime officials to pay particular attention to collecting "information on political and social backgrounds." The regime could then "select the most prominent elements, concentrate on them and their activities, and thus work on winning them over to the ranks of the Party." In doing so, Saddam hoped to appropriate their status and thereby enable the regime to co-opt others.

The regime bombarded these select religious actors with Ba'thist propaganda on religion, attempting to convince them of the validity of its interpretations of Islam and Arabism. As Saddam recognized, and as subsequent chapters will demonstrate, transforming the religious landscape would not be simple or easy. To be effective, the Ba'thists, including Saddam, needed not only to properly adhere to Party ideology but also to present themselves as pious believers and as good Muslims. Thus, the regime created five prerequisites for Ba'thists who would work on winning over religious activists. It stressed the following:

a) The importance of attending the mosques and seeking to demonstrate a proper appearance and a decent social standing.
b) Choosing an outlook from which it is possible to act within religious circles.

c) Giving the necessary financial aid [to religious leaders] . . . through the Ministry of Endowment and Religious Affairs.

d) Designating a comrade to oversee the people in the schools and the villages.

e) Understanding the importance of religious occasions and participation in them.[38]

Saddam's plan to win over influential religious actors in Iraq highlighted two important features of the regime's relationship to the Iraqi religious landscape at the beginning of Saddam's presidency. First, and most importantly, these were the policies of a regime that was on the outside looking in. In other words, it had not penetrated the religious landscape and had little control over religion in Iraq. As opposed to later regime plans that discuss how the Ba'thists would rely on their supporters in the religious establishment, the religious leaders discussed in the regime's plans from 1979 to 1980 were clearly not tied to—and certainly not loyal to—the Ba'thist regime. The entire purpose of this plan was to begin co-opting these religious leaders so that they would be tied to the regime in the future. Second, the regime's preference was not to eliminate religion as a prominent aspect of Iraqi society. Rather, the regime wished to control religion by enforcing a Ba'thist interpretation of Islam that would legitimate Ba'thist rule and marginalize its opponents. Accordingly, Ba'thists who worked with religious leaders were instructed "to expose them to the interpretation and outlook of the Party especially toward religion and the performance of religious rituals."[39] By highlighting what the Ba'thists considered to be an intrinsic and necessary link between Islam and Arab nationalism, Saddam felt that the regime could win religious supporters and undermine Islamist and sectarian opposition. At the same time, the regime also attempted to limit the influence of religious leaders and institutions outside of its control. If Iraqis listened to such religious leaders or attended such institutions, the regime feared that they could be influenced by sectarian or Islamist interpretations of Islam that would threaten the regime by undermining the unity and stability of the country.

Some dissident religious groups, especially among the Shi'is, were even promoting Islamic revolution and violence against the regime.

Because the Ba'thists did not yet control most religious leaders and institutions in the country, the regime's public policies sometimes falsely gave the impression to outsiders that it was simply attempting to limit religious activities in the country. However, reading the regime's public statements in light of its internal records makes clear that such impressions were mistaken. The regime wished to limit participation in religious activities outside of its control while promoting religious activities it did control.[40]

The regime had to be very careful in its approach to religion. Saddam's wariness about this topic was not new. In his landmark 1977 speech, "A View on Religion and Heritage," cited earlier, he declared, "our Party . . . is always on the side of faith"; but he also cautioned against promoting that idea too forcefully. Saddam warned that a reactionary opposition was "using religion for political purposes." And because Saddam was unable to control religious discourse, he wanted to "avoid clashing with them directly and in a traditional manner." He feared that such a clash would "consolidate the stand" of this religious opposition and "create a psychological barrier between the Party and its ideology on one hand and certain sections of the population on the other."[41] In other words, it would allow Islamists to paint the regime as anti-religious and thus delegitimize it among large sections of the Iraqi population. As such, the regime needed to prevent a full-blown clash with the religious opposition. In such a conflict, authoritative religious actors beyond the regime's control could define the terms of the conflict and smear the Ba'thists as the enemies of Islam.

Consequently, the Ba'thists needed to balance between their desire to invoke their interpretation of Islam and the danger of doing so too forcefully. This dynamic predated Saddam's rise to power in Iraq. Aflaq himself had recognized a similar problem earlier in the century. In 1956, he argued, "we are not ignorant that our view [on religion] requires effort and caution several times that of the communist view, which shrinks from the problem in that it denies it completely." Accordingly, Aflaq understood that employing religion as part of his ideology was inherently problematic and difficult. The communists, he suggested, had a much easier task because they could simply attempt to keep religion out of the public sphere. If they were successful in doing so, their legitimacy could not be threatened by religious actors. However, as mentioned previously, Aflaq rejected the communists' atheism. This left him arguing for an interpretation of Islam that most traditional Islamic authorities vehemently rejected. It was a dangerous position, and he recognized it as such; but he also understood the need to work toward transforming what he considered to be the widely accepted, yet reactionary, discourse on religion into what he viewed as a progressive, nationalist, religious discourse. On the issue of religion, he argued, "there is a vast distance which will necessarily remain very tense between the sick and negative situation that we live in, and the other goals of our ideas." He also recognized that when it came to religious matters, there was a need for "sufficient courage and complete vigilance in order to ascertain all the causes of corruption in the current situation, and to fight them unrelentingly."[42] It would be difficult to find better words to describe how Saddam perceived his task in 1979.

However, Saddam's plan was also complicated by the fact that in the early years of their rule, the Iraqi Ba'thists spent most of their time and resources attempting simply to stabilize their regime. They did not have the manpower or institutional resources to deal with religious issues effectively. As a result, they often had little recourse other than repressing problematic religious actors and ideas. As mentioned before, during the late 1960s and much of the 1970s, they had downplayed the importance of religion in the thought of canonical Ba'thist theorists such as Aflaq to avoid ideological clashes over Islam. Accordingly, many rank and file Ba'thists were unaware of, or disinterested in, their Party's teachings on religion. This lapse on the part on the nascent Ba'thist regime made the issue of religion even more dangerous. Most Ba'th Party members—like most Iraqis—were religious. The regime leadership feared that Ba'thists who did not completely understand the Party's position on religion could fall prey to the opposition's propaganda and adopt what the regime considered to be the wrong interpretation of Islam. As a result, Party members could begin to believe that the regime's stance was anti-Islamic, or they could adopt sectarian attitudes that would turn them against each other and threaten social cohesion more generally.[43] Thus, a major part of the Saddam's plan to control religion was to indoctrinate Ba'thists on the Party's official position toward religion. This indoctrination on the Party's core teachings toward religion was necessary not only to protect the regime from an internal threat but also to facilitate its efforts to spread a Ba'thist interpretation of religion that was non-sectarian.

Indoctrination, however, would take time. Therefore, when the regime implemented Saddam's plan in 1979, only specially designated Ba'thists were permitted to work in the religious sphere. Unlike their peers who worked in other areas (e.g., with workers or women's organizations), Ba'thists who operated in mosques or coordinated with religious leaders received additional background checks and had to be individually approved by the Party Secretariat in Baghdad.[44]

These efforts to penetrate the religious sphere and to persuade religious leaders and the youth about the "truth" of Ba'thist interpretations of religion—and especially of Islam—continued throughout the decade. Year by year, and district by district, the regime slowly but steadily "escalated," as Saddam put it, the Ba'thists' presence in Iraq's religious landscape.[45]

CONCLUSION

As a committed Ba'thist, and a disciple of Aflaq, Saddam possessed a fairly developed interpretation of Islam and an innate propensity to instrumentalize it politically. In the late 1970s, this propensity combined with local factors such as the need to fend off the rise of domestic Islamist movements and the Iranian revolution, as well as Saddam's desire to entrench his authority by assuming the presidency. The March 1979 plan that Saddam initiated during the High National Security Council was designed to address all of those factors.

The plan inaugurated a process that completely transformed the relationship between religion and state in Iraq. However, it would be a mistake to interpret the 1979 plan as a blueprint that carefully laid out the regime's policies for the 1980s, 1990s, and 2000s. There is no evidence that Saddam anticipated how his policies would manifest in the coming decades. He certainly did not foresee the so-called Faith Campaign, which as we will see in later chapters, defined those policies in the 1990s. Instead, the plans that Saddam put forth in 1979 should be understood as stemming from a deeply ingrained impulse to shape Iraqi society in a way that was beneficial to his regime and detrimental to his adversaries. This plan was designed to accomplish that within Iraq's religious landscape.

As the following chapters will show, some aspects of the plan worked better than others. Saddam's Ba'thist ideology emphasized the concept of Arab unity and downplayed sectarian differences. The Ba'thist regime was inclined to create a single strategy for dealing with religion among Iraq's various sects. It quickly realized that doing so was untenable. Iraq's Shi'i religious landscape had its own particularities, and the regime would have to adjust accordingly. The next two chapters discuss the regime's plans to penetrate the Iraqi religious landscape generally and then the particular policies that the Ba'thists had to adopt to deal with Shi'i institutions and sectarianism.

Co-opting and Coercing Religion
in Saddam's Iraq

Saddam's decision to take control of religious affairs in Iraq, which he revealed during the March 1979 meeting of the High National Security Council, proved felicitous. The following month, Iran officially became an Islamic Republic and Ayatollah Ruhollah Khomeini steadily consolidated his power. Iran's new leaders did not hide their intention to spread their brand of revolutionary Islamism beyond Iranian borders. Neighboring Iraq was home to the most important Shi'i shrines and had a large Shi'i majority. It was, therefore, a logical first target. Saddam, who became president of Iraq in July 1979, felt increasing pressure from the country's Islamist opposition. He accused the Iranians of interfering in domestic Iraqi affairs, which he considered to be a violation of the 1975 Iran-Iraq peace treaty. This, combined with Saddam's assumption of Iranian weakness after a year of revolutionary upheaval, led him to invade Iran in September 1980. The assault initiated a calamitous eight-year war between the two states.

The Iran-Iraq War presented a number of challenges for the Ba'thists. Khomeini and his followers in Iran pummeled the Iraqis with propaganda depicting Saddam's regime as anti-Islamic and they openly sought to in-flame Iraq's Islamist opposition. The Iraqi Ba'thists were forced defend themselves on Islamic terms. However, they did not turn to Islamism. Instead they relied on the Ba'thist tradition of reverence for Islam and their insistence that unlike communists, Ba'thists were believers. Promoting such ideas, without putting the regime's legitimacy into the hands of untrusted religious authorities, required a delicate balance. More than rhetoric or ideology, the regime needed to develop a cadre of religious leaders who would defend it and promote its version of Islam. That required a process of institutionalization and bureaucratization, which, fortuitously, was aided by emergency measures and mobilization linked to the war.

Detailing of this process is necessary not only to understand how Saddam responded to the increased threats and opportunities of the war with Iran but also because the system that the Ba'thists put in place during the first decade of Saddam's presidency was designed to shape the country's religious landscape in a manner that would promote Ba'thist interpretations of religion—while at the same time stifle Islamist and sectarian actors who the regime felt would tear apart Iraqi society. The regime's system for controlling the religious landscape provided the foundation for Ba'thist policies during the 1990s. And the destruction of this system in 2003 was an important factor in unleashing religious insurgencies in the country.

INSTITUTIONALIZATION

The plan that Saddam had put forth during the March 1979 meeting of the High National Security Council formed the foundation of Ba'thist policies toward religion. During that meeting, Saddam began a process of institutionalization, which would link Iraq's religious actors to the state, the Ba'th Party, and the security services. Saddam ordered the formation of Party councils to organize students, teachers, and university professors. These counsels cooperated with the regime's security services. Their primary mission was to "engage with elements [of society] that have religious preferences and try to win them over to the Party."[1]

Such a strategy was assisted by broader institutional reforms to help the regime, and Saddam in particular, to gain control over religion in Iraq. In 1979, Saddam changed the name of the Ministry of Endowments to the Ministry of Endowments and Religious Affairs, giving it a broader mandate. In 1981, he formalized his control over it by reorganizing the bureaucracy so that the Ministry of Endowments and Religious Affairs reported directly to the presidential office.[2] In 1982, he further consolidated his control over the ministry by appointing one of his closest and most loyal advisors, Abdullah Fadil, as the Minister.[3] During this period, as Ofra Bengio has observed, "Financial allocations for the ministry were boosted, and young men replaced older officials."[4] This new cadre was explicitly loyal to Saddam.

In 1981, the regime also implemented "The Law of Service in Charitable and Religious Institutions," which stated that one was only permitted to work as a religious leader after passing an exam in front of the "Special Committee for Work as an Imam in the Mosques." This law was meant to ensure the loyalty of religious leaders, but it also caused considerable frustration. As the regime was fairly new to working in the religious sphere, it did not have enough information on most of Iraq's imams and sermongivers. Thus, the Ba'thists had no way to ensure their loyalty. Consequently, many mosques were left without religious leaders.[5]

In the early 1980s, Saddam also created committees for religious awareness (taw'iya diniyya) throughout Iraq.[6] These committees were composed of religious leaders loyal to the regime and were established at the local level, with several of them in each province. They were designed to institutionalize, bureaucratize, and thus better control religion. Through them, the regime kept an eye on religious trends in all corners of the country and communicated directly with religious leaders about which practices and ideas were acceptable and which would be punished. These committees also provided the topics that sermon-givers were required to discuss during Friday prayers. As a rule, all mosques in Iraq were required to give the same regime-dictated sermon on Friday; and then, if necessary, sermon-givers were permitted to discuss local issues. But these local topics, as well as any modifications to the sermon, needed to be approved by the committees.[7] In organizing the religious leaders into committees, the regime also created institutions that could speak more authoritatively in favor of Saddam's rule. These complemented the regime-controlled "leagues of Islamic scholars," which were organized at the provincial level. Thus, the Iraqi press often publicized the statements of these committees and leagues: not as the opinions of individuals but as the Islamic scholars of Baghdad, or the religious committee of Mosul or Basra.[8] Doing so afforded these statements of support a greater sense of authority.

The regime encouraged Islamic scholars to join these committees as a way of co-opting them. The Ba'thists hoped these scholars could then be used to raise support for, and diminish opposition to, their Party. Saddam made this policy explicit in a 1984 presidential decree that ordered regime officials to "approach the men of religion that you see as most influential among the people. Urge them respectfully to join the religious awareness committees and inform them that they can benefit from membership in them. Then activate these committees by having them meet directly with the citizens on religious occasions."[9]

The benefits Saddam mentions in this decree included not only prestige and authority but also financial rewards. Considerable sums of money were available to those who were willing to assist the regime. As such, the regime did not always need to actively co-opt religious leaders. In some cases, religious leaders themselves sought to enter the regime's system of control and thus reap its benefits.

A 1982 letter to the regime from one such enterprising group of Kurdish religious scholars in northern Iraq underscored this point. The authors of the letter began by stating that the majority of religious scholars in their area had "announced their loyalty to the political leadership since the eruption of the [Ba'thist] revolution." And they condemned "Khomeini the devil, and his spiteful gangs." They argued, moreover, that in periods of trouble, the religious leaders in the area had used their mosques and their pulpits to defend the Ba'thist revolution. They had also held televised symposiums to support Iraq's soldiers. Doing so, they argued, helped to solidify the ranks of the army. After establishing their loyalty and support for the Ba'thist regime, the authors of the letter then discussed the establishment of a regime-funded religious awareness committee in their area. However, they claimed that the head of the committee was not well-known either intellectually or socially, and thus the committee was failing. A more effective role, the authors argued, had been played by other religious scholars and sermon-givers in the mosques. They then stated that in order not to waste money, and to better serve the war effort, the funds that were allocated to the religious awareness committee should be reallocated to "the well-known men of religion" in the area (by which they meant themselves).[10]

This letter highlighted a number of phenomena that typified the Ba'thists' attempts to work in the religious sphere in the early 1980s. When the regime first endeavored to set up religious institutions and find religious leaders who were both loyal and influential, it struggled to do so. The regime had little experience in this arena. Its supporters were not typically religious leaders and did not possess traditional religious educations. In the early years of Saddam's presidency, as this letter described, the regime populated many of its new religious institutions with Party loyalists as opposed to influential and well-known religious leaders. Nevertheless, as the letter also demonstrates, religious leaders learned fairly quickly that joining these institutions provided real benefits and that the only real requirement was demonstrating loyalty to Saddam's regime. Hence, in the letter, the authors left no doubt about their support for the Ba'thist regime; and in exchange for financial support, they offered their legitimacy and influence.

MOBILIZATION DURING THE IRAN-IRAQ WAR

The regime's attempt to gain control of religious discourse in Iraq was necessary to counter the Iranian brand of revolutionary Islam that some Ba'thists feared could metastasize in Iraq. However, as much as the conflict with Iran threatened to incite problematic interpretations of Islam,

it also provided the Ba'thist regime with opportunities to map and penetrate Iraq's religious landscape. Between 1980 and 1988, Iraq fought a long
and bloody war with Iran. Iraq mobilized much of its population for the
war effort, increasing the size of its military by 350%.[11] With this came a
greater need for military chaplains. This chaplain corps consisted mostly
of Islamic (both Sunni and Shi'i) scholars and sermon-givers. Their primary purpose was to provide religious guidance to the soldiers fighting on
the front lines, reassuring them that their cause was just and Islamically
acceptable. Of course, the regime also used these religious leaders in its
propaganda. To demonstrate Iraq's Islamic credentials, the Iraqi press ran
feature stories about the chaplains and their role in the war.[12]

Yet, the expansion of the army's chaplain corps also played an additional, easily overlooked role in the regime's policy of encroachment on
the religious sphere. An applicant wishing to become an army chaplain
was required to provide extensive information to the regime. This included
which schools he had attended and his employment history. The regime
investigated his father, brothers, and uncles, whether he had ever been
convicted of a crime, and if he had belonged to any political parties or organizations. Following the investigation, regime officials then completed
a form on each applicant outlining, among other things, his "political orientation"; "personal characteristics"; "the reputation of his family"; his
"integrity"; and whether he had "any relatives, to the third degree, who
had committed crimes."[13] This was invaluable information for a regime
attempting to understand and control the religious landscape.

As the war progressed, the number of religious leaders in the Army
increased considerably. They formed a unit called Muhammad's Guard,
and regime reports show that up to 2,000 of them at a time were operating on the front lines.[14] Sometimes, especially during the early years of
the war, Shi'i scholars were sent into captured Iranian territory to express
their support for Saddam and to denounce Khomeini to the local population.[15] By the final years of the war, the Minister of Endowments and
Religious Affairs, Abdullah Fadil, claimed that there were 4,250 men of religion in the Army.[16] For the regime, this meant that it now had thousands
of religious leaders who had been through extensive background checks

and could be trusted. Some of these chaplains came from families with a tradition of religious scholarship. Therefore, the investigations unearthed important information about larger networks of scholars and helped the regime to map Iraq's religious landscape.

THE POPULAR ISLAMIC CONFERENCE

Most of the cases discussed thus far deal with local or low-level religious leaders. However, the regime also established a system to co-opt religious scholars who possessed—or sought—a national or even international reputation. The most important institution in this system was the regime-sponsored Popular Islamic Conference in Baghdad. This conference was attended by well-known and well-respected Islamic scholars from around the world. They came together in Baghdad because either they or the states they represented disliked Khomeini's Islamic revolution and had aligned with Saddam in his war against it.

The Ba'thists had very little experience in dealing with these international Islamic networks. Therefore, they turned to Saudi Arabia, which was assisting Saddam in his efforts to bring down the Iranian regime. The Saudis dispatched Ma'ruf al-Dawalibi, an ex-Syrian Prime Minister who had been spearheading Saudi Arabia's Islamic diplomacy. Tapping into Saudi networks, he helped bring 280 religious scholars and activists from 50 countries to Baghdad for the first Popular Islamic Conference in April 1983.[17] Then, in 1985, over 300 participants—including the head of the Saudi-sponsored Muslim World League, an official Egyptian delegation, the Moroccan Minister of Endowments, and the director of the Deobandi Dar al-'Ulum in Karachi—attended the Second Popular Islamic Conference.[18]

Having attracted a number of well-known Islamic leaders from around the world, these conferences provided the regime with a means to entice prominent Iraqi religious scholars as well. Participation in the conference was prestigious, came with financial rewards, and allowed one to rub shoulders with influential figures from all over the Islamic world. In return, the only sacrifice the regime asked of Iraq's religious leaders was to forego their political independence. All participants, both Iraqi and foreign, were required to support Saddam's regime and blame Iran for the continuation of a war between Muslims, which, as the participants repeatedly pointed out, is explicitly forbidden in the Qur'an (verse 49:9).[19] The more ambitious Iraqis also filled leadership positions at the conference in which they made sure to guide the discussion in appropriate directions. Saddam actively sought the support of Iraq's Sunni and Shi'i Arabs as well as Kurds; but as the conference was directed at countering Khomeini's Islamically themed propaganda, he was especially keen to include prominent Shi'i scholars.

Chapter 3 will deal specifically with the regime's relationship to the Shi'i religious establishment, but here it is worth stating that Saddam invited the leading Shi'i scholars in Iraq, such as Ayatollah Abu al-Qasim al-Khu'i and prominent members of the Hakim family, to join the conference. However, citing their insistence on remaining apolitical, they all refused. The regime had feuded, often violently, with the Hakim family for over a decade, and this rebuff brought the relationship to a boil. The next month, 90 members of the family were arrested. Several of them were executed in front of their relatives.[20]

Unable to attract senior Shi'i scholars, the regime offered the conference's money and prestige to lesser-known figures from prominent families. In doing so, the Ba'thists hoped that whereas these scholars may not have been as well known, their family names would invoke the authenticity and authority that the regime desired. A prime example of this phenomenon was 'Ali Kashif al-Ghita'. Although he had not distinguished himself as a scholar in his own right, he came from the Kashif al-Ghita' family, which was one of the most important scholarly Shi'i families of the 19th and 20th centuries. The regime and 'Ali Kashif al-Ghita' used this for their mutual benefit. The regime gained the support and blessings of a Shi'i scholar from an immediately recognizable and highly respected family, and 'Ali Kashif al-Ghita' received prestigious titles and financial rewards. In 1981, when the regime had required a fatwa from a Shi'i authority denouncing Khomeini as a heretic, 'Ali Kashif al-Ghita' had provided one.[21] Now, in 1983, the regime called on him once more, this time to convene the Popular Islamic Conference.[22]

The regime's difficulty in finding prominent, traditionally trained, yet trusted religious scholars was not limited to the Shi'is, however. It had trouble in this regard even among Sunni Arabs. Thus, the Secretary-General of the conference for most of the 1980s, Bashshar 'Awwad Ma'ruf, was not a traditional religious scholar; rather, he was a secular Ba'thist historian of Islam. Ma'ruf would lead the Ba'thist efforts in the Islamic sphere throughout the 1980s, and he typified the type of official on whom the regime based its religious policies during the period.

Born into a prominent middle class family in 1940, Ma'ruf had benefited from the new, secular, state education system in mid-20th-century Iraq. His father was a lawyer and ensured that he received the best possible education. Ma'ruf excelled at every level, graduating from high school with honors in 1960. He entered Baghdad University that year where he studied Islamic history, eventually earning a BA (1964), MA (1965), and PhD (1976). As was customary for ambitious young scholars in Iraq, Ma'ruf also spent significant periods studying abroad. However, unlike traditionally trained Islamic scholars who traveled to centers of Islamic learning—such as Mecca, Medina, or al-Azhar in Cairo—Ma'ruf went to Germany to study history at Hamburg University and then to the secular Cairo University in Egypt. Thus, socially and educationally he had more in common with secular Ba'thists—whose base of support was firmly entrenched in the newly urbanized middle class—than he did with traditional Islamic scholars who continued to attend study circles in religious seminaries and mosques. Tellingly, he wore a suit and tie, not the garb of a religious scholar, and some more traditional Iraqis even questioned whether or not he prayed regularly.[23]

Ma'ruf helped the regime reach out to religious Iraqis. His background allowed him to integrate comfortably into secular Ba'thist circles, and indeed, he joined the Party. Yet, his deep knowledge of Islamic sources and history also garnered him respect among religious leaders. Under his leadership, the regime increased the scope of its work within Iraq's religious landscape. By 1987, participants in the Popular Islamic Conference alluded to its increasing role in Iraqi affairs. The Minister of Endowments and Religious Affairs, Abdullah Fadil, stated that it had recently expanded and was now assuming a major role in confronting Iraq's challenges. Ma'ruf al-Dawalibi, who was now named the chairman of its executive committee, praised "the Iraqi government's limitless aid to the organization."[24] Official Iraqi media began to refer to it not only as a Popular Islamic Conference, but as the "Popular Islamic Conference Organization" (PICO), and the regime granted it a building in Baghdad to be used as a permanent headquarters.[25] PICO then held numerous symposiums and began publishing books on Islam. In addition to providing the regime with potent propaganda, these new PICO endeavors created even more incentives with which to draw Iraqi scholars into a system of rewards in exchange for loyalty.

Most of the "scholarship" that PICO produced during this period sought to demonstrate the heretical and even un-Islamic nature of Khomeini's Iran. It linked Iran's Islamic Revolution to sectarian movements, especially among the Persians, throughout Islamic history.[26] Though the regime attempted to prevent it, the discourse at these events sometimes included coded language and only semi-veiled sectarian attacks on Shi'ism in general.[27]

COERCION AND CONTROL

The processes of institutionalization, bureaucratization, and co-optation were pervasive throughout Iraq during the 1980s. By employing these tactics, the regime made considerable headway penetrating Iraq's religious landscape. However, these efforts were obviously more effective in some areas than others. Some religious leaders—among both Sunnis and Shi'is—opposed Saddam and refused to work for the regime, no matter what benefits it offered. Also, in the Shi'i areas of Iraq, religious scholars were less dependent on state finances and thus were less easily enticed by financial rewards. In situations in which the regime encountered resistance to its penetration and control, it resorted to more coercive tactics.

In the 1980s, the regime's main hurdle to controlling religion in Iraq was regulating religious leaders who had previously enjoyed some degree of independence from the state and who had no desire to sacrifice their beliefs or conscience. Believers who saw the regime's policies as an assault on their religion could be particularly difficult to tame.[28] This became especially problematic for the regime when these religious leaders worked in mosques that enjoyed independent financing—especially if the financier lived abroad and was therefore beyond the regime's control—and were not managed by the Ministry of Endowments and Religious Affairs. As the regime worked to gain control of the religious landscape in the 1980s, it encountered this problem quite regularly. Therefore, a pillar of its strategy was to bring all Iraqi mosques under the control of the ministry, eliminate independent or at least un-vetted financing of religious institutions, and enforce compliance among all of Iraq's religious leaders. To accomplish this, Ba'thists regularly attended the various mosques in their areas and reported what they found to the Party hierarchy.

Examining one such encounter between a Ba'thist and a non-compliant sermon-giver illuminates this process and helps to clarify the regime's policies. In March 1986, a Ba'thist attended a local Sunni mosque for the Friday sermon in Baghdad. He was dismayed to see that the sermon-giver "did not call for our [Ba'thist] leadership or for the victory of our army over its enemies despite the fact that he was instructed to do so." The Ba'thist approached the sermon-giver and informed him that it was necessary to discuss these issues in his sermons. The Ba'thist also emphasized the sermon-giver's duty to convince people to donate to the Iraqi Army and assist it in the fight against the Persians. The sermon-giver responded that he had not been instructed to do so. The Ba'thist assured him that he did not need explicit instructions on these matters because the Qur'an itself clearly mandated that he support the Ba'thist regime against its enemies. The sermon-giver acquiesced and stated that he would do as instructed in his sermon the following week.

The next week, the Ba'thist returned to the mosque for the Friday prayer, but again the sermon-giver did not discuss the required topics. Instead he lectured those in attendance on hypocrites (*munafiqun*), which was a thinly veiled attack on the Ba'thist regime's appropriation of religion. Moreover, the sermon-giver did not use the microphone in the hope of hiding his sermon from those outside the mosque. The Ba'thist then had another, slightly sterner conversation with him. The next week the sermon-giver stood up and announced that he would no longer give sermons. This was undoubtedly a protest against the Ba'thist's continued attendance. Nevertheless, the sermon-giver continued to live in the mosque. In fact, he had just built rooms for himself and his new wife.

The Ba'thist submitted a handwritten report about his encounter with the sermon-giver to his local Party office and pointed out, additionally, that the Ministry of Endowments and Religious Affairs did not own the mosque in question. He believed it had a private owner who lived outside Iraq.[29] A Ba'thist official then typed a report highlighting the important elements of the encounter. The report was forwarded up the Party's chain of command, first to the Baghdad Bureau (*tanzim*) and then to the Party Secretariat. The Secretariat contacted the Ministry of Endowments and Religious Affairs, informing it that the sermon-giver had demonstrated "a lack of commitment to the Party's guidance" and instructed it to "take the appropriate action."[30]

In cases such as this, the Ministry of Endowments and Religious Affairs worked with the security services to arrest the rogue sermon-giver and identify the financier of the mosque. If the ministry could not vet and control the financier (as in this case because he was residing abroad), it confiscated the mosque and brought it under the ministry's direct management. As this case aptly showcases, however, the regime's first inclination was not to resort to violence. The sermon-giver was given several opportunities to comply. If he had done so, the regime probably would have continued to view him with suspicion. The black mark against his record would not have been expunged, and he would not have been eligible for a position in one of the regime's religious institutions discussed previously. Yet, as long as he remained compliant, he would have been permitted to continue preaching.

Even after his arrest, there was still a possibility for redemption. Saddam favored psychological manipulation as a means to win over potential enemies. As Wendell Stevenson and Kanan Makiya have each shown, one particularly Machiavellian tactic that Saddam employed was to have the regime sentence a transgressor to death; then at the last moment, Saddam would intervene, not only pardoning the condemned man but restoring him to his previous position and sometimes even promoting him. This would create a personal debt to Saddam for one's life and livelihood.[31] As such, the regime's archives contain lists of imams and sermon-givers who were sentenced to death and then pardoned.[32] Although of course, the regime did not hesitate to carry out the grisly task, or worse, when it felt there was no alternative.[33]

CHRISTIANS

Thus far, this chapter has focused on Islamic institutions and Muslim religious leaders. It should be stressed, however, that the regime also applied its strategy of co-opting and coercing to Iraq's Christian minority. Similar to its policies toward Islam, the regime offered financial assistance to loyal Christian religious leaders and built new religious centers through which it could institutionalize Christianity in Iraq.[34] The regime then co-opted Christian leaders both to help control Iraq's Christian population and to bolster Iraqi propaganda. In the early 1980s, the Iraqi press regularly carried stories claiming "Christian men of religion are not immune from Khomeini's persecution," and that "Christian men of religion denounce Khomeini's actions and his corrupt regime." In such instances, Iraqi Christian leaders discussed the dangers that Khomeini's Islamic revolution posed to their community and to their co-religionists in Iran.[35]

Despite these media portrayals, Iraq's Christian leaders often attempted to preserve their independence and were not always willing to integrate into the regime's authoritarian system. Thus, to co-op or coerce—whichever the situation called for—Iraqi Christianity, the regime relied on Christian Ba'thists who lived and worked in the community. In the Ba'th Party archives, for example, one finds files on Christian Ba'thists who were instrumental in surveying the Christian religious landscape and reporting on its religious leaders. These Christian Baʻthists were also in-dispensable in the regime's penetration and management of churches as well as Christian social and religious clubs.[36] Yet, although these Baʻthist Christians were certainly more capable of operating in Christian circles than were Muslims, they were not always welcome.

In 1983, for instance, one such Christian Baʻthist reported that he had attended a two-day festival held by the Syrian Orthodox community. This festival was held after "the historic decision of the Revolutionary Command Council to grant cultural rights to Assyrians." However, he was surprised to find that there were no slogans or banners at the festival celebrating the Revolutionary Command Council's decision. The opening ceremony, for example, only dealt with Syrian Orthodox themes. This was especially troublesome because the man who delivered the opening address was instructed to speak about the regime's decision. The Christian Baʻthist was dissatisfied and he made his displeasure known to the bishop.

Later, the same Christian Baʻthist attended a youth seminar held by the Church. At this event, he alerted the same bishop that a number of prob-lematic people were in attendance. Apparently they were members of a non-political Christian organization that therefore did not openly support the Baʻthists. Despite this, the Christian Baʻthist was "surprised that the bishop defended them." Then, to make matters worse, he reported that the bishop "accused me of trying to sabotage the sect by spreading the ide-ology of the Party in its ranks. Accordingly, he told me not to interfere in the affairs of the sect." The bishop then decided to suspend the seminar as long as the Baʻthist remained in attendance.

The Christian Baʻthist, however, refused to back down. He continued to speak with the attendees and he also gave the bishop a number of or-ders: (1) The bishop must support the Party and the Baʻthist revolution in his blessings, and he must ensure that all religious organizations—including the one whose members were present at the event—supported the Party. (2) These religious organizations needed to hold elections and select people who would carry the responsibility for the sect and the homeland (*watan*). Although he does not explicitly say so, it is clear that in these "elections," regime loyalists would be "elected." And finally, (3) it was necessary to "culturally indoctrinate and raise the consciousness of the youth on the issues of patriotism (*wataniyya*) and progress." These are the same tactics that the regime applied to Islamic leaders and institutions discussed previously. The regime preserved religious institutions wherever possible, but it stripped them of their independence. Through these policies, the regime also hoped to bring Iraqi Christianity into its system of control.

Nevertheless, as the Ba'thist reported, "The bishop refused to comply, and he began to close the doors of the archdiocese and the churches so that the seminar could not be held for three consecutive weeks." The bishop understood the regime's tactics, and if he could not keep the seminar independent, he at least wanted to prevent it from becoming an instrument of the Ba'th Party. The Christian Ba'thist attempted to persuade him, but, as he reported, the bishop "continued stubbornly in not holding the seminar."

The Christian Ba'thist ended his report by stating that the bishop was against the Ba'th Party, and for good measure, he accused him of having connections with the Muslim Brotherhood. He then stated that the regime needed to replace some of the Christian organizations and that elections needed to be held for them. Through these elections, the regime could insert Ba'thists or their allies into the leadership and thus control the organizations. Finally, the regime needed to inform the bishop that the youth seminar would no longer be permitted.[37] The Christian Ba'thist's report was then forwarded to the security services (*al-amn al-'amm*) so that it could deal with the transgressors and enforce his recommendations.[38]

As this incident demonstrates, the regime's strategy for controlling Christianity was similar to its approach toward Islam. It wished to use existing institutions because they possessed the authority that the regime coveted. The regime hoped to hollow out these institutions and then fill them with loyalists. These loyalists would transform the institutions into components of the Ba'thist regime. The regime only resorted to coercion when Christian religious leaders resisted its "recommendations," as they, along with their Muslim counterparts, often did. As such, the Christian Ba'thist spent three weeks attempting to convince the bishop to restart the youth seminar. The Ba'thist did not wish to destroy the seminar but rather to control it and to use it. Only after concluding that he could not co-opt the bishop did he shut his seminar down.

CONCLUSION

Saddam's general strategy for penetrating the Iraqi religious landscape, which was outlined in this chapter, would contribute greatly to his regime's capacity to instrumentalize Islam politically. The regime employed this strategy continuously throughout the 1980s. It gradually worked to identify mosques, churches, and religious leaders who on one hand were trustworthy and should be supported, or on the other hand were suspect and thus needed to be dealt with in some fashion. In doing so, it worked diligently to bring Iraq's religious landscape under its control and to eliminate independent religious activity throughout the country.

Co-opting and Coercing Shi'ism

The previous two chapters laid out Saddam's general strategy to co-opt and coerce the religious landscape in Iraq during the 1980s. During that process, his regime wished to downplay the role of sects in the name of "unity"—which was one of the pillars of Ba'thist ideology. As such, the plans outlined in chapter 2 attempted to apply unified policies to Sunnis and the Shi'is—as well as religious minorities such as Christians—in Iraq. However, the regime's aversion to recognizing sects was an ideological preference that did not always address the realities of Iraqi society or the prejudices of Ba'thist leaders. Thus, although the regime intended to apply its policies uniformly to all Iraqis, it was often less successful among Iraq's majority Shi'i population.

Shi'is and Sunnis have different conceptions about some basic principles of Islamic belief and history, which made it difficult for the Ba'thists to impose a unified interpretation of Islam. The regime also faced a number of other problems in southern Iraq that frustrated their strategy of applying a single policy to all religious leaders and institutions. The income of Shi'i religious scholars, for example, came directly from their followers through a religious tax, which required all Shi'is to pay one-fifth of their salary to the religious establishment. This tax did not exist in traditional Sunnism. Sunni scholars were, therefore, much less financially independent and much more susceptible to the regime's financial overtures. The Shiʿis of southern Iraq also had long-established religious seminaries, particularly the *hawza* in Najaf, which were among the holiest and most prestigious centers of Shiʿi religious learning in the world. The regime could not easily lure away Shiʿi students by constructing new religious schools under Baʿthist control or replace scholars who were educated in these venerable institutions with those educated in regime-sponsored schools. Furthermore, Shiʿi rituals include large public commemorations, which tend to bring the masses out into the streets. These commemorations could, and sometimes did, turn into sectarian political rallies in which the regime felt compelled to intervene.

Hence, the means that the regime employed to control the religious landscape in other areas of Iraq were not easy to replicate in the Shiʿi regions. Moreover, because southern Iraq contained Shiʿism's holiest sites and centers of learning, the Iraqi Shiʿis were deeply connected to the wider Shiʿi world through pilgrimages and the presence of large numbers of foreign students. Iraq's Shiʿi scholars were especially closely linked to Shiʿism's other important center of learning in Qom, Iran. The transnational character of Iraqi Shiʿism—particularly because of its strong ties to Iraq's chief adversary, Iran[1]—was problematic for a regime that insisted on controlling everything within its borders.

Thus, despite the regime's preference for a single unified policy toward all Iraqis regardless of religion or sect, it was forced to adapt to the realities on the ground. This chapter will focus on the distinct policies that the regime used to gain control over Iraqi Shiʿis and indeed, though less successfully, Iraqi Shiʿism during the 1980s. In line with the regime's general strategies toward religion during this period, its penetration of Shiʿi institutions helped shape the religious landscape and develop the regime's institutional capacity. Thus, the regime's actions discussed in this chapter laid the groundwork for the policies that the regime enacted during the last decade of Saddam's rule.

THE BA'THIST VIEW OF IRAQI SHI'ISM
AND SECTARIANISM

Before discussing Saddam's policies for gaining control over Iraq's Shi'i religious landscape, it is important first to outline the ideological foundation on which those policies rested. For some time, much of the secondary literature on Iraq depicted Saddam's policies as overtly sectarian.[2] This narrative has been challenged by more recent scholarship, much of it based on the regime's internal records, which present the regime's actions in a less sectarian light.[3] However, the regime's records are not perfect sources, and there are reasons to believe that they do not present an accurate picture of the role that latent sectarianism played in the formation and execution of Ba'thist policies.

The Ba'thists attempted to present their interpretation of Islam as "traditional" and "normal" rather than sectarian.[4] However, concepts and practices that seemed ordinary or even generic to members of one sect could appear deviant to members of other sects. Sunnis dominated the Arab Middle East and the Ba'th party under Saddam. Therefore, the generic Islam that the regime promoted often had a Sunni bias. Even secular and non-observant Sunnis frequently held ideas about the basics of Islamic history that had a clear Sunni slant. The Sunni version of Islamic history was not only reinforced in religious schools but also in secular histories of the region and in popular culture.

Certain core aspects of Ba'thism are tied to these traditional Sunni understandings of Islam and could be interpreted as inherently problematic for Iraqi Shi'is. The Arabic term "Ba'th" is best translated as "resurrection." Early Ba'thists chose this name as a reflection of their desire to resurrect the golden age of Arab Caliphates. This was problematic for orthodox Shi'is who considered the first three Caliphs as well as later Islamic empires to be illegitimate usurpers of divine authority. The Ba'thists' pan-Arabism was also problematic for some Iraqi Shi'is in that it transformed them from a majority in Iraq to a minority in the larger Arab world. Finally, unlike in post-2003 Iraq, where there are two ministers of religious endowments (one Sunni and one Shi'i), in Ba'thist Iraq there was only one. His position was designed to represent all Muslims; but in practice, he, along with other senior religious leaders in the regime, was always Sunni. And, whereas the regime paid tribute to Shi'i sensibilities by zealously glorifying Ali, its official publications also insisted that all the Rashidun Caliphs be honored—a practice that is inherently anti-Shi'i.[5] Other standard Shi'i practices such as making pilgrimages on foot or displaying images of Imams were also outside the boundaries of what the regime considered "normal." Thus, although the regime's polices did not use overtly sectarian language, they often favored Sunni practices over Shi'i practices.

Analyzing sectarianism in Saddam's Iraq is complicated by the regime's taboo against discussing it openly. As others have noted, the terms Sunni and Shi'i are conspicuously absent from the regime's records.[6] This was almost certainly due to a prohibition against discussing certain topics that violated official Ba'thist ideology. However, in some rare cases, one is able to circumvent such taboos. For example, Iraqi Ba'thists who lived abroad wrote regular reports back to the Party Secretariat in Baghdad. The authors of these reports (possibly because they were living outside the regime's all-encompassing system) did not always adhere to the regime's taboos and jargon. They spoke about regime violence more directly than did reports from inside Iraq, and they did not always use the designated euphuisms. At times sectarian language seeped into their reports as well. For example, a senior Iraqi Ba'thist in the United Arab Emirates filed a report on an Iraqi dissident who was encouraging "Shi'i" Iraqi merchants to oppose the regime.[7] A similar report from inside Iraq would never have used the term "Shi'i" to describe these merchants. That disparity suggests Ba'thists were clearly aware of sectarian divisions and acted accordingly, even if they did not discuss doing so openly.

Because it was forbidden for Ba'thists to use sectarian language, it can be difficult to determine what role sectarianism played in the regime's actions. For example, when the regime deported thousands of Shi'is from southern Iraq during the early 1980s, claiming that they were Iranians, most outside observers considered "Iranian" to be a crude euphemism for "Shi'i."[8] Yet, even in the Ba'th Party's most secret correspondences, regime officials depicted the problems in southern Iraq as a struggle between Iraqi Arabs and foreign (mostly Iranian) forces.[9] The status of an Arab or Iranian in southern Iraq was complicated by the fact that it had been a border region between the Ottoman and Persian Empires. People with deep roots in the region had multiple citizenship statuses, and many Arab Shi'is in southern Iraq did not possess official Iraqi national identity cards. When this ambiguity is combined with the regime's taboos against describing Iraqi Shi'is as Shi'is, it becomes difficult to determine how much trust to put in the regime's sources that depict the deportations in ethnic (Persian vs. Arab) terms as opposed to sectarian (Sunni vs. Shi'i) terms.

Nevertheless, as Fanar Haddad has argued, policies and actions that at first may have seemed sectarian sometimes had other causes. Practices favoring Sunnis were often just Saddam favoring those with whom he enjoyed close ties. These were mostly Arabs from the region around his hometown of Tikrit who happened to be Sunnis. Thus, political appointments were less about sectarianism than about loyalty and trust.[10] Further, it is problematic to suggest that because Ba'thism at times seems to have a built-in Sunni bias that it is inherently incompatible with Shi'ism. Such assumptions assume a static interpretation of Shi'ism and Shi'i identity that always outweighs other identities, such as Arabism, territorial nationalism, or class. Such ideas are also ahistorical in that many of the early leaders of the Iraqi Ba'th Party—including its first Secretary-General, Fuad al-Rikabi—were Shi'is,[11] and that Shi'is continued to hold senior positions in the Iraqi Ba'th Party until the regime's demise in 2003.[12]

Moreover, taboos and ambiguities cannot always explain the lack of sectarian discourse in the regime's records. In some important incidences, the regime appears to have been genuinely unconcerned with Sunni-Shi'i sectarianism among Arabs. For example, the questionnaires that Iraqis filled out during security investigations for sensitive positions asked for one's "nationality" (i.e., Kurd or Arab) and "religion" (i.e., Muslim or Christian), but did have a place to mark whether one was Sunni or Shi'i.[13] Likewise, the regime sometimes took inventories of Ba'th Party members who were Kurds so that the regime could closely monitor them. There were no equivalent inventories of the Shi'is in the Party.[14] These forms and policies make clear that the regime did not officially target Shi'is *as* Shi'is. At times critical decisions about security were made without the knowledge of whether someone was Sunni or Shi'i. Moreover, as Dina Khoury explains, "most of the upper echelons of the local party cadres were drawn from long-time residents."[15] Thus, in Shi'i areas, officials who have been accused of having an anti-Shi'i bias were themselves Shi'is. This phenomenon is also reflected in the trove of oral histories that have been recorded since the fall of the regime.[16]

Thus, whereas sectarianism certainly existed in Iraq during the 1980s and it almost certainly influenced the regime's actions, it must be emphasized that this was not the intention of senior Ba'thist officials. The Ba'thist Party's internal records showcase a system where (at least *de jure*) Sunnis and Shi'is were treated equally, even if this probably was not the case in practice. It should also be noted that although official discourse on Islam in Saddam's Iraq had a Sunni bias, it was not orthodox Sunnism. Ironically, the person who had the most profound influence on Saddam's view of "true" Islam was neither a Sunni nor a Shi'i but rather the secular Christian, Michel Aflaq.

As the remainder of this chapter will make evident, the regime relied on this Ba'thist interpretation of Islam—emphasizing Arabism, belief in God, and performing what Ba'thists considered traditional religious rituals—to counter accusations of sectarianism and to depict religious opposition to the regime in southern Iraq as Persian rather than as Shi'i.[17] The regime feared that the Iranian-backed opposition had strategically tied itself to the Shi'i religious leadership and that Iran had infiltrated traditional Shi'i institutions such as the *hawza* as well as Shi'i religious ceremonies during the holy month of Muharram. These institutions and ceremonies had deep roots in Iraqi society and in traditional Shi'ism. If the regime wished to maintain any level of Islamic legitimacy and avoid outright confrontation with its Shi'i population, it could not simply destroy them. This was particularly important during the 1980s, as the majority of foot soldiers in Saddam's army during the Iran-Iraq War were Shi'is.

MUHARRAM COMMEMORATIONS

Shi'i uprisings against the Ba'thist regime began in the mid-1970s when Iraqi security forces interrupted a religious procession during the holy month of Muharram.[18] These processions were part of larger Muharram ceremonies in which the Shi'is commemorate the Battle of Karbala and mourn the martyrdom of the Prophet Muhammad's grandson, Husayn. They climax on the tenth day of Muharram, known as the 'Ashura. During these ceremonies, large crowds assemble to march and to recite the Qur'an in remembrance of Shi'i martyrs.

Any unauthorized gathering of large numbers of people is inherently dangerous to an authoritarian regime. The fact that these gatherings had already exploded into anti-regime demonstrations in the past made them even more troublesome. Though this unrest had several causes—not all of them sectarian or religious in nature—the Ba'thists feared that the Iranians intended to undermine their regime by "employing religious celebrations" to, among other things, spark sectarianism; spread anti-regime rumors; sabotage Iraq's military, political, and economic sectors; and to "carry out assassinations of Ba'th Party officials and people affiliated with the security services."[19] Thus, whatever their cause, Saddam feared that these events, if not properly managed, could become a real threat to his rule. If he hoped to gain control over religion in Iraq, he felt that he needed to prevent these religious ceremonies from being "exploited" by Iran and the Islamists "for political goals."[20]

With Saddam's ascension to the presidency and the increased emphasis he put on religious affairs, the regime began to formulate more structured approaches to handling the Muharram ceremonies. First, it was necessary for it to create security plans for each province and to coordinate the efforts of the Ba'th Party, the military, and the various security services. Accordingly, the regime created special unified councils for monitoring all areas of interests. These councils were also responsible for "diagnosing hostile elements" and putting them under particularly tight surveillance so that they could not exploit the events.[21]

The regime was extremely cautious when implementing any security plan. The provincial plans ordered "the security services to create active agents from among the good Ba'thists, who were not susceptible to outside influence, to form headquarters that will back up the Party Headquarters as a reserve force for dealing with emergency situations." These forces were under the command of Party officials and were in constant contact with the provincial governor and the Party chain of command.[22] Other Ba'thists were issued weapons and directed to guard important and vulnerable locations throughout the province such as gas stations, electric power stations, various communication infrastructure, mosques, shrines, and other municipal, religious, and security buildings.[23]

All incidents were to be handled calmly and with strict discipline. To that extent, Party officials were ordered to select Ba'thists who were "good, calm, and understand the religious character of the region." They would work with the security services, who would return repeatedly to the shines and religious centers to continuously monitor any negative phenomena and the "hostile people" who tried to exploit them.[24] As discussed in previous chapters, the regime maintained tight controls over which Ba'thists were permitted to engage in religious affairs. The same policy was applied when dealing with the Muharram ceremonies.[25]

During the ceremonies, the regime hoped to promote a Ba'thist understanding of Islam and thus diminish Iranian and Islamist influences. The Ba'thists were especially keen to warn the citizens against the practices of "hostile client forces," which tended to be Islamists who Ba'thists sources depict as Iranian backed reactionaries. Ba'thists and security forces assigned to deal with religious matters attempted to counter Iranian influences by "creating general awareness among the citizens, helping them to reject sinful practices in society, to understand the true nature of religion, and to understand the principles of the Party concerning religion."[26] In the discourse of Ba'thism, "backward" and "sinful" meant Iranian and Islamist, while the "essence" or "true nature" of religion was, of course, the Ba'thists' Arabized interpretation of it. Thus the regime's outlook toward religion in the early 1980s is clearly discernible from these documents. It considered the opposition's claims (that Ba'thism was anti-Islam) to be demonstrably false, and thus the regime strove to undermine the opposition's attacks not only by denouncing them as foreign but also by emphasizing Ba'thist views of religion.

The regime believed that the best means of accomplishing its goals in Shi'i areas was through control of the *husayniyyat*—the halls that the Shi'is use for commemoration ceremonies during the month of Muharram. The regime designated official Qur'an readers and preachers in every *husayniyya* as well as in Shi'i mosques.[27] The regime then circulated the lists of the approved individuals among the security services along with orders to prevent all others from performing these roles.[28] Ba'thist officials also organized "meetings with the sermon-givers to tell them to raise enthusiasm [for the regime] and to denounce the racist Iranian aggression." Specifically, they ordered these preachers to denounce "the leader in Tehran" and to praise Saddam.[29] Similarly, the Union of Women of the Najaf Branch of the Party held meetings with female readers of the Qur'an to relate "what is required of them" during these occasions.[30]

To further diminish the chance of unrest, the regime sometimes restricted the presence of youth at the reading circles, only permitting older men (*kibar al-sinn*) to attend.[31] The security services also "set the time for ending the *husayniyyat* [reading] circles at nine in the evening." However, the regime did permit some flexibility for those who cooperated with it on these matters. This, in turn, provided extra incentive for following the guidelines.[32] Finally, to prevent large crowds from forming, the regime forbade the use of loudspeakers except inside the mosques and *husayniyyat*, and attempted—though less successfully—to restrict the distribution of food to crowds or to marchers in processions.[33]

These restrictive measures were paired with regime-sponsored ceremonies and propaganda that glorified the Ba'thist regime and depicted it as a champion of Shi'ism. In addition to the preachers and Qur'an readers who "repeatedly praised the party, the revolution, and the Victorious Leader, Saddam Hussein,"[34] the regime ordered "the Directorate of the [Religious] Endowments of the province to hoist two large black flags to commend the sacrifice of Imam Husayn" and "to aggrandize the redemption of his descendent the Victorious Leader Saddam Hussein (may god preserve him)."[35]

AYATOLLAH AL-KHUʼI AND THE SOURCE
OF EMULATION

To effectively gain control of Iraqi Shiʻism, the regime had to do more than simply control and manipulate Shiʻi ceremonies during Muharram. As in other areas, the Baʻthists hoped to control religion by controlling religious leaders and through them, religious discourse. However, as mentioned previously, the regime's strategies of co-opting and coercing proved less effective among the Shiʻis. The independent institutions and finances of Iraqi Shiʻis enabled them to take a stand and demonstrate that they were willing to suffer or even die rather than compromise their beliefs.

The Baʻthists thought that the position of the senior Shiʻi religious scholar (the source of emulation) had been politicized in the early 20th century, and that Iran had effectively gained control over it. During the 1980s, the senior Shiʻi scholar in Najaf was the Iranian-born Ayatollah Abu al-Qasim al-Khuʼi. Much to the regime's consternation, al-Khuʼi remained apolitical and refused to publicly support either side in the Iran-Iraq War. The regime reports argued that al-Khuʼi was "hostile to the Party and the revolution." However, by hostile, the regime did not mean that he openly denounced Saddam and the Baʻthists. Had he done so, he would have certainly been eliminated. Al-Khuʼi's views and actions were more subtle. This was made clear in a report that listed the "hostile" acts for which al-Khuʼi was guilty. The list not only provides insight into al-Khuʼi's stance toward Saddam but is also a good guide to the regime's perception of what actions or beliefs warranted concern. It begins:

1. Al-Khuʼi and his sons continue to speak Farsi.
2. He tries to avoid following the official regulations concerning religious occasions and holidays.
3. He "embraces non-Arab elements, especially Persians . . ." and he offers Persian students and men of religion financial support.
4. "Al-Khuʼi's position toward our just Party and against the evil Iranian enemy is not clear and not understood to a certain

extent at this time." And he does not express his views on the war despite the aggression of the Iranians and the cooperation between Khomeini and the Zionists.

5. Al-Khu'i and his entourage encourage sinful/mistaken practices and thus encourage sectarianism.

6. His organization contains some students of religious studies who have avoided their military duty.[36]

7. He tries to increase the number of Pakistanis, Afghans, and some of their families in Iraq.

8. He pays salaries to the families of "escapees and deserters."

9. A delegation he sent on the Hajj met with delegations from Iran and the Arab Gulf states.

10. He works with the Hakim family members even though some of them have been imprisoned.

11. He does not attend memorials for the martyrs of the war.[37]

These complaints represent the regime's view of al-Khu'i during the 1980s. As the list made apparent, the Ba'thists' main concerns were that he was not an Arab or a proponent of Arabism, and that he did not openly support the regime or its war with Iran. The regime had no respect for the tradition of political quietism within Shi'ism. Ba'thists considered the role of religious leaders as essential in maintaining morale during the war. Al-Khu'i, however, refused to play his part. He remained independent, both in his behavior and in his contacts to the broader Shi'i world.

Unsurprisingly, the regime closely monitored al-Khu'i and the network of Shi'i scholars under his patronage. Belonging to al-Khu'i's network was not in itself condemnable. In fact, the Ba'thists actively recruited his disciples. Some of al-Khu'i's followers even worked for the regime and in the Ministry of Endowments and Religious Affairs. One regime study from 1985 listed 65 men of religion who were part of al-Khu'i's network but were loyal to the "Party and the revolution." As such, the Ba'thists distinguished between al-Khu'i's followers who supported the regime and those who they suspected of disloyalty. The Ba'thists were aware that some of al-Khu'i's followers refused to associate with other Shi'i scholars who were loyal to Saddam. Predictably, the regime considered such scholars to be suspect. One could also raise the regime's suspicion by not participating in various activities to support Iraq during the Iran-Iraq War, or by having Islamist relatives, especially if they were members of an Islamist party.[38] In some cases, the regime had demonstrated its willingness to assassinate senior religious scholars in Iraq. In 1987, it killed al-Khu'i's son-in-law and his son-in-law's brother for their refusal to condemn the Iranian assault on Basra. The bodies were dumped unceremoniously at al-Khu'i's house.[39]

Efforts to monitor and control al-Khu'i's network were often ad hoc. Regime officials would simply write whatever derogatory information they had on the Shi'i scholars in a memo or on a blank piece of paper. Unlike similar regime reports in the 1990s,[40] there were no standardized forms requiring specific information. In this period, each official created his own system and determined what was relevant to report.

BA'THIFICATION OF SHI'I RELIGIOUS SCHOOLS

In the early to mid-1980s, the regime began to develop larger, more systematic plans for dealing with Shi'i seminaries. The regime was, to put it mildly, suspicious of their independence and often accused them of being controlled by Iran. One report argued that "weakness of the state" prior to the Ba'thists coming to power in the 1960s permitted the *hawza* to be manipulated by colonialism, international oil companies, and Iran, among other nefarious forces. Moreover, because of this manipulation and control by outside forces, the *hawza* had spawned political organizations that mislead the people by disguising themselves "under the cover of religion."[41] As the Ba'thist regime built its institutional capacities, and thus strengthened the state, it wished to bring the Shi'i seminaries under control or to eliminate them.[42] At one point, senior regime officials even suggested "moving the *hawza* from Iraq to Iran."[43] However, the regime's inclination to keep traditional institutions in place, and then to co-opt them, prevailed. It instead decided "to strengthen the role of the *hawza* in order to serve the march [of the Ba'th] and the revolution."[44] In doing so, the Ba'thists could feed off the authority and perceived authenticity of these institutions while employing them for the regime's purposes. This was a long and complex process, the fruits of which will be seen in later chapters covering the 1990s.

However, gaining control of the *hawza* was no simple task. Shi'i scholars closely guarded their independence and were willing to suffer considerably to maintain it. Because the regime was unwilling to eliminate them, it needed to find other means to bring them under its control. One of the most important policies the regime implemented in that regard was to take charge of the *hawza*'s finances. On one hand, the regime seized the endowments that the Shi'i religious leaders had amassed and that they used to maintain their independence from the state.[45] On the other hand, the regime itself began supporting the *hawza* financially and thus attempted to "reduce their dependency" on foreign funds (especially from Iran).[46]

The Ba'thists also used their control of Iraqi border and immigration policy to influence Shi'i religious institutions. In the late 20th century, even traditional institutions such as religious seminaries were required to work within the modern nation-state system. Therefore, all foreign students traveling to Iraq to study at these seminaries required state-issued visas. The regime ordered the special security services in its embassies to investigate the political and social background of every potential student and thereby limit who could study in Iraq. The embassies then forwarded the approved students' information to the security services in Iraq; and as one report argues, "in light of this information, cooperation with these students [while] they are in the country is possible." Further, the regime only offered them a limited visa, and thus required the students to take part in continuing reviews. Extensions or renewals of the visas required that they continue to cooperate.

The regime assessed that these students were vulnerable because "for the most part," they "come from circles which need financial support, and therefore [the regime] can provide this for them." In doing so, the Ba'thists felt that "it is possible to influence [the students] and to supply them with ideas on the Islamic religion and its luminous essence." In other words, the regime hoped to indoctrinate them with Ba'thist interpretations of Islam. But, "as for the students who deviate from this approach, there residency will be revoked and they will be sent back to their countries." This provided the regime another way to reduce Shi'i independence.

For Iraqi students studying in traditional Shi'i seminaries, the regime took a different approach. It chose 20–30 specific students and concentrated on giving them a proper "Party education" (read indoctrination) and on making them into "good comrades who are acquainted with religious matters." After these students had been won over, they were then used to spy on and control the others. When these students graduated, they were put on the budget of the Ministry of Endowments and Religious Affairs and sent to the various provinces to serve as men of religion. They would then help spread Ba'thist interpretations of Islam among the general population and to keep an eye on other Shi'i scholars who were not working for the regime. A select few of the Iraqi students were also used to manage the foreign students. As one report stated, a small group of Iraqis—"3 or 4 of the students from each province accepted in these schools in Najaf and Karbala"—was "chosen meticulously and soundly by the Party and security services." These students became "a means to facilitate" the activities just outlined for the foreign students both in the classroom and more casual settings.

The regime hoped "the final outcome of applying the above" would be "the strengthening of the *hawza* in Iraq and its future management." Importantly, this would be "carried out by Iraqi men of religion themselves and by not giving other nationalities (*jinsiyyat*) the opportunity to change them."[47] This point also highlights one of the regime's underlying assumptions about the problems it faced in southern Iraq. Because Ba'thists viewed the opposition as stemming from the Persians' age-old dislike of Islam's Arab roots, and from their inability to properly understand Islam's canonical Arabic sources, the regime insisted on the Arabization of the religious curriculum in Shi'i religious schools. In doing so, they hoped to neutralize Persian influences. The regime also formed a special committee composed of representatives from the Ministry of Information and the Ministry of Endowments and Religious Affairs to oversee "the wording of books, and volumes, as well as the approved curriculum for teaching in the religious schools." The report noted that these restrictions not only applied to the textbooks but to all books. Thus the committee recommended "the confiscation and destruction of religious books published by Persian elements, which contradict Islamic law and the essence of religion."[48] In instituting these policies, the regime hoped to create a "unified" curriculum among all religious schools in the country, regardless of sect, and to eliminate any school that attempted to preserve its independence from the regime.[49]

MEDIA AND CULTURAL INDOCTRINATION

In the mid-1980s, the regime also developed media and "cultural indoctrination" (tathqif) policies in its plan to control the hawza, the Shi'i religious establishment, and the lay Shi'i population. These efforts relied on the Arab Shi'is' nationalistic and patriotic sentiments. The Ba'thists attempted to demonstrate that religious tendencies coming out of Iran were "hostile to the Arabs, and the Islamic religion"; and further, that Iran intended to divide the Arabs and Muslims in the Arab Homeland (watan).[50]

The Ministry of Endowments and Religious Affairs worked with the media and the Ministry of Information to create and propagate Ba'thist religious propaganda. They were ordered to "adopt a cultural and media program" that followed Saddam's example in exhibiting "true religion" and exposing harmful distortions. More specifically, they were to broadcast television series and movies that highlight "the Arab-Islamic heritage"[51] and that (1) demonstrate the truth about Persian views of religions, their distortions of its principles throughout history, and their intentions now; (2) showcase "the ancient and modern position of the Persians toward Arabs, citing their mistreatment of the caliphs, the Prophet's family, and his companions;" and (3) equate them with the Zionists, as both of them have evil intentions against the Arab world.[52] The regime assessed that this type of programing "had a positive psychological effect on the citizens." Through it, the Party hoped to successfully "culturally indoctrinate" the masses, and keep them away from "sinful practices which are alien to the essence of religion."[53]

Developing a coordinated approach to implement these plans took several years. Yet by the mid-1980s, Saddam's ideas had been converted into a steady stream of propaganda that saturated the Iraqi population. In 1984, the system was largely in place; and Saddam praised the Iraqi press for its "excellent role" in depicting "our just nationalistic (*qawmiyya*) battle." He then decreed that the media continue broadcasting religious films and television series that "research the essence of the Arab-Islamic heritage" and that demonstrated "the Persian aggression on the Arab-Islamic heritage throughout history." These programs were required to clarify the Ba'th Party's position on the issue of religion and to emphasize that the Party had strengthened the "heritage of the Orient (*mashriq*) for the Nation (*umma*)," though the regime's records express concerns over whether it was able to successfully convey this message in the early years of the decade.

Saddam was especially keen to tie traditional Shi'i Islam to the concepts of Arabism, loyalty to the regime, and steadfastness in the battle against Iran. Thus, he was adamant that the Iraqi media "express the pure values of the Arab character including sacrifice for the sake of principle . . ."; and that the "characteristics of Imam Husayn are strengthened by adherence to these Arab values." Saddam ordered the media "to demonstrate that elements vindictive toward the Arab Nation (*umma*), especially the fire-worshiping (*majus*) Persians, are attempting to distort the values of Islam and Arabism, and especially the Arab character."[54]

Accordingly, it should come as no surprise that during the early to mid-1980s, the Iraqi press gave considerable coverage to "large celebrations" in Najaf, which the regime held in memory of Imam Husayn, and to mark the birthday of his father, Imam Ali.[55] Media reports on these events highlighted the role of Saddam, the Ba'th Party, and the Ministry of Endowments and Religious Affairs in promoting Shi'i Islam.[56] Thus, as these regime policies demonstrate, Saddam and the Ba'thists did not wish to prevent large Shi'i ceremonies: they actually encouraged some of them. Instead, their policy was to eliminate all manifestations of Shi'ism that lay outside of their control while at the same time promoting a regime-sponsored, pro-Ba'thist Shi'ism.

CONCLUSION

The regime did not wish to destroy Shi'ism or Shi'is. Instead, it worked meticulously and over several years to bring Shi'i scholars and institutions under its patronage and control. At the same time, it infiltrated Shi'i ceremonies, co-opting them for spreading a Ba'thist interpretation of Islam that it hoped would be both acceptable to the Shi'i masses and legitimize Ba'thist rule in Iraq. Thus, although the regime developed specific polices to deal with Iraqi Shi'is, its intentions were basically the same as its intentions when dealing with Sunnis and others in Iraq's religious landscape. These policies allowed the regime to control discourse and drive dissent out of the public and political spheres.

Suppressing the Islamist Opposition

Previous chapters dealt with the Ba'thist regime's strategy to co-opt and coerce religious leaders into supporting the regime in Iraq. This was the regime's preferred method of penetrating and controlling Iraq's religious landscape. However, co-optation and coercion were not always viable means to deal with religious actors in Iraq. Some Iraqis held ideas about religion that the regime considered intolerable. Most Iraqis who fell into this lamentable category were members of various Sunni and Shi'i Islamist political parties. Membership in any political organization other than the Ba'th Party necessarily resulted in harsh regime responses. The fact that Iraq was fighting an Islamist regime in Iran and attempting to manage an independent religious revival in Iraq, which at times had manifested as a violent insurgency, made Iraqi Islamist parties even more dangerous.

Iraqi Islamists were sometimes difficult to distinguish from pious but non-political Muslims. They also had a long history in Iraq and spanned a number of ethnicities and sects. All of these factors made them difficult to uproot. However, the regime was quite relentless in confronting them. Although it never completely succeeded in cleansing Iraqi society of Islamist parties, the progress that it made in driving them underground and out of Iraqi politics during the 1980s proved vital to shaping Iraq's religious landscape in a way that would permit the regime to employ religion more actively in its political strategies during the 1990s.

IRAQI ISLAMISTS

Among Sunnis, the two most important Islamists groups during the 1980s were the Muslim Brotherhood and Hizb al-Tahrir. Both of these groups were dominated by Sunni Arabs. In northern Iraq, a small Turkmen Islamic party existed; and in the mid-1980s, the Kurdish Islamic Party was formed.[1] However, neither the Kurdish nor the Turkmeni Islamist parties attracted much of a following.

By contrast, the Muslim Brotherhood[2] did enjoy significant support in Iraq. The Brotherhood is a Sunni Islamist movement that was founded in Egypt in the 1920s. In the 1940s, a Sunni Arab Iraqi named Muhammad Mahmud al-Sawwaf traveled to Egypt and met the Brotherhood's founder, Hassan al-Banna. When al-Sawwaf returned to Iraq, he founded the Iraqi branch of the organization.[3] The Muslim Brotherhood flourished in Iraq, attracting traditional Sunni Muslims who were concerned about the rise of communism in the country. They pushed for a reformist rather than a revolutionary approach to Islamizing Iraqi society and curbing secular reforms. In resisting the rise of leftist politics in Iraq, the Brotherhood felt solidarity with Shi'is and even reached out to the senior Shi'i scholars in the *hawza*. However, sectarian differences prevented them from cooperating.[4]

In 1960, the Iraqi Brotherhood officially registered to participate in elections as the Iraqi Islamic Party. It clashed with various authorities throughout the decade. When the Ba'th Party came to power in 1968, the new regime initiated a brutal campaign to crush the Brotherhood, and members of the Iraqi Islamic Party were forced underground or into exile. In 1971, the regime arrested large numbers of Muslim Brothers, including most of the organization's leadership.[5] The Iraqi Islamic Party was disbanded, but the Muslim Brotherhood continued to operate covertly in mosques and other religious organizations.

Like the Muslim Brotherhood, Hizb al-Tahrir is a Sunni Islamist political party tied to a larger transnational network. It was founded in the 1950s by a Palestinian named Muhammad Taqi al-Din al-Nabhani (d. 1977), and it maintained branches throughout the Arab world. The Iraqi branch of Hizb al-Tahrir was founded by Abd al-Aziz al-Badri in the 1960s. It was never as strong as the Muslim Brotherhood, and it had a tendency to splinter into smaller movements, but it continued to have a significant following when Saddam became president in 1979. Hizb al-Tahrir differed from the Muslim Brotherhood in several significant ways. Perhaps most importantly, it wanted to overthrow the government and was against an educational or reformist strategy. Although it was a Sunni party, it was able to attract Shi'i supporters and cooperated with the leadership at the *hawza* in Najaf.[6] Sunni Islamists in the Muslim Brotherhood and Hizb al-Tahrir would continue to menace Saddam when he ascended to the presidency, but the threat they posed to his Ba'thist regime paled in comparison to that posed by their Shi'i counterparts.

A number of Shi'i Islamist parties were operating in Iraq when Saddam became president. The Da'wa Party was the oldest and most important. Other significant groups included the Mujahidin and the Islamic Action Party. The Da'wa Party, like the Muslim Brotherhood, had formed in the 1950s as a reaction to the rise of communist and leftist movements in Iraq. It had close ties to the senior Shi'i religious scholars in the Najaf *hawza*. The ideas of Ayatollah Muhammad Baqir al-Sadr, which attempted to bridge the gap between Shi'ism and modern politics, became an inspiration and central feature of the Da'wa Party's ideology. The party's goal was to undo secular reforms in Iraq and instead, create an Islamic state governed by Islamic law. Like the Muslim Brotherhood, the Da'wa Party faced a wave of severe repression when the Ba'thists came to power in 1968. However, unlike the Muslim Brotherhood, which remained largely non-violent, the Da'wa Party fought back. It played a pivotal role in several Shi'i uprisings during the 1970s. Then, in support of Khomeini's Islamic revolution in Iran, the party launched a full-scale insurrection in southern

Iraq in the late-1970s and early 1980s. Throughout the 1980s, the party was involved in several violent attacks against the regime and attempted to assassinate senior Ba'thist officials.

Other Shi'i parties, such as the Islamic Action Party and the Mujahidin, were much smaller than the Da'wa Party and were tied to specific scholarly families. The Islamic Action Party was associated with the Shirazi and Mudarrisi families. The Mujahidin were connected to the Hakims.[7] These parties were independent and often maintained slight ideological differences with Khomeini's understanding of an Islamic State. For example, whereas followers of the Islamic Action Party agreed with Khomeini that Shi'i religious scholars should hold political power, they disagreed with his conception of a single scholar holding absolute authority.[8] Nevertheless, they generally supported Iran during the Iran-Iraq War. Furthermore, despite their ideological differences with Khomeini, these Iraqi Shi'i Islamist parties drew inspiration and received considerable aid from revolutionary Iran. In November 1982, the exiled Iraqi Ayatollah, Muhammad Baqir al-Hakim, announced the formation of the Iranian sponsored umbrella organization known as the Supreme Council for Islamic Revolution in Iraq (SCIRI), which the Iranians used to both support and coordinate the actions of Iraq's Shi'i Islamists.[9] These Shi'i Islamists were often prone to violence, and in the Ba'thists' view, they posed an intolerable threat. Unlike other religious Iraqis whom the Ba'thists wished to co-opt and coerce into supporting the regime, Saddam considered the Islamists to be beyond the pale.

The regime relied on its Ba'thist understanding of Islam in the fight against Islamism. Because the Ba'thists interpreted Islam to be an Arab religion and inseparable from the imperatives of Arab nationalism, they viewed the Islamists' tendency to put religious identity above Arabism as a distortion of the true religion. More specifically, they considered Islamism to be an Iranian perversion of Islam, which racist, anti-Arab, Iranian nationalists were employing to undermine the Arab nation. These ideas were not only present in Ba'thist propaganda but also in the secret reports that the Ba'th Party and the security services regularly filed on the opposition.[10] Such reports depicted Shi'i Islamists such as the Da'wa Party and the Islamic Action Party not as Shi'i but as Iranian or at minimum as agents of Iran. The regime's documents almost always inserted the word "client/agent" ('amil) in front of their names. For example, the Da'wa Party was normally referred to as "The Client Da'wa Party," and regime reports claimed that the Da'wa Party had been backed by the Iranians since its founding. As one report argued, "this support aims to make the Da'wa Party a fifth column that can effectively achieve Persian aspirations in the eastern areas of the Arab Homeland."[11] Interestingly, the Ba'thist applied similar logic to the Sunni Islamist organizations, such as the Muslim Brotherhood and Hizb al-Tahrir, which it also referred to as "clients" of unnamed hostile foreign powers.[12]

TRACKING AND CONFRONTING THE ISLAMISTS

The regime began keeping track of the opposition almost as soon as it came to power. However, in the 1960s and early 1970s, neither the security services nor their reports were as systematic or comprehensive as they would become during Saddam's presidency. Thus, although one does find references to the Muslim Brotherhood, the Da'wa Party, and even Baha'is (the regime considered Baha'is to be a Persian heresy and therefore a threat) in its domestic intelligence reports from the early 1970s, they are sporadic and unorganized.[13] It was not until 1978–79—just as Saddam made his move on the presidency—that the reports became more formalized.[14] From that point forward, in another sign of the regime's increasing entrenchment—as well as the centralization and professionalization of security and intelligence services—regime officials were required to file detailed biannual reports on all opposition movements. These reports listed specific activities of each group and were supplemented by reports from local Ba'th Party branches, which gave the exact numbers of known opposition members in each geographical area. These reports also cross-referenced this information with that of previous yearly reports and thus demonstrated trends in opposition activity.

Because the regime had several security and intelligence services acting independently, it could cross-check the reports to ensure that no organization reported false information. As such, the *jihaz al-mukhabarat* and *al-amn al-'amm* both submitted similar biannual reports titled "Activities of Political Movements," or occasionally "Activities of Hostile Movements" (the regime considered any "political" movement to be necessarily "hostile" and would thus use the terms interchangeably). As mentioned, these reports were in addition to regular intelligence reports that the Party branches submitted on the opposition.

Some researchers may be wary of these documents. After all, a system that punished security officials for not finding and eliminating "the enemy" necessarily incentivized false confessions and fabricating records. Indeed, since the fall of the regime in 2003, numerous Iraqis have come forward to explain that they were horribly tortured and forced to give false confessions during the regime's campaign against the Islamist opposition.[15] In many of these cases the defendants were assigned a lawyer who instead of defending them would insist on their guilt and request that the court punish them harshly.[16] These cases probably skewed the regime's records to some extent. Nevertheless, there are good reasons not to dismiss the regime's records altogether. First, the larger narrative that they provide generally correlates with what independent, outside researchers observed during the period.[17] An Islamist uprising undoubtedly occurred in Iraq during the late 1970s and early 1980s. Then, in the early 1980s, the regime violently suppressed it. The regime's records reflect those events. Moreover, the regime understood well that security officials in Iraq had an incentive to distort the records. Such distortions were not helpful to high-ranking regime officials who required a clear picture of what was occurring in the country. Therefore, the regime leadership put in place a system of checks to help ensure that the information they received was accurate.

As mentioned previously, the regime leadership received reports on opposition groups from two intelligence services and the local branches of the Ba'th Party. If one organization attempted to misrepresent problems in its area of responsibility, it would be immediately obvious to the Ba'th Party Secretariat, which reviewed and compared all the reports. For example, because the Party branches and the security services were responsible for maintaining control and eliminating the opposition, no one wished to submit a report that showed gains for the opposition. Occasionally, some officials did attempt to cheat the system. In one report from 1983, a Party official gave the correct number for the active opposition in his area but inflated the numbers from previous years so that the opposition's gains would seem less dramatic than they actually were. The Party Secretariat quickly understood what had occurred, and in a very curt exchange, demanded not just a correction but an explanation on why the discrepancy had occurred. The Secretariat gave the Branch two days to provide a sufficient explanation.[18] The regime's archives did not preserve the outcome of this incident, but one can assume it was not pleasant for the errant Ba'thist official. However unpleasant it may have been for those in the system, this series of cross-checks was beneficial for a regime that desired accurate information. They also help researchers attempting to understand what occurred in Iraq during that period.

CONTAINING THE UPRISING

In line with the regime's wish to downplay sectarianism, the earliest reports on the opposition did not distinguish between Sunni and Shi'i Islamists. For example, reports from the late 1970s had a section titled "The Muslim Brotherhood and other Islamists," which included the activities and the membership numbers for the Da'wa Party.[19] Later, as the Ba'th Party apparatuses and regime security services became more organized and rigorous, they began to distinguish between the various Islamist movements. This distinction was also warranted because from 1978 to 1982, the Muslim Brotherhood and other Sunni Islamists remained only a minor nuisance; but as the Islamic revolution erupted in Iran and the Iran-Iraq War began, the Shi'i Islamists emerged as a formidable force. For example, the reports from these years showed considerable growth (sometimes more than a 20% expansion in membership) of the Da'wa Party.[20] This fact should dispel the notion that regime officials were unwilling to report bad news. At the beginning of the 1980s, the regime faced a crisis in southern Iraq, and its records clearly reflected that.

In response to this crisis, the regime launched a brutal campaign of repression. In 1980, the regime famously arrested and executed Ayatollah Muhammad Baqir al-Sadr and his sister Bint al-Huda. It also assassinated numerous members of the Hakim family, which had produced a number of important Shi'i scholars in the 20th century and continued to dominate the *hawza* when Saddam became president. Six members of the Hakim family were executed, and 100 were detained in 1983. Ten more were killed in 1985; and later in the decade, the regime assassinated Mahdi al-Hakim (a grandson of Ayatollah Muhsin al-Hakim, d. 1970) while he was on a trip to Sudan.[21] Hundreds of lesser known Da'wa Party members were also executed in a mass campaign; and thousands of Shi'is, whom the Ba'thists claimed were Iranian nationals, were deported.

To facilitate this repression, the regime created new legal and procedural frameworks. Perhaps most importantly, the regime made membership in the Da'wa Party a capital offense. These legal and procedural adjustments assisted the security services in their campaign to combat Islamists and Islamism. For example, an Iraqi Shi'i related that he first encountered the regime's repressive apparatuses in 1975. He was attending a religious gathering and one of the other attendees was an undercover agent from the security services. The agent had the entire gathering arrested. Following this first incident, the Iraqi Shi'i was arrested twice more in the late 1970s, but the regime released him because it had nothing with which to charge him. Following legal changes in 1981, the situation was different. It was easier for the security services to charge suspected Islamists and the penalties were much harsher. Thus, when the same Iraqi Shi'i was arrested again in 1982, he spent ten years in prison. He was only released in 1992, probably as part of the general amnesty.[22] He was fortunate to have survived. Many of his counterparts did not. His story was one of thousands of cases in the well-documented battles between the regime and the Da'wa Party.[23]

As mentioned in previous chapters, during this period the regime developed a cadre of officials who specialized in religious matters. With regard to security, Iraqis who were interrogated by the security services noted that special investigating officers "knew all about the Da'wa Party" and "knew the [Da'wa] Party members."[24] The Revolutionary Courts, which tried cases involving Islamists, also had special judges. One judge in particular, Muslim al-Jaburi, was well known to the defendants and travelled all over Iraq to try cases involving Islamists.[25]

Iraqis who suffered under this system gave numerous reasons why they were persecuted. A woman was arrested for writing a letter to her husband in which she included a phrase alluding to the victory of God in an eminent conquest. Others faced harsh consequences when they returned to pray at a mosque after the regime had warned them against it. The regime also targeted young men who attended unauthorized gatherings or who were "considered as outside the Ba'th Party's power."[26]

The Ba'th Party records reveal numerous battles between Ba'thists and Shi'i insurgents, as well as the regime's harsh tactics such as raids on hospitals.[27] Iraqis who were arrested have since discussed brutal torture that included the use of electricity, rape, starvation, and being hung from the ceiling in positions that ripped apart their limbs.[28] Despite the sectarian narratives that have surrounded the regime, much of the torture and fighting against Shi'i Islamists in southern Iraq was carried out by other Shi'is. Some Shi'i Ba'thists loyal to Saddam infiltrated groups such as the Da'wa Party and acted as covert regime agents. For example, one Ba'thist officially left the Ba'th Party in 1980 so that he could "gain the trust" of Islamists. Working from within the ranks of the opposition, he was able to carry out various espionage operations as well as assassinations and arrests.[29] Other Shi'is recount that Shi'i Ba'thists arrested or even killed members of their own family for joining the Da'wa Party.[30]

Though the Sunni Islamists were never as great a threat as their Shi'i counterparts, the regime unleashed a similarly harsh campaign against them. The regime reports showed Hizb al-Tahrir continuing its operations against the regime in Iraq, supposedly with the assistance of its sister branches in Kuwait and Jordan.[31] The regime also feared that the Iraqi Muslim Brotherhood was supporting Khomeini and his Islamic revolution. The state security services reported that religious leaders sympathetic to the Brotherhood did not mention the Iran-Iraq War in Friday sermons despite the fact that all sermon-givers were required to call for Iraq's victory in the conflict. Furthermore, the Muslim Brotherhood instructed its members not to participate in regime-sponsored events, such as the Popular Islamic Conferences, which the regime saw as vital in its campaign against the Iranians.[32]

The regime's response to such defiance was severe. As Osama Tikriti, a leader of the Iraqi Muslim Brotherhood later recalled, the Ba'thists executed large numbers of the Iraqi Muslim Brothers in 1980–81. The campaign against the Brotherhood continued throughout the 1980s. Later in the decade, 72 members of the Brotherhood were arrested, and 52 received various sentences during a major wave of repression.[33]

Nevertheless, these brutal tactics were only one side of the regime's strategy. The regime was willing to employ violence, but that was not its first inclination. It preferred to win over the opposition through more subtle tactics. The regime had a number of techniques at its disposal. In addition to crude methods such as blackmail and threats, Aaron Faust has argued that the regime "advocated including people who might have reason to oppose the Ba'thist State in its activities so as to block other political movements from influencing them."[34] And, as previously noted, Saddam often attempted to gain the loyalty of adversaries through having the regime sentence them to death and then personally pardoning them. Using this technique, he hoped that those who owed him their lives would not actively work against his rule and sometimes would even be converted into his supporters. Saddam felt that by acting more strategically he could eliminate the opposition while at the same time avoid creating even more enemies among the families and tribes of the condemned.

The regime's records show that these less violent tactics had mixed results. On one hand, it was not uncommon for Da'wa Party members who had been arrested and then pardoned to later return to subversive activities.[35] On the other hand, a report from 1984 in which the regime documented its efforts to deal with "fugitives" classified captured opposition members as either "arrested" or "repented" (nadiman). Thus, in the regime's estimation, it was able to convince at least some of its opponents (those who had "repented") to give up their opposition.[36] Other reports presented to Saddam at the end of the 1980s show significant successes in the regime's efforts to win over its adversaries. These reports classified Islamists into four categories: (1) "fugitives," (2) those who have been "sentenced" and were thus presumably in custody, (3) those who had been "neutralized," and (4) those who were performing "patriotic (*watani*) activities" (in other words, they were working for the regime). A 1989 report stated that the Da'wa Party had 3,299 known members, of which 821 were fugitives, 2,051 had been sentenced, 206 had been neutralized, and 221 were conducting patriotic activities.

Thus, although the regime was never able to win over most Islamists, it was able to pacify some, and more importantly, to turn a significant number of them into active agents. Having over 200 Da'wa Party members working for the regime from within the opposition was a significant victory. The regime adeptly employed them to spy on and undermine its adversaries. It should also be noted that similar ratios applied to Sunni groups such as the Muslim Brotherhood and "other political movements that used religion as a cover." However, these were on a much smaller scale. By the end of the 1980s, the Muslim Brotherhood had—in the regime's estimation—been reduced to less than 100 active members 28 fugitives, 20 sentenced, 28 neutralized, and 11 conducting nationalist activities.[37]

Through a combination of violence and these more subtle tactics, the regime was able to steadily gain control over the Islamist insurgency that accompanied the Iranian revolution. Unlike earlier reports, the records from 1982–84 show the number of active Islamists leveling off and even decreasing in some areas. The regime's records generally confirm the widespread independent assumptions that the regime had crushed the uprisings in the first year or two of the 1980s.[38] Nevertheless, the Ba'thists still struggled to maintain control of some regions, especially in the marshes along the border with Iran.[39]

THE ISLAMIST OPPOSITION'S DEMISE

Despite these gains, the regime was only able to limit, but never completely eliminate, the Da'wa Party or other Islamists. The Ba'thist records show that insurgents and opposition parties continued their activities against the regime. Even in the mid-1980s, during the height of the regime's crackdown, the Ba'thists suspected that Da'wa Party members were still working in the *hawza*, and the security services continued to catch young Shi'i Islamists gathering information on vital sites in Iraq. There were constant attempts to assassinate Iraqi officials, especially men from the intelligence and security forces, and Islamist insurgents carried out various bombings and suicide attacks throughout Iraq.[40] One 1986 report from the Director of Military Intelligence even uncovered a plan to assassinate Saddam during a visit to southern Iraq.

The Ba'thists feared that Islamists also indoctrinated Iraqis, making them more susceptible to the propaganda of what the regime termed "the fire-worshiping (*majus*) Persians." To the regime's dismay, Iraqi officials often found Islamists carrying photos of Muhammad Baqir al-Sadr and what the Ba'thists described as "Khomeini the Anti-Christ" (*khumayni al-dajjal*).[41] Even more disconcerting was that, as one report acknowledged, some soldiers fighting on the frontlines during the Iran-Iraq War had been "affected by religious propaganda" and were surrendering to the Iranians as a result.[42] In addition to soldiers, the Da'wa Party competed with the Ba'thists in attempting to win over the youth.[43] Regime officials often discovered graffiti and Da'wa Party slogans on the walls of schools. Da'wa Party supporters would also sometimes write their slogans on small pieces of paper, insert them inside plastic balls, then throw them into the schoolyards so that children playing would pick them up.[44]

However, as significant as these events were, they were manageable. Unlike periods of crisis in the early 1980s, in the middle years of the decade, the regime felt it had established control. This success gave the regime a clearer picture of the opposition and its membership. Thus, although intelligence reports showed an increase in the number of known Da'wa Party members from 1984 to 1985, they noted that this was a result of the security services and the Ba'th Party apparatuses gaining more information, not an increase in Da'wa Party membership or activities. The actual number of Da'wa Party members decreased.[45] In 1986, the reports began to show a substantial decline in the number of Da'wa Party supporters; and by 1987, if the reports are to be believed, membership in the Daʿwa Party was almost half of what it had been in 1985.[46] During this period, the regime believed it had successfully undermined Shiʿi Islamists and its intelligence reports gloated that groups such as the Daʿwa Party had entered a "period of despair."[47]

In the regime's assessment, three general explanations accounted for this success: (1) the most basic reason for the decline in Daʿwa Party supporters was because the regime had "assassinated" so many of them; (2) the regime was successful in its various attempts either to neutralized them or to convince them to leave the Daʿwa Party; and finally, (3) The regime assessed that much of the opposition had fled Iraq.[48] Thus, although the regime was never able to eliminate its adversaries completely, it was able to instill order and reduce the opposition's activities to a manageable level.

This control came at a cost. Despite the regime's preference for winning over the opposition instead of simply executing them, it had nevertheless resorted to widespread violence and killings. This created a problem, as the scale of the violence meant that many Baʿthists—especially among the Shiʿis—had friends and relatives who had been arrested, tortured, or killed by the regime. Saddam feared that the opposition could use this to turn these Baʿathists against him. Thus, the regime was forced to implement policies for monitoring and controlling the Baʿthists who in turn had been tasked with monitoring and controlling the general population. This led to a system of spiraling authoritarianism. For example, in 1987, Saddam ordered a special investigation and assessment of each full Baʿth Party member with a relative who had been executed by the regime. This assessment would determine if the member was at risk of being exploited by the opposition and, therefore, whether he could remain in the Party. A less stringent assessment was conducted on full Party members who had family members sentenced to prison and on those below the rank of full member.[49] Moreover, the regime sometimes made examples of security officials who did not strictly abide by the rules. In 1986, for example, it executed an intelligence officer for failing to report that his uncle and cousins were in the Daʿwa Party.[50]

Having installed an effective system of repression, Saddam then used the end of the Iran-Iraq War in 1988 to further entrench his regime and apply more pressure on the remnants of the opposition. With the end of the war, Iran was keen to maintain the ceasefire, so it became a less welcoming haven for Iraqi opposition.[51] The loss of Iran as a base of operations devastated the already depleted Islamist insurgency in Iraq. The regime capitalized on this situation to crush the opposition's strongholds in the marshes along the Iraq-Iran border. During the war, these regions had been extremely difficult to control. The terrain was almost impossible to navigate; and because the marshes bordered Iran, insurgents could easily flee back and forth between the two countries. Moreover, they could count on a steady flow of supplies and manpower from Iran. The conclusion of the war put an end to that situation. In August 1988, as the ceasefire was coming into effect, the Ba'thists seized the opportunity to reestablish their rule over the marshes.

The regime launched a major operation to "purify the marshes" beginning at 5:00 AM on August 8th and ending "with the last light" on August 9th. As the regime's after-action report stated, "the operation took place under civilian leadership," with the secretaries general of the Party Branches in operational control. Major contingents from the security services, the police, the army, and the air force supported the Party apparatuses. The regime named the operation, "Exploitation of Victory" (*istithmar al-nasr*), as it was meant to capitalize on Iraq's supposed victory in the Iran-Iraq War. The reports on the operation claimed that it was "successful" not only in achieving "direct results" but also in providing "the required deterrence." In carrying out collective punishment, Saddam hoped to dissuade the residents of the marshes from allowing their region to be used as a safe haven again. As such, the regime acted in a particularly ruthless manner. In addition to arresting 43 deserters and 170 suspects, those carrying out the operation also "burned and destroyed" 378 houses, 45 huts, and 516 boats; killed 67 deserters; burned two piles of munitions, one motorcycle, 32 piles of metal, and three barrels of oil; seized huge amounts of ammunition, a car, and a few motorcycles; destroyed four water pumps, one plow, one store of wheat; and so on and so on.[52]

Such operations in the marshes coincided with mass arrests in other Shi'i areas of Iraq. Iraqis claimed dozens of families were uprooted and either imprisoned or exiled to Iran. A Shi'i scholar, Amir Ali Yasin al-Tamimi, recalled that everyone in his town—including himself—who had a fugitive in their family were rounded up on August 18th, 1988. A total of 45 families in his town were arrested with him, his mother, and his sisters. The following February, after months of torture, they were all sent to Iran and told they would be executed if they returned.[53]

RESULTS FROM A DECADE OF OPPRESSION

The regime's overt violence was part of a larger and ultimately unachievable strategy of completely eliminating Islamists, and indeed all independent political influences from Iraqi religious institutions. It wanted to extract Islamists from Iraqi religious life and in doing so, separate them from the general population. As mentioned in earlier chapters, Iraqi counterinsurgency doctrine in the early 1980s was based on Mao's idea that insurgents "live among the masses like fish in water, and when the two are separated, great harm is done to the insurgents."[54] This was particularly important in Shi'i regions. The Ba'thist regime claimed that the Da'wa Party and other Islamists were Iranian agents, but it also clearly recognized that they had embedded themselves in traditional Iraqi Shi'i institutions.

Though the regime preferred to leave traditional religious institutions in place, this outcome was not always feasible. If Islamist influences could not be extracted from a religious institution, it was indeed eliminated. Through a combination of repressing Islamists and co-opting non-political Shi'is, the Ba'thists were able to close many of southern Iraq's independent religious schools. For example, one 1988 report stated that "there were 19 religious schools in Najaf and Karbala until the year 1985 and as a result of the continuous cultural indoctrination, the number of schools in Najaf was reduced to two and they disappeared altogether from Karbala."[55] Moreover, the reports from this period were optimistic that the regime would eliminate or co-opt the remaining independent religious schools altogether in the near future.

Shi'is who lived in southern Iraq during this period have generally confirmed the accuracy of these reports,[56] as have independent investigations by the United Nations. As one such investigation in 1992 argued, "The number of clergy at Najaf had been reduced from eight or nine thousand twenty years ago to two thousand 10 years later and 800 before the uprisings in 1991."[57] By design, those Shi'i scholars who remained were much more likely to support or at least not openly oppose the Ba'thist regime. In addition to such repression, the Ba'thists promoted scholars loyal to Saddam and the Party. Thus, at the end of the 1980s, the Ba'thists exercised considerable influence in the *hawza* and were able to monitor its activities much more effectively.

One can also observe the regime's successes in eradicating Islamist influences in its reports on the Muharram ceremonies. The regime's policies toward these ceremonies during the late 1980s remained largely the same as they had been earlier in the decade. The Party and security services continued to closely monitor potentially hostile elements and prevented people from carrying out "practices that do not fit well with the development and advancement of our beloved Iraq." Designated Ba'thists also continued to hold seminars and worked to "culturally indoctrinate" the Party apparatuses as well as "the popular councils, the citizens, and the men of religion." As they had done in the past, representatives from the Ministry of Endowments and Religious Affairs met with Shi'i men of religion prior to the events to discuss what was expected of them. Likewise, the regime maintained its focus on using "television and radio programs." It did so "by choosing speakers from among the men of religion to explain the historical importance of this occasion and the role of *shu'ubiyya* and the Persians in deviating from the truth as well as introducing practices that are not appropriate for Arabism and religion and that have no connection to history." The only real change was—now that the war had ended—the regime wished to glorify its "victory" over the "Zionist Persian enemy" and emphasize that it was achieved "under the leadership of the Man of Peace, Descendent of (Imam) Husayn, Comrade, Struggler, Saddam Hussein (may God preserve him)."[58]

The real difference between the Muharram ceremonies in the early 1980s and those in the latter years of the decade was not the regime's approach to them or its policies; rather, it was the success that the regime had in implementing its plans. For example, the tone of the reports from the early 1980s was one of concern. They had expressed a fear that "[Islamist] elements which are vindictive toward the nation (*umma*), especially the Persians, continue their efforts to distort Islam, the values of Arabism, and particular Arab characteristics . . ." and that these hostile elements were exploiting the ceremonies to sabotage the regime. Also, the Party had been concerned that it needed to further clarify its position on religion to the people and to emphasize that the Ba'th Party would strengthen "the heritage of the Orient (*mashriq*) for the Nation (*umma*)."[59]

Conversely, the tone of the 1989 reports was much more positive. The Party cooperated much better with other official apparatuses, and together they were able to limit potentially disruptive activities. For example, the "condolence meetings" for men, which in the past had been exploited by the opposition, no longer took place. Likewise, the regime reduced the condolence meetings for women—which were much less dangerous—to a few cases for which it had given special permission. The regime was also successful in controlling the youth more generally, for example, by preventing them from riding around on motorcycles. And, finally, whereas previously the Ba'thists worried that they had not been able to successfully present the Ba'thist views on religion and Islam effectively, by the end of the decade they felt that they were successful in doing so.[60] It should come as no surprise, therefore, that others who have examined the Ba'th Party's files on the Muharram ceremonies have noted that "the regime succeeded in keeping them under control . . . even benefiting from them at times"; and, moreover, "by 1989, the [hostile] practices had almost ceased completely."[61]

Although the regime's policies had larger repercussions in the Shi'i areas of Iraq, it should be noted that they were not targeted solely at the Shi'is. The regime worked to eliminate Islamists and other opposition movements from schools and religious institutions in Sunni areas as well. As members of the Iraqi Muslim Brotherhood have reported, the leadership of the organization was forced out of Iraq. For the remainder of Saddam's presidency, it would operate in exile, mostly in the United Kingdom. Those Brothers who remained in Iraq were forced to conceal their membership in the organization. By the end of the 1980s, the regime reports indicated that members of the Muslim Brotherhood in Iraq were driven underground, and its members were wary even of using private telephones to call each other for fear of the regime's security services.[62] As in Shi'i areas, the regime saw itself in a battle with the Sunni Islamists over the loyalty of the youth. Thus in addition to mosques, schools were an important area of conflict. One regime report from 1989 lists teachers who were to be removed from their positions. A total of 61 teachers were listed, over half of which (34) were dismissed because they were members of or sympathetic to the Muslim Brotherhood.[63]

CONCLUSION

The regime's ability to crush much of the Islamist opposition in Iraq was a pillar of its strategy for penetrating and transforming Iraq's religious landscape. Pervious chapters have discussed Ba'thist attempts to coerce and co-opt religious leaders into supporting the regime. The reduced presence of Islamists diminished the competition that these newly co-opted scholars faced. Perhaps even more importantly, the removal of Islamists opened space for new religious actors, who, as chapter 5 will detail, the regime spent much of the 1980s creating. However, Islamists were never eliminated completely from Iraq; the remnants of the Islamist movements that were discussed in this chapter continued to operate underground. As later chapters will discuss, the Ba'thists had to commit considerable resources toward keeping them out of the public sphere in the 1990s. This fact had significant repercussions not only for the final years of Saddam's rule but also following the American-led invasion in 2003 when the system that kept these movements out of Iraqi politics was destroyed.

Addressing the Limits
of Coercion and Co-optation

B y the mid-1980s, it became clear to the Ba'thist leadership that their policies of coercing and co-opting religious leaders resulted in two major problems. First, they simply did not have enough trusted religious scholars to shape Iraq's religious landscape in the manner that they had hoped. Second, the religious leaders who they had managed to coerce and co-opt were unreliable, and they often subtly resisted the Ba'thist interpretations of Islam that the regime attempted to impose.

THE DEARTH OF TRUSTED RELIGIOUS LEADERS
IN THE 1980S

The regime's strategy of encroachment on Iraqi religious life discussed thus far was fairly successful in limiting who could act as a religious leader in Iraq. This success, however, came with its own challenges—the most problematic being that there simply were not enough acceptable religious leaders to fill the necessary positions. Often the regime attempted to fill this void with secular Ba'thists who could speak intelligently about Islam. The Popular Islamic Conference Organization's secretary general, Bashshar 'Awwad Ma'ruf, has already been mentioned, but he was not alone. The regime's files on Ba'thists who wrote about the Party's relationship to Islam in the early 1980s show them to be secularly educated intellectuals who often specialized in Arab nationalism.[1] Their views on religion mirrored the regime's contorted view. Thus they spoke of religion being "dual-natured." In other words, it was both a powerful tool and potentially dangerous. For example, in a 1983 article titled "The Ba'thist View of Religion," a pair of secular Ba'thist intellectuals explained that although the Ba'th was not a religious party, it was a "movement inspired by Islam, its renewal and its revolution." Yet, they continued, "the dual-nature of religion and the sensitivity in dealing with it in Arab society, especially lately, has caused the problem of religion to be one of the most dangerous problems present in modern Arab society."[2]

Ba'thist intellectuals who wrote tracts such as this were useful to the regime, but only to a certain extent. On one hand they provided the regime with carefully considered ideas on religion. Aware of both the benefits and pitfalls of mixing religion with politics, they skirted a fine line between the two. They portrayed the Ba'th Party as a champion of Islam and the religious opposition as extremists. Yet, on the other hand, the influence of these intellectuals was limited. They taught at universities, attended seminars, and sometimes wrote in newspapers, but they did not lead prayers or give Friday sermons. They were not the custodians of the Islamic tradition, and thus lacked authority on religious matters.

In fact, in the early 1980s, there was a severe dearth of traditional religious leaders whom the regime trusted in Iraq. In the regime's archives, for example, one finds requests to modify the increasingly strict restriction on who could become a religious leader because, as one letter to the regime read, "many of the mosques suffer from a lack of Imams." Such requests were invariably denied, but they provided a clear indication of the Ba'thist regime's lack of confidence in much of Iraq's religious landscape. As a result, it was unable to populate religious institutions with its supporters or effectively propagate its message on religion to the Iraqi people as a whole.[3]

Further complicating matters for the Ba'thists, the Islamic scholars who they were able to co-opt and coerce into assisting the regime had already developed their own views on religion. Their interpretations of Islam did not always coincide with the regime's official narrative of Ba'thist Islam. Unlike scholars who were openly hostile to the Ba'thists, or who refused to cooperate, religious leaders and secular Islamic intellectuals who worked with the regime erected a façade of Ba'thism around a set of ideas that were sometimes counter to the regime's desires.

This phenomenon is perhaps best illustrated by the interaction between the regime and semi-co-opted elements of the religious landscape on the issue of sectarianism. Despite the Ba'thists' effort to highlight their beliefs about Arabism and unity between Sunnis and Shi'is, secular institutions controlled by the state were not the ideal setting to champion such ideas. Narratives of Sunnism, Shi'ism, and sectarianism are closely tied to discourses on Islam. Therefore, the custodians of Islamic discourse (i.e., traditional religious scholars) could offer arguments that were much more authoritative than the propaganda of a secular regime. However, neither traditional Sunnis nor traditional Shi'is shared the Ba'thist desire to minimize the theological boundaries between sects. Doing so was a serious challenge to their creeds.

Nevertheless, with the onset of the Iran-Iraq War, the regime desperately needed reputable Islamic scholars to counter Iran's Islamically themed propaganda. They actively sought the support of Iraq's Sunni and Shi'i Arabs as well as its Kurds. As outlined in earlier chapters, the Ba'thists were especially keen to include prominent Shi'i scholars but had difficulty in doing so.[4] Behind closed doors, Ba'thist officials acknowledged that those Shi'i scholars who were willing to assist the regime, such as 'Ali Kashif al-Ghita', were more symbolic than authoritative and thus not very effective.[5]

The real support for the regime's attempts to appear Islamically legitimate came from Sunnis who despised Iran and often disliked Shi'ism in general. For example, the First and Second Popular Islamic Conferences in 1983 and 1985 would not have been possible without help from Ma'ruf al-Dawalibi, who represented the sectarian Sunni regime in Saudi Arabia.[6] The Saudis ensured that attendees at the conferences included ardently anti-Shi'i delegates such as the director of the Deobandi Dar al-'Ulum in Karachi.[7] Indeed, militantly sectarian Sunnis in Pakistan would emerge as an important international ally for Saddam, even as he attempted to limit the spread of their sectarian ideas inside of Iraq.[8]

Likewise, the Iraqi religious leaders who openly cooperated with the regime were mostly Arab Sunnis. Many of them did not share Ba'thist views of Islam, but they were willing to help Saddam combat what they saw as a Shi'i threat emanating from Iran. Even Bashshar 'Awwad Ma'ruf, who was probably the single most important Iraqi responsible for propagating regime-sponsored Islamic discourse, held sectarian views that senior Ba'thists found very problematic.[9] As an official representative of the regime, Bashshar 'Awwad Ma'ruf was well aware of Saddam's aversion to overtly anti-Shi'i arguments. In public and at regime-sponsored conferences, he normally adhered to Ba'thist stipulations about the legitimacy of Shi'ism. For example, in seminars discussing Khomeini's theory of Islamic Government, he claimed that Khomeini's ideas were "offensive to the Shi'is, to the Sunnis, and to all Muslims."[10]

Nevertheless, Bashshar 'Awwad Ma'ruf secretly despised Shi'ism, and he wrote a number of polemical attacks against Shi'is under the pen name Muhammad Bundari.[11] His resort to a pen name highlights two important points. First, it demonstrates that the regime did not support the propagation of anti-Shi'i views. Hence, Bashshar 'Awwad Ma'ruf could not publish such arguments under his real name. Second, it shows that support for the regime did not necessarily translate into complete support for its view on Islam. This latter point is relevant because although Sunni scholars associated with the regime were careful to pay lip service to official Ba'thist discourse, they sometimes found subtle means to express their true views. For example, books published by Sunni scholars on behalf of the regime in the 1980s sometimes highlighted the fact that Khomeini viewed the Caliphs Abu Bakr, 'Umar, and 'Uthman as sinners who had gone against explicit verses of the Qur'an and usurped power.[12] These views were not unique to Khomeini, however. They are mainstream Twelver Shiʻi beliefs, and such books represented an attack on Shiʻism more generally. Some sectarian Sunni scholars who worked for the regime, and therefore could not express their sectarian views publicly, employed this type of argument as a coded critique of Shiʻism.

On close examination, it is possible to detect these tensions in the way that sectarian Sunni scholars negotiated the fine line between their sectarian beliefs and the discourses that the Baʻthist leadership considered acceptable. At times they would overstep the regime-imposed boundaries but then quickly realize their mistake and retreat back into a safer discourse. For example, the University of Baghdad's College of Shariʻa hosted a conference on "Religious Extremism" (*Tatarruf al-Din*) in 1986. The dean of the college opened the conference by making clear that the discussion would focus on Khomeini's followers as religious extremists who threatened the unity of the nation (*umma*).[13] The speakers then attempted to tie Khomeini's ideas to "fringe" (and in the eyes of the Baʻthists, illegitimate) movements throughout Islamic history.[14]

However, Rushdi Muhammad, who was a professor of religion in the faculty of Shariʻa, took his argument one step further. Citing a more stringent stream of classical Sunni scholars, such as Ahmad ibn Hanbal and Ibn Taymiyya, he condemned the "Persians" for their tendency to form secretive organizations. He then criticized all political organizations based on the idea of the Imamate as an "inherited spiritual authority."[15] This was not simply a critique of Iranians. The essence of Shiʻism is belief in the Imamate as an "inherited spiritual authority." Elsewhere in his remarks, his anti-Shiʻi sentiments were laid bare. He traced the idea of religious extremism back to those who opposed the early caliphs, explicitly singling out the Kharijites and the Shiʻis.

Nevertheless, he appears to have understood that he crossed a regime-imposed red line. He then quickly mentioned something that he termed "Arab Shiʻism." He presented this brand of Shiʻism as legitimate and distinguished it from other forms of (presumably) Persian Shiʻism by stating that Arab Shiʻis were intensely criticized by "foreign elements."[16] Yet he never explained what the Arab Shiʻis believed, or how they differed from other

Shi'is in their opposition to the early caliphs. Most likely, his remarks were simply an attempt to appease the Ba'thists and thus to avoid attracting unwanted attention from enforcers of regime ideology. Again, this episode highlights the problems of a strategy consisting of co-opting and coercing religious leaders. These religious leaders had their own motivations for supporting the regime, and at times they could be counterproductive. In this case, religious leaders who were supposed to promote a Ba'thist Islam that would unite the Iraqi people against the Iranian enemy were instead fomenting sectarianism, which threatened to divide the country and push its Shi'i majority into the welcoming hands of Iranian Ayatollahs.

High-ranking regime officials were aware of this problem. In one 1988 report, the Director of Iraqi Intelligence (*al-mukhabarat*) was particularly concerned about ensuring the "good intentions" of "some of the more zealous among our friends (among academics and men of religion)[17] with respect to Khomeinism as a sectarian, political phenomenon, and to Shi'ism as a legal school within the domain of the Islamic Shari'a."[18] Yet, the regime had little recourse. It did not have alternative religious leaders who could speak authoritatively about Islam.

CREATING RELIGIOUS LEADERS

At first, Saddam responded to the lack of acceptable religious leadership by proposing that Ba'th Party members, who were committed to the Party's ideology, could fill positions in religious institutions. In September 1984, he issued a presidential decree stating, "Party comrades who wish to become men of religion will be chosen with the proper specifications and competencies to perform the mission of influencing the minds of the citizens. This is a Party duty and the responsibility for it lies with the Party."[19] The regime sent appeals to each province, requesting the Party bureaus (*tanzimat*) to nominate "competent" Ba'thists who desired to take part in this "mission." The bureaus submitted lists containing each candidate's name, party rank, birthday, profession, and the name of the departments in which he had worked. Then they were to send the candidates to the

Ministry of Endowments and Religious Affairs for training beginning on December 2, 1984.[20]

However, the Ba'thist rank and file consisted mostly of secular nationalists who were not interested in becoming religious scholars. The responses to this request, therefore, were nowhere near adequate. Some offices wrote back simply stating, "We wish to inform you that there are not any comrades in our bureaus that wish to work as men of religion."[21] Of the regions that did produce volunteers, the numbers were not inspiring. The entire Central Region of Iraq only produced three volunteers: two from the province of al-Anbar and one from Diyala. Salah al-Din, Saddam's home province, did not produce any volunteers.[22] Moreover, the caliber of the Ba'thists who did volunteer was not high. None of those listed possessed a background in Islamic studies. Many were teachers, some were in the military, and some had random backgrounds such as one "agricultural engineer."[23]

By the mid-1980s, the regime responded to these setbacks by adding another layer to its strategy. In addition to co-opting and coercing religious leaders or having Ba'thists attempt to fill the gaps, the regime decided to create its own seminaries to train religious scholars. In doing so, it could address two problems at once. On one hand, it could increase the number of loyal scholars in mosques and various religious institutions. On the other hand, the regime could fully indoctrinate these budding religious leaders with Ba'thist ideology on Islam and weed out those who had other agendas.

The regime had inherited a few institutions, such as the College of Shari'a and Fiqh at the University of Baghdad, and it worked to bring them under its total control. The Party created committees to regulate who these institutions accepted.[24] In doing so, the regime ensured that its graduates who worked in the religious sphere could be trusted. Yet, these existing institutions could not produce enough new scholars to fill the void left by the regime's restrictive policies.

In 1985, the regime tried a different, eventually more successful, approach by creating the "Institute for the Preparation of Imams and Sermon-Givers," which would supplement the existing religious schools.

In addition to producing a higher number of acceptable religious leaders, this new institute also allowed for even stricter control over the students. The regime created a separate, more rigid acceptance procedure that was handled on the ministerial level and coordinated by the Ba'th Party. Thus, this process was administered by officials who were higher ranking than those who handled admissions at other universities and institutes. The regime implemented these additional restrictions, its documents reveal, "to ensure the desire of the student and his loyalty to the revolution."[25] In 1986, the institute began accepting applications for what would later become known as the Saddam Institute for Imams and Sermon-Givers. Both of the applicant's parents were required to be Iraqi (mainly to prevent students of Iranian ancestry) and to undergo an extensive background investigation. Further, the students needed to be graduates from a state high school or an official Islamic institute. This ensured that the regime knew what the students had been taught. No one who had received an education independent of its control could enter the institute.[26]

In 1988, the Minister of Endowments and Religious Affairs, Abdullah Fadil, put forward an even more ambitious plan. He hoped to create a world-class Islamic university in Baghdad. The minister stated that the idea of an Islamic university initially came from the executive committee of the Popular Islamic Conference Organization as well as many of "our friends" who conduct Islamic work to counter Khomeini. These friends were almost certainly wealthy Gulf Arabs, and he affirmed that they had already pledged to support the project financially.

The minister believed that the new Islamic university would be "very useful," as it would "support the political, creedal, and educational goals [. . .] of the Mujahid President Leader, Saddam Hussein, for creating a [proper] understanding of Islam and thwarting the propaganda of Khomeini." It could help to ameliorate both problems that the regime faced in its attempts to shape a religious landscape capable of promoting its strategic goals. With regard to the lack of acceptable scholars, the new university would "create an Islamic leadership both inside and outside Iraq that will spread the proper Islamic understanding of the Arab spirit of Islam." Despite funding from Gulf Arabs, the minister also felt that the regime could maintain tight controls over the university's curriculum. Thus, the "young active leadership" that the university produced would "agree with the ideas of the President Leader (may God preserve him)." This cadre of Islamic leaders would fight "sectarianism, theological particularism, and *hakimiyya* (politicization of religion)[27] that in the near and distant future will threaten the powerful foundations of our intellectual work in the domain of Islam."[28] Thus, the minister believed the university could create a cadre of loyal religious leaders who would be a powerful instrument in fighting sectarianism and the Islamist opposition, while at the same time promoting Ba'thism and legitimizing the rule of Saddam. The minister presented his plan to the presidential office, which in turn requested assessments from the Iraqi Intelligence Service (*jihaz al-mukhabarat*) and the Ba'th Party's Secretariat.

The Director of the Iraqi Intelligence Service and the Director General of the Office of the Party Secretariat responded with lengthy reports. Both reports recommended moving forward with the project; but because they understood that the regime's efforts in the religious sphere were often subtly undermined by Islamic scholars who did not wholly accept Ba'thist ideology, they emphasized the need to have the university conform to "the views of the Party and the revolution in interacting with religion." In addition to fears about sectarianism, the Office of the Secretariat wished to counter critiques of Arab nationalism and socialism that were sometimes voiced by religious leaders. Islamists in particular often described these pillars of Ba'thism as foreign imports, labeling them reprehensible innovations (*bida'*). Thus, the Secretariat's report asserted that the university should "emphasize that the Arab-Islamic civilization is a humanistic civilization that interacts with other world civilizations in a positive way." The Director of the Intelligence Service also cautioned against Islamist views, arguing that it was necessary for any cultural project in Iraq to be conducted "in the general framework and for the purposes of developing nationalism (*qawmiyya*) and to interact positively with the general politics of the state."

Yet, the regime hoped to isolate more than just Islamist and sectarian views. It wished to eliminate all foreign and independent influences.

Both reports expressed wariness about the idea of outside funding. The Director of the Intelligence Service argued that when accepting foreign funding, it was also imperative to (1) "strengthen education policies in a framework defined by the documents of the Party and the revolution," (2) "avoid the imposition of conditions by foreign organizations that offer funding," and (3) ensure that Iraqis are in charge of the budget and administrative matters. The Office of the Secretariat echoed this view, cautioning that financial support coming from abroad must "not be bound by any conditions and have no influence over educational policy."

To ensure that the graduates of the university would fully adopt the regime's ideology, both reports also discussed in detail the methods of controlling students. Most importantly, the regime needed to manage the "conditions of acceptance and define the preparation of the students." The Office of the Secretariat suggested accepting young students who had not yet attended a university. They would be easier to mold, and thus the regime would have less difficulty "building the loyalty of these students to Iraq and the Arab nation [umma]." The reports also discussed the need to develop a plan to keep the students loyal to Saddam and tied to the regime after they graduated.

Finally, the Office of the Secretariat cautioned that it might be necessary to disassociate the university from the Popular Islamic Conference. To be most effective, the regime needed to "prevent any governmental status from being attributed" to the university. Although this was officially the regime's policy toward the Popular Islamic Conference as well, the Office of the Secretariat was concerned that it had become associated with the regime. Hence, the Party Secretariat argued that the Popular Islamic Conference should only be involved if it "does not carry any governmental status."[29]

Following the recommendations in these reports, the regime opened the university later in 1988 under the name "Saddam University for Islamic Studies." It closely managed who studied and worked at the university, and it strictly controlled the curriculum. The regime once again turned to its leading official on Islamic issues, Bashshar 'Awwad Ma'ruf, who was named the university's first president. Although he was also

PICO's Secretary General, the regime was careful not to associate the new university with the Popular Islamic Conference. And despite Saddam's name in its title, the regime asserted that the university was independent.

The system of control that the university implemented was mirrored by the Saddam Institute for the Preparation of Imams and Sermon-Givers. They both focused on ensuring that all students and staff were loyal to the regime and possessed the correct political orientation. Saddam had originally hoped to limit acceptances to the university and the institute to Ba'thists, but this policy was impossible to implement because too few Ba'thists applied. He eventually acquiesced, ordering the institute and university to accept the Ba'thists first and then "clean students."[30] Therefore, the regime only considered applications from students and staff who came from acceptable backgrounds. Their political tendencies were listed either as Ba'thists, supporters of the Party, or independents with no derogatory information against them. No supporters of any other political movement were considered. Additionally, the applicants could not have familial ties with opposition political parties, and very few of them had any relatives living abroad.[31]

Every potential student or employee was required to complete a form detailing his education, party affiliation, relatives, military service, whether he had been in prison, and so forth. One question asked, "Do you have relatives up to the fourth degree who have previously been convicted of involvement in political parties?" Others inquired, "Do you have relatives who live outside the country? Who are they and what are the reasons that they live there? What are their addresses and employment? Was their exit from Iraq legal?"[32] If the university wished to accept a student or offer a staff position, it forwarded this information to the Party Secretariat. The Secretariat then sent it to local Party branches responsible for the geographic areas in which the applicant had lived or worked. The branches conducted an investigation. They filled out another, more detailed form on each applicant. These again dealt mostly with the applicant's political tendencies and participation in the Ba'th Party. They also discussed his level of studies and the political orientations of his family and friends. These forms were sent back to the Party Secretariat, which made a determination about the applicant's acceptability. It then informed the university.[33]

Because the university understood that only politically acceptable students and staff would be approved, it only considered applicants who met the regime's criteria. Thus the Party approved the vast majority of applications it received. However, the applicants also understood that there was a political test involved. Sometimes, if applicants did not meet the regime's expectations, they would lie. In doing so, they could make it past the university's initial check, but the Party would reject them.

For example, one man applied for a minor staff position at the university. He met all of the professional qualifications for the job and the university wanted to hire him. He filled out the form on his family's background and political orientations. He listed himself as a Ba'thist with the Party rank of Advanced Supporter. The university was pleased and sent a memo to the Party Secretariat stating that it had a vacant position and wished to nominate this man to fill it. The university listed his qualifications and attached the form with his information. The Party Secretariat located his local branch and forwarded the package to it. After conducting an investigation, the branch sent the results back to the Secretariat. Not only was the man not a Ba'thist, he had also "refused to volunteer" for one of the regime's pet projects. This Orwellian terminology—implying that volunteering was not voluntary and someone could, therefore, "refuse to volunteer"—says a good deal about the nature of the regime. The Secretariat wrote to the university, rejecting the application. It did not give a reason. It simply stated that "we do not support" his nomination.[34]

CONCLUSION

As will be shown in the following chapters, the Saddam University for Islamic Studies and other similar institutions became the foundation on which Saddam built his Faith Campaign in the 1990s and early 2000s. These institutions were the culmination of a much larger process that Saddam had begun in the late 1970s. The first decade of Saddam's presidency had been marked by the ever-deepening encroachment of the Ba'thist regime into all spheres of Iraqi society. The religious sphere was no exception. However, the "dual-nature" of religion, as some Ba'thists termed it, offered both unique challenges and unique opportunities. Accordingly, upon his assumption of the presidency, Saddam set out both to neutralize the dangers posed by religion and to exploit its potential benefits. Interestingly, he did not attempt this, as many have assumed, by modifying his own view of religion or Islam. Instead, he worked diligently to impose his Ba'thist ideas of religion onto Iraq's religious landscape and attempted to eliminate all who opposed that process. The ends of this strategy were clear (regime control of religious discourse in Iraq), yet the means to achieve it were not always as effective as the regime would have liked. Nevertheless, as later chapters will demonstrate, the combination of the coercion, co-optation, and creation of Islamic leaders succeeded to a much greater degree than has been acknowledged in the literature on Iraq. Consequently, Saddam was able to employ religion very effectively during the 1990–91 Gulf Crisis and throughout the final decade of his rule.

PART II

The Gulf War and Its Aftermath
1990–1993

Continuity and Change
in the Gulf War

On August 2, 1990, Saddam sent shockwaves through the international political system by invading his oil rich neighbor to the south—Kuwait. The crisis alarmed other Gulf Arab monarchies who feared they could be Saddam's next targets. Saudi Arabia hastily requested military support from its longtime ally, the United States. On August 10th, and then on September 5th, Saddam again raised eyebrows in the West by delivering what became known as his first and second "jihad speeches." Western observers in the media and in academia interpreted these speeches as a major ideological shift for Saddam's regime. Saddam continued to make such gestures in the coming months, culminating in January 1991 with his placement of the words "God is Great" on the Iraqi flag. Many outside observers interpreted these actions as a sign that the once militantly secular president of Iraq was now calling for holy war. Yet, as this chapter will demonstrate, these claims have been overstated. Neither the so-called jihad speeches, nor Saddam's other Islamized rhetoric during the 1990–91 conflict represented an abrupt ideological shift. Rather, they were a natural continuation of his regime's rhetoric and of decades-old Ba'thist thinking.

This does not negate the fact that certain developments occurred in Ba'thist methods of instrumentalizing religion during the conflict. Yet, as this chapter will also show, these developments were not ideological in nature. They are better understood as a corollary to the regime's project to bring the Iraqi religious landscape under its control.

CONTENT OF SADDAM'S ISLAMIC RHETORIC

In the so-called jihad speeches of August and September 1990, Saddam did indeed employ religious rhetoric. Addressing the Arabs in the first speech, he declared, "your nation is a great nation. God chose it to be the nation of the Qur'an. After choosing it throughout the various stages of history, he honored it with the task of upholding the principles of all the divine missions and being the preacher and keeper of the principles, values and wisdom contained in them." He then implored Arabs and Muslims to rise up in the name of Islam against the evil infidel armies that threatened Iraq.[1] He continued this line of argument again in his second speech on September 5th: "It is your turn, O Arabs, to save the entire human race, not only yourselves. Your turn has come to show your values and to highlight the meanings of the message of Islam in which you believe and which you practice."[2]

These speeches took much of the world by surprise. Western observers had been accustomed to viewing Ba'thist Iraq as a secular bulwark against Iran's Islamists regime. They were amazed to hear all this talk of God and holy war. An op-ed in the *Times* of London on August 14, 1990, typified this reaction. It argued that Saddam "rose to power as a Ba'thist: that is, a member of a secular, modernising socialist movement within the Arab world." However, something dramatic and unexpected had suddenly occurred: "The crisis in the Middle East did not start out as a holy war; far from it," the op-ed argued; yet, "Holy war came to the Gulf last Friday," on August 10th, with Saddam's first jihad speech. The author of the op-ed found Saddam's religious rhetoric highly unusual. After all, he maintained, "During the Iran-Iraq War, [Saddam] was the object of the kind of rhetoric he is now hurling at King Fahd [of Saudi Arabia]. Until fairly recently, his appeal was based mainly on 'the Arab nation', rather than on Islam."[3] Other Western media outlets ran similar analyses. An article in the *Washington Post* carried the headline: "Once-Secularist Saddam Discovers Benefits of Moslem Piety,"[4] and newspapers ranging from *The New York Times* to *The Guardian* argued that until the Gulf Crisis, Saddam had been the leader of a "proudly secular government," but that he had suddenly turned to Islamic radicalism.[5] Academic treatments of the Gulf War also tended to adopt this narrative, sometimes arguing that "Saddam found religion" around the time of the Gulf Crisis and that the jihad speeches of August 10th and September 5th were a critical turning point.[6]

However, comparing Saddam's rhetoric during this period with Ba'thist rhetoric from earlier periods shows that it was not as novel as it was sometimes portrayed. This is an important point because, as will be shown later, it suggests that the regime's instrumentalization of these ideas were not rooted in ideological transformations. Rather, they were rooted in the development of its institutional capacities to propagate its ideas.

Saddam had always seen Islamic and Arab history as intertwined. Islam, in his view, was the religion of the Arabs. The people and the religion could not be separated. In that sense, the jihad speeches and Saddam's rhetoric during the crisis reflected the same official position on Islam that his regime had articulated since at least the 1970s, and probably earlier. For example, in the jihad speeches, despite all the discussion of God and holy war, Saddam was clearly addressing the Arabs. He began his statements with "O Arabs." The Arabs, he argued, were the "nation of the Qur'an" and had been "chosen" by God. Saddam called on the Arabs to live up to "the meanings of the message of Islam in which you believe and which you practice." It was in this sense that he invoked Islam—as the religion of the Arab people, not as an independent or primary identity. When he did mention Muslims, it almost always followed his call to Arabs.

Similarly, as he had done previously, Saddam depicted seemingly Islamic symbols such as Mecca in light of their role in Arab-Islamic history and not simply as religious symbols divorced from Arabism. During the Iran-Iraq War, for example, official Iraqi propaganda had denounced "the leader in Tehran" for the "abuse of holy symbols in Holy Mecca."[7] During the Gulf Crisis, instead of attacking Khomeini, Iraqi propaganda denounced the Saudis and Americans for their abuse of the city. Very little had changed in this accusation, except, of course, the perpetrator of Mecca's abuse.

Not all of Saddam's militantly religious rhetoric can be attributed to a conflation of Islam and Arabism, but this more ardent Islamic rhetoric was not new either. For example, ten years earlier, in 1981, he had addressed a group of foreign ministers from Muslim states at a summit in Baghdad. On the issue of Palestine, Saddam exclaimed, "The first Muslims had fought under the leadership of our Great Prophet (Peace be upon Him), and after him under his Caliphs and his companions, against aggressive and corrupt empires." He then continued: "As the descendants of those great men, believing in the glorious message of Islam (*risalat al-Islam*),[8] today we shoulder the responsibility of jihad for those principles."[9] Thus, jihad and religious militancy were not new for Saddam. There was no substantive difference between such statements from the early years of Saddam's presidency and his most aggressive religious rhetoric during the Gulf War.

Nevertheless, it is easy to see how such rhetoric could lead outside analysts to question whether Saddam was adopting Islamism. This is even more understandable because some of Saddam's statements in this period seemed to resemble arguments made by Islamist reformers in the Muslim Brotherhood and similar organizations. A key component in the thought of these Islamist reform movements during the 20th century was a call for an Islamic revival based on the return to Muhammad's teaching and the founding generation of the religion (*al-salaf*). Similarly, Saddam lamented that "Islam . . . has been transformed into a state of routine and bureaucracy, practiced by the majority according to the technical device of the minority" and that religious guidance had been "stripped of the . . . basic spirit." Saddam also suggested that the true spirit of Islam should be revived by returning to Islam's roots and by studying "the action of the Prophet Muhammad."[10]

However, a close reading of the intellectual heritage of Ba'thism, and Arab nationalism more generally, reveals that a more likely source for Saddam's views was the Ba'th Party's founder Michel Aflaq—whom Saddam himself claimed was the inspiration for his ideas. Like other Arab nationalists of the mid-20th century, Aflaq claimed that Islam had been corrupted. Therefore, he called for a "reform" (*islah*) of the religion based on a return to the Prophet Muhammad's example and to a proper understanding of the earliest Islamic sources. In the 1940s and 1950s, Aflaq insisted, "all the influence that Islam imparted on civilizations after its conquests is from the seeds planted in its first twenty years," but that memories of this period "had atrophied among the Arabs after hundreds of years."[11] As Saddam would do during the Gulf Crisis, Aflaq bemoaned this state of affairs and drew attention to "the contradiction between our great past and our disgraceful (*al-ma'ib*) present."[12] Accordingly, Aflaq's solution was not to do away with religion but to reform it by returning it to its original state. The Ba'thist revolution, Aflaq argued, "carries the seeds" of this "reform." Therefore, Aflaq maintained that Ba'thism was a "return to a clear and sound religion which is completely applicable to its original goals."[13] As such, Aflaq claimed to rely on the earliest sources such as the Qur'an and the Sunna of the Prophet, rather than on later jurisprudence. Although there was some overlap between Aflaq's rhetoric and certain elements of Islamist thought, Aflaq was a severe critic of Islamism and a staunch opponent of Islamists. Saddam clearly sided with Aflaq in these disagreements, and Saddam's rhetoric during the Gulf War should be seen in light of what Aflaq had espoused in the mid-20th century rather than a dramatic shift toward Islamism.

INSTRUMENTALIZING ISLAM IN THE GULF CONFLICT

Throughout the 1980s, Saddam had worked to neutralize independent religious discourse in the country. By 1990, his regime was fairly confident that it had succeeded. Accordingly, Saddam felt free to promote his views on religion more explicitly. It is important to note, therefore, that the Gulf Crisis does not represent a change in Saddam's understanding of

Ba'thism. The important change—and this is one of the more insightful contributions of the Iraqi archive—is that Saddam felt confident enough to express more openly and forcefully the positions to which he had been inclined since at least the 1970s. This point is critical not only for understanding what would occur during the Gulf Crisis but also during the final decade of Saddam's rule.

Despite the reporting in Western media during the Gulf War, the Ba'thists' references to Islam were not sudden or unprecedented. Previous chapters have already recounted that as the regime gradually gained control over the Iraqi religious sphere, it slowly began to instrumentalize Islam. Co-opted religious leaders spoke out on behalf of the regime and new institutions such as the Popular Islamic Conference Organization produced a range of intellectual content that reinforced the Ba'thist discourse on Islam. By the mid-to-late 1980s, the regime's increasing control over religion in Iraq mirrored an even more overt instrumentalization of it.

Near the end of the Iran-Iraq War, as Ofra Bengio has argued, Saddam "doubled his efforts to harness religion to the cause of the war and to manipulate religion for political purposes." For example, the operation to retake the al-Faw Peninsula was named "Blessed Ramadan" and was retroactively dated to the first day of the Islamic holy month of Ramadan.[14] Perhaps most famously, the Anfal Campaign against the Kurds in the latter years of the Iran-Iraq War was named after the eighth Sura of the Qur'an, which describes a battle between early Muslims and pagans. This fit well into Ba'thist interpretations of Islam because the Ba'thists viewed the early Muslims as Arabs fighting for an Arab religion. Thus, if the modern Kurds opposed the Ba'thist Arabs, they were the enemies of Arabs and of their religion, Islam. The Kurds were, therefore, the modern equivalent to the enemies of the early Muslims in the Qur'an. The regime also assigned Islamic names to its weaponry. In 1988, it began using its own version of the Scud-B missile that it named al-Husayn, after the Shi'i Imam.[15] This, of course, was also a double entendre. "Husayn" referred both to the name of the Shi'i Imam and to Saddam himself. It therefore helped to link the Iraqi president to great Arab-Islamic heroes of the past. In fact, official Iraqi rhetoric often blurred the line between them. In some cases, Iraqi propaganda even began to attribute supernatural powers to, or even to partly deify, Saddam. In May 1988, one Iraqi newspaper reported that an Iranian bombardment had destroyed all the buildings in a particular area. Only walls bearing a picture of Saddam remained standing.[16]

Although these were not the first instances in which Saddam had employed such symbols, these examples highlight how Islam became increasingly prominent as Saddam's regime penetrated Iraq's religious landscape. As the Ba'thists co-opted, controlled, and filled many positions of religious leadership in the country, Saddam began to employ these religious leaders more actively in his political strategies. This control, and the parallel instrumentalization of religion, continued steadily in the two years between the end of the Iran-Iraq War and the beginning of the Gulf Crisis.

The Western press may have been surprised by Saddam's Islamized rhetoric during the Gulf Crisis, but an analysis of Iraq's Arabic media prior to the crisis clearly demonstrates what was coming. The *hajj* season prior to the conflict (in June 1990) was a case in point. By that time, relations between the Iraqi regime and the Gulf Arab monarchies had already become tense. Saddam attempted to utilize the Islamic institutions and networks that he had built during the 1980s to claim the mantle of Islamic legitimacy. For example, on June 27th, Iraq's main daily, *al-Jumhuriyya*, dedicated its front page to promoting Iraq's position vis-à-vis the Gulf Arabs. In this section, the editors included a headline and a brief article about a meeting during the *hajj* between the Saudi-based president of the Popular Islamic Conference Organization and Abdullah Fadil, the Iraqi Minister of Endowments and Religious Affairs. The two Islamic leaders praised Iraq for its support of Islamic activism and thus portrayed Saddam as a leader worthy of respect from an Islamic perspective. That this was included in a section dedicated to undermining the Gulf Arabs demonstrates how the Ba'thists had integrated religious discourse into their international political strategies. The next day, the paper continued with the same theme, highlighting Abdullah Fadil's meetings with his Egyptian and Jordanian counterparts, all of whom lauded Iraq's commitment to Islamic cooperation between their countries.[17]

Earlier in the month, Saddam had addressed a Popular Islamic Conference held in Baghdad, and he had employed the same Islamic rhetoric that would shock Western observers several months later. Saddam welcomed his guests from around the Islamic world by stating that "Baghdad was built by the Muslims and it was founded on a virtuous foundation. . . . It should always be in the service of the faithful wherever they are, and in the service of the nation of Islam." He then launched into attacks on his enemies in the West and in Israel, using Islam and Arabism as his primary point of departure: "For what is this injustice compared to all the injustices that have happened to Arab holy sites, and Muslim holy sites, nay, the believers' holy sites."[18] Thus, despite the attention they have received, neither the jihad speeches, nor Saddam's Islamized rhetoric during the remainder of the Gulf Crisis, represented a sudden shift in Saddam's views on Islam.

In fact, the Iraqi press even published analyses of Saddam's speech that made clear his views on Islam had not changed. One lengthy article from June 29th, 1990, for example, highlighted that Saddam's statements were a reflection of the decades-old Ba'thist view that Arab nationalism (*qawmiyya*) and Islam were intimately linked.[19] These were essentially the same arguments and explanations that the Ba'th Party's founder, Michel Aflaq, had made in the 1940s and 1950s and that Iraqi Ba'thists had echoed throughout Saddam's rule. This Arab nationalist interpretation of Islam may have been a nuanced stance—one that the regime felt obligated to explain over and over again—but it was one to which Saddam was clearly committed, and had been for some time.

Importantly, the instrumentalization of Islam to this degree was only possible because the regime had worked to neutralize independent religious leaders and thus independent religious discourse in Iraq. By the time Saddam invaded Kuwait in August 1990, he had put a system in place to control and manipulate Iraqi discourse on religion. During the Gulf Crisis, as Jerry Long points out, Iraq's religious leaders acted "in concert with the regime."[20] Long continues: "In looking . . . at establishment Islam within Iraq, one quickly notes how its message exactly parallels that of other agencies in government." In fact, the rhetoric of Iraqi religious leaders "reflected both the current wartime parlance of the government

and traditional Ba'thist influence." Further, their "words bear a remarkable resemblance to those of Saddam himself years before."[21] This was
not the result of happenstance. The regime was able to successfully coordinate this messaging through the religious institutions that Saddam
had established over the previous decade. As Long notes, "when Saddam
gave a message on jihad, as he did on 10 August, the Popular Islamic
Conference, the National Assembly, 'Holy Mecca Radio' (a clandestine
Iraqi broadcast aimed at Saudi troops), and Abdullah Fadil, the Iraqi
minister of [Endowments] and Religious Affairs, immediately gave parallel and equally vigorous calls to holy war." And of course, "The news
media carried the same message without deviation, writing editorials that
squared exactly with what the regime had said and done."[22] More surprising, however, were the reactions of local religious leaders throughout
Iraq. In a sign of how deeply the regime had penetrated Iraq's religious
landscape, Long observes that "Religious dignitaries in the provinces likewise supported the regime, and they did so in terms similar to those of
the commission of senior Iraqi ulama and with similar adulations."[23] The
regime also used the Christians it had co-opted in Iraq to garner support
abroad among international Christian organizations.[24]

Saddam was even able to break—at least partially—some of the most
ardently independent Shi'i scholars in the Najaf *hawza*. The Ba'thists
detained Ayatollah al-Khu'i and forced him to issue a pro-Ba'thist fatwa
in August 1990. Al-Khu'i proclaimed that it was not permissible to "seek
support from heretics against Muslims."[25] Of course, the Ba'thists claimed
that they were good Muslims and that their Saudi enemies were heretics.
Even in periods of great distress during the Iran-Iraq War, the regime had
not previously been powerful enough to arrest al-Khu'i or force him to say
anything on their behalf (even something as ambiguous as the preceding
statement). Clearly the regime's prior inability to coerce him had not
stemmed from a lack of desire but rather from a fear of the consequences.
By 1990, the regime felt sufficiently comfortable with its control over Iraqi
Shi'ism to attempt such a bold move.[26]

The coordinated instrumentalization of religion that Long observed
during the Gulf Crisis is also clearly evident in the regime's internal

records. The regime's strategic and operational plans often discussed a "psychological aspect" of the conflict in which Iraq would undermine its enemies by bombarding them with propaganda. In the regime's planning, this propaganda was explicitly designed to "emphasize jihad for God's sake in order to expel the American invaders and their allies," as well as to "create hatred and hostility by all Muslims" for the Americans and their allies. To do so, the regime instructed it officials to "emphasize that the Islamic holy places are being violated by foreign forces who entered the holy land and defiled the Ka'bah and the Prophet's grave." Although these were military plans, they integrated all elements of state power. Religious propaganda was handled primarily by the Ministry of Endowments and Religious Affairs. After receiving its orders from the military, the Ministry of Endowments and Religious Affairs then commanded Iraq's religious leadership into action.[27] In that sense, the regime's documents confirm the deliberate and coordinated nature of Iraq's religious propaganda, which Long and others had observed during the Gulf Crisis. However, before the release of the regime's internal documents, even the most astute outside observer could not have known the extent to which this coordination resulted directly from a decade of coercing, co-opting, and creating religious leaders.

CONCLUSION

The Gulf Crisis was a period of transition for the regime but not of major ideological shifts with regard to Islam. The Ba'thists basic outlook toward religion remained the same throughout the conflict, and—as will be discussed in the coming chapters—afterward. Accordingly, the focus on the regime's supposedly dramatic ideological shifts concerning Islam during the 1990-1991 conflict has been misplaced. Instead, to understand the regime's increased instrumentalization of Islam, one needs to investigate the authoritarian structures that were necessary for Ba'thist ideology to operate. The transformation that had occurred in the regime's relationship to the religious landscape over the previous decade was the key factor in explaining the rise in religious rhetoric. This transformation resulted in the regime's increased capability to control religious discourse in Iraq. Accordingly, what many outside observers mistook for the regime's adoption of a more Islamic outlook, was actually a reflection of the regime's comfort as well as its ability to instrumentalize its understanding of Islam more fervently.

Nevertheless, whereas the increasing instrumentalization Islam in Ba'thist politics was not primarily ideological in nature, it did have significant ramifications for the relationship between religion and politics in Iraq. The regime would lose much of its international standing and financial resources following the war. Many of the policies it had enacted in the 1980s would not be viable in the 1990s. Yet, as later chapters will demonstrate, the religious landscape that the regime had shaped in the 1980s was not destroyed by the war, and the benefits derived from the regime's activation of this landscape during the 1990–1991 crisis foreshadowed the way in which the Ba'thists would instrumentalize religion in the coming years.

Iraq's Religious Landscape in the Wake of the Gulf War

The Gulf War may not have marked a major turning point in the regime's understanding of religion, but the war and its aftermath were extremely traumatic both for the regime and for Iraqi society. Such trauma necessarily had significant impacts on religion and politics in Iraq as well as on the regime's policies toward religion. As this chapter will demonstrate, these changes resulted from shifts in Iraq's geopolitical position in relation to its neighbors as well as to the regime's continued efforts to penetrate and control Iraq's religious landscape.

THE GEOPOLITICS OF WAHHABISM

Although the Gulf War shifted the geopolitical landscape in the region, prior to the war, Iraq had been allied with its Gulf Arab neighbors against the perceived threat of Iran. During and after the war, the Iraqi regime perceived the greatest geopolitical threat to be its Gulf Arab allies. Because Islam had been instrumentalized politically by most of the regional actors, the crisis also sent ripples through Iraq's religious landscape. Saudi Arabia was particularly important in this respect. The modern Saudi state traces its origins to an 18th-century alliance between the Saudi family and the founder of what has become known as the Wahhabi or salafi[1] movement. This alliance between Wahhabi religious scholars and Saudi political rulers has provided Islamic legitimacy for the modern Saudi state, now in its third manifestation.[2] In the mid-to-late 20th century, Saudi Arabia began supporting likeminded or at least sympathetic Sunnis Islamists throughout the Islamic world as a means of influencing regional politics.[3] It is not surprising, therefore, that increased tensions between Iraq and Saudi Arabia coincided with a rise in Sunni Islamist and Wahhabi agitation inside Iraq. For example, shortly after Iraq's invasion of Kuwait, Iraqi intelligence began documenting Wahhabi attempts to smuggle religious propaganda into Iraq. Under interrogation, some of these Wahhabi infiltrators claimed to have acted on the instructions of religious scholars in Saudi Arabia.[4]

Other intelligence reports from the period stated that the "Wahhabi movement" was secretly operating in Iraq and that, whereas their main focus was spreading their creed, Wahhabis supported Saudi Arabia and were known "to use terror against those who disagree with them." Iraqi intelligence also feared that because the Wahhabis were adamantly opposed to Shi'ism and Sufism, they were likely to inflame what the regime saw as dangerous sectarian divisions within Iraq. Furthermore, the intelligence reports noted that the Wahhabis did not fear the regime's coercive techniques or long prison sentences. In fact, Wahhabis viewed them as a necessary sacrifice and accepted them as their inevitable fate. Thus, the Ba'thists found their usual coercive tactics to be inadequate.[5]

Of course, religiously based Sunni opposition movements had existed in Iraq prior to the Gulf Crisis. Iraqi intelligence had reported on other Sunni groups such as the Muslim Brotherhood in the 1980s. The Brotherhood differed from the Wahhabis in a number of ways. First, it was an overtly political organization with a defined structure and leadership. The Wahhabis, on the other hand, were loosely connected believers who adhered to a particular creed. They were not a clearly defined political organization with membership and a hierarchy of leadership. Another important distinction was that although the Ba'thist regime in Iraq often suspected Iran and/ or Syria of supporting the Iraqi Muslim Brotherhood, there was no clear patron–client relationship. The Wahhabis, on the other hand, were clearly supported by, and for the most part loyal to, Saudi Arabia.

Despite this history, the threat of Wahhabi infiltration during the Gulf Crisis was a new phenomenon. The regime's files in the early and mid-1980s mention Wahhabis as a threat, but they only do so sporadically.[6] The regime's more systematic intelligence reports on domestic opposition did not mention Wahhabis or Salafis during that period.[7] Even as late at 1989, documents presented to Saddam only discussed "the Muslim Brotherhood and political movements that use religion as a cover." The documents failed to mention either Salafis or Wahhabis by name. Even though they were not technically a political organization, one can assume that they fell under the ambiguous category "other political movements that use religion as a cover."[8] The next year, that would change. In August 1990, a report prepared for Saddam on the Wahhabis suggested that they were a clear threat and gaining influence.[9]

It is worth mentioning, however, that the problems the Wahhabis posed during the Gulf Crisis were significantly different from those the regime had faced in its interactions with Shi'i and Sunni Islamists during the previous decade. At the beginning of the 1980s, the regime had very little influence over Iraq's religious landscape. Thus it worked to penetrate space that was hitherto outside state control. In doing so, it encountered entrenched Islamists as well as independent and uncooperative religious leaders. Intelligence reports from the Gulf Crisis (and afterward, as will be discussed in subsequent chapters) presented a new problem. Sunni Islamists, and Wahhabis, were encroaching on space that the regime had already conquered. Thus, the Ba'thist strategy began to focus more on maintaining the regime's authoritarian grip rather than establishing it. In other words, instead of working to penetrate Iraq's religious landscape, the Ba'thists began to focus on keeping others out.

Despite some tactical differences in the regime's approach toward Wahhabis, its experience with Shi'i Islamists in the 1980s provided it with tried and true methods for dealing with a foreign-backed religious opposition. Special care was taken to prohibit anyone with Wahhabi sympathies from attending the military academies or other sensitive educational institutions.[10] The Ba'thists also began depicting Wahhabism as heretical and a reprehensible innovation that had little to do with true Islam—just as they had done to Khomeini and his followers in the 1980s. The regime then removed books that "delve into Wahhabi thought" from markets and bookstores. Furthermore, the Ministry of Culture and Information was ordered "to strengthen its censorship of texts which contain the ideas of this [Wahhabi] movement and prevent their circulation." The Ministry of Education and the Ministry of Higher Education and Scientific Research conducted "a survey of the libraries in their colleges, institutes, and schools—especially if they were Islamic." They then removed all "books, especially from this and [other] movements which are not permitted to be distributed." The regime combined these actions with a massive and hitherto unprecedented effort to survey every mosque in the country and to root out all Wahhabi elements. This would set a precedent that dramatically increased Ba'thist control over religion.

The regime's tactics were not just defensive (i.e., identifying and eliminating problematic elements). By this time, it had developed its own cadre of loyal religious scholars who were willing to toe the Ba'thist line. It used them not only to contradict Wahhabis arguments but also to aggressively spread Ba'thist interpretations of Islam. In doing so, the regime hoped to fortify the population against Wahhabi proselytization. For example, the regime ordered the Ministry of Endowments and Religious Affairs to "increase the Qur'an teaching sessions which are under its direct guidance" and to "assign imams and sermon-givers in the mosques to degrade this [Wahhabi] movement and to expose its harmful intentions during their sermons."[11]

RELIGIOUS INSTITUTIONS IN THE WAKE
OF THE GULF WAR

The ramifications of Iraq's move against the Wahhabis and their Gulf Arab patrons went far beyond countering certain theological arguments. It sent tremors through Iraq's official religious establishment. In the early 1980s, when Saddam began actively instrumentalizing Islam, he had done so with the aid of the Saudis and other Gulf Arabs. Thus, several of Iraq's most important Islamic institutions were closely linked to a Saudi–Wahhabi establishment that the Ba'thists now portrayed as heretical.

For example, during the Gulf Crisis, Saddam continued to rely on the Popular Islamic Conference and the Islamic scholars that it brought together. In December 1990, Iraq announced that it would hold a Popular Islamic Conference in which "350 Muslims from around the world will gather in Baghdad six days before the U.N. deadline [for Iraq's withdrawal from Kuwait] . . . in a show of support for President Saddam Hussein."[12] The conference was held as planned on January 9–11, 1991. It should not be forgotten, however, that the Popular Islamic Conference was originally a joint Saudi–Iraqi venture. The Saudis obviously took issue with Saddam's use of the conference to oppose Saudi interests. Therefore, they held their own shadow Popular Islamic Conference in Mecca on the same dates as its Iraqi counterpart. Delegates to the Saudi conference included prominent Saudi scholars, the Sheikh of al-Azhar, and importantly, the chairman of PICO's executive committee, Ma'ruf al-Dawalibi. Unsurprisingly, the Saudi Popular Islamic Conference declared that Iraq's invasion of Kuwait "violated the very principles of Islam," and that religious scholars who supported Saddam were "committing a sinful act."[13]

Another related religious institution that the Saudis had helped create in Iraq was the Saddam University of Islamic Studies. Though this university claimed to be independent, it was originally an offshoot of the Popular Islamic Conference. It enjoyed financial support and religious legitimacy from the same Saudi and Gulf Arab sources. As recently as two months prior to Iraq's invasion of Kuwait, the university remained a joint project between Iraqi Ba'thists and Gulf Arabs.[14] The 1990–91 crisis irrevocably altered that relationship and thus had obvious repercussions for the university's funding.

The university's senior leadership acknowledged this setback in internal correspondences. In the months after the war, the new president of the university, Muhammad Majid al-Sa'id,[15] bluntly stated that it was "suffering from many problems and constraints."[16] Most of these difficulties were financial and material. There were also organizational inconsistencies inherent in the university's original plan. Officially, the plan called for the university to be independent; but in reality, the regime maintained tight control over it. When al-Sa'id became president, he seems not to have realized that this supposed independence was a farce.

To remedy these "problems and constraints," he asked that the Iraqi regime—as opposed to the Gulf Arabs—address the university's financial and material needs. He also requested that the Ministry of Endowments and Religious Affairs loosen its grip over the university's internal affairs.[17] Saddam responded with a presidential decree authorizing a new board of trustees—devoid of the Gulf Arabs who once prominently sat on it—and granting the faculty and staff of the university increased privileges. The decree also ordered an expansion of the university's campus through the construction of new buildings and the commandeering of some existing buildings in the area. Saddam then pledged to provide all the university's financial and material needs, though tellingly, he did not mention the idea of increased independence. The regime would maintain its iron grip on the university until the end.[18]

The prestige of Saddam University for Islamic Studies actually increased after it lost Saudi funding. By all accounts it emerged as an important center for Islamic learning in the early 1990s. As Amatzia Baram has argued, the university's "students were hand-picked and, with a select teaching staff and generous budgets, it was, indeed, an elite school." Furthermore, "when the president of the university needed funds he could go directly to the very top and receive all that he needed."[19]

Nevertheless, it must be stressed that although the university was an important tool that Saddam used to implement his religious policies, it did not represent a new outlook toward religion or political Islam. In fact, the purpose of the university in the 1990s was to undermine Islamists. As its new president argued, one of the primary purposes of the university was to undermine "the intellectual campaign and creed of Islamists." Similar to their Ba'thist predecessors in the late 1970s and early 1980s, the university's leadership continued to view Islam as dual-natured—in other words, as both potentially useful but also potentially threatening. Thus, whereas in 1983, Ba'thist intellectuals had argued that "the dual-nature of religion" made Islam both the "inspiration" for Ba'thism and "one of the most dangerous problems present in modern Arab society,"[20] in 1992, al-Sa'id similarly argued that the dual-nature of religion meant that the Saddam University for Islamic Studies could not be a normal or traditional university. Indeed, he asserted, the Islamic university carried a specific message (risala), "but it is [both] a dangerous and a great message."[21] Thus, it needed to be treated with particular sensitivity. This meant that the regime would make the university a centerpiece of Iraq's political strategies, but at the same time the Ba'thists would devote considerable time and resources to ensure that those who maintained interpretations of Islam that could potentially undermine the regime were kept off of the campus.

In that sense, not only did the university's view of Islam remain unchanged from earlier Ba'thist interpretations, its mission in the 1990s remained the same. Al-Sa'id's report on the university made clear that its purpose was to promote a Ba'thist interpretation of Islam as well as to create cadres of domestic and international Islamic leaders who would support Saddam and his regime.[22] Thus, the Saddam University for Islamic Studies was not intended to empower Iraq's religious landscape but rather to control it.

The fate of the Popular Islamic Conference and the Saddam University for Islamic Studies highlights an important transformation that had taken place in the relationship between the Ba'thist regime and Iraq's religious landscape. When the Ba'thists were forced to decouple these two institutions from their Saudi and Gulf Arab sponsors, they were able to do so with little to no complications. In the early 1980s, the Ba'thists could not effectively operate these institutions on their own. They had limited experience in religious affairs, and there were not nearly enough trusted Islamic leaders to run them. A decade later, however, Saddam had created a critical mass of reliable religious scholars. He also had a bureaucracy in place to control them. Henceforth, he no longer required outside assistance in matters of religion.

SECTARIANISM IN IRAQ AFTER THE GULF CRISIS

Just as the regime's changing relationship with Wahhabis and their Saudi sponsors transformed religious institutions in Iraq, developments among the Shi'is during and immediately after the Gulf War affected the regime's approach toward controlling religion in Iraq.

In the wake of Iraq's defeat and expulsion from Kuwait, the international community encouraged the Shi'is of southern Iraq to rise up and overthrow Saddam. This encouragement was not accompanied by material support, and Saddam brutally crushed the rebellion. In the process, his regime destroyed several southern Iraqi cities and condemned untold numbers of Shi'is to prisons or mass graves. The uprising in southern Iraq that followed the 1991 Gulf War produced a number of myths about the regime's policies and actions. Too often, historians have accepted these myths uncritically.[23] As a result, the standard narrative of Iraqi history usually presents the regime, and Saddam in particular, as shifting to harsh anti-Shi'i policies in the aftermath of the 1991 crisis.[24] The two most prominent myths surrounding the regime's policies in 1991 highlight this point. The first myth posits that regime forces who put down the uprising were motivated by anti-Shi'i sentiments and that they prominently employed slogans such as "no Shi'is after today." The second myth states that in April 1991, Saddam penned a series of seven anti-Shi'i articles in the official Ba'thist newspaper, *al-Thawra*.[25] Scholars of Iraq have argued that these *al-Thawra* articles became the basis of Iraqi policies toward Shi'is and Shi'ism for the remainder of Saddam's rule. Nevertheless, a close examination of these two myths seriously challenges their historicity.

The first myth—that the regime officials who put down the uprising were motivated by anti-Shi'i sentiments—cannot be disproved, but it needs to be destabilized. The facts surrounding this myth are murky. The Shi'i opposition claimed that the regime acted in a blatantly sectarian manner in suppressing the 1991 uprising. However, many supporters of the regime dispute the basic facts of such claims. No concrete evidence exists to support either side.[26] Nevertheless, some circumstantial evidence challenges the idea that it was a strictly sectarian affair. It is true

that Saddam sent his Republican Guard south to help put down the uprising, and that the Republican Guard largely consisted of soldiers from
the Sunni regions surrounding Saddam's hometown of Tikrit. However,
these were not the only regime elements involved in suppressing the uprising. Some Shi'i clans such as Banu Malik of Basra and a clan from the
area of Hamza in Qadisiyya supported the regime and fought on behalf of
the regime to crush the rebellion.[27] Moreover, one of the highest ranking
regime officials directly involved in putting down the uprising was a
Shi'i—Muhammad Hamza al-Zubeidi,[28] and one of the Republican Guard
divisions was commanded by the Shi'i general 'Abd al-Wahid Shannan Al
Ribabat.[29] It is difficult to imagine that these Shi'is were promoting slogans
such as "no Shi'is after today."[30] This does not preclude the possibility that
some Sunni soldiers did so. However, their actions were probably due to a
breakdown in discipline rather than official policy.

The second myth posits that the April 1991 articles in *al-Thawra* were a
major turning point in Saddam's approach to Iraq's Shi'is. The articles in *al-
Thawra* did depart from the regime's official stance on Shi'ism. In some cases,
they seem to blame Shi'ism for the uprisings and the Shi'is for betraying
the regime. The simple fact that they employed the term Shi'i in a political
sense was a deviation from the regime's public and private discourse in the
1980s.[31] That this series of articles appeared in the official newspaper of the
Iraqi Ba'th Party is certainly important, but one needs to be careful about
what conclusions to draw. The articles did not indicate who had authored
them. The Shi'i opposition attributed them to Saddam. Doing so allowed
them to paint him as openly anti-Shi'i and thus to foster discontent among
Iraq's Shi'i majority. Despite the lack of any evidence, Western scholarship
on Iraq has continually repeated this rumor.[32] And because the articles were
attributed to Saddam, most scholars of Iraq have assumed that they were
a major turning point in his views on Shi'ism.[33] However, no evidence has
emerged to suggest that Saddam actually wrote the articles, that they reflected his views, or that they became the basis of the regime's policy. In fact,
a closer analysis suggests that the opposite is true on all accounts.

Iraqis familiar with Saddam's writings have argued that these articles deviate significantly from Saddam's prose in terms of style and vocabulary.[34]

Moreover, in private conversations, Saddam continued to adhere to his earlier ideological inclinations that had a Sunni bias but were meant to transcend the Sunni–Shi'i divide in the name of Arab unity.[35] He does not appear to have had a change of heart with regard to sectarianism. Finally, evidence from the regime's archive overwhelmingly demonstrates that the regime did not adopt these overtly anti-Shi'i views as the basis of its official policies.

Instead of interpreting these events as a shift toward overtly sectarian policies, the regime's internal records suggest that they were the outward manifestations of internal regime struggles over the ongoing process of Ba'thist penetration into Iraq's religious sphere. Senior regime officials were aware that some of their "friends" working in the Iraqi religious sphere during the mid-to-late 1980s held views on Shi'ism that were not completely in line with the regime's official ideology. At times, as previous chapters have shown, elements working on behalf of the regime spread a clearly anti-Shi'i message. However, the regime had little recourse. There simply were not enough religious leaders in Iraq who were willing to support Saddam. Consequently, as long as these scholars paid lip service to Ba'thist ideology and did not openly foment sectarianism, the regime tended to overlook some of their infractions. The 1991 uprising in southern Iraq enflamed sectarian animosity on both sides of the Sunni–Shi'i divide. Some Sunnis saw the uprising as a betrayal of the regime by the Shi'is. In turn, Shi'is interpreted the regime's harsh tactics in putting down the uprising as a Sunni assault. After these events, the regime was no longer able to ignore the issue of sectarianism. Therefore, it attempted to enforce its ideological boundaries more actively.

Following the Gulf War, the most prominent official to make the case against attacking the Shi'is and the need for reform within the regime was the Minister of Endowments and Religious Affairs, Abdullah Fadil. In January 1992, the Iraqi military drafted a plan to deal with the Shi'i insurrection in the south. It included a suggestion that the Ministry of Endowments and Religious Affairs hold a conference in which senior Iraqi religious scholars would counter Khomeini's theory of Islamic Government (*wilayat al-faqih*). The conference would also work to discredit exiled Iraqi religious leaders such as the Iranian based Ayatollah Muhammad Baqir al-Hakim.[36]

The Ba'th Party Secretariat forwarded the plan to Abdullah Fadil. In his response, Abdullah Fadil acknowledged that Khomeini's ideas represented reprehensible Persian innovations and that they were a threat to the regime. However, he argued that in countering the insurrection, the regime had given the Iranians and the foreign media an opportunity to describe the Iraqi Ba'thists as Sunni sectarians who wanted to eliminate Shi'ism. He then suggested that "under the present conditions," the regime should not further "inflame" this sentiment by attacking Shi'i religious leaders. Doing so, he insisted, would only strengthen the Iranian regime and its supporters.[37]

Abdullah Fadil thus subtly acknowledged that the anti-Shi'i views of some Ba'thists were a liability to the regime. The articles in *al-Thawra* were an example of these problematic views toward Shi'is. Far from adopting those views, Saddam would heed Abdullah Fadil's advice. The threat of sectarianism strife, combined with the increased capacity of the Ba'thist regime to operate in the religious sphere, finally gave Saddam the impetus to eliminate some of the problematic sectarian elements within the regime-sponsored religious leadership. Most prominently, he decided that Bashshar 'Awwad Ma'ruf's sectarian inclinations were a liability. Citing Ma'ruf's negative stance on Shi'ism, Saddam stripped him of his titles, dismissed him from his official positions, and then exiled him to Jordan.[38] Other Sunni scholars who had ties with the former ally and now enemy, Saudi Arabia, were also marginalized. Ma'ruf al-Dawalibi (who had helped found the Popular Islamic Conference) and the rest of the Saudi contingent were no longer welcome or willing to help.

The regime also stepped up its efforts to repress sectarianism within the ranks of the Ba'th Party and the security services. In 1992, everyone in the Army received a letter stating that they were not permitted to speak about Sunnism or Shi'ism. The regime ordered the intelligence services to monitor and punish anyone who violated the order.[39] In the regime's records, one also finds incidences of such stipulations being implemented and enforced on the ground. For example, in reports on the Shi'i Muharram

ceremonies during the 1990s, one finds orders to report violations of regime policies "without expressing prejudice toward any Islamic ritual."[40]
In other words, the regime attempted to limit anti-Shi'i statements and
accusations by Sunni Ba'thists who were tasked with controlling potentially disruptive Shi'i ceremonies. However, the fact that the regime felt it
necessary to give such an order suggests that elements of the Party were
"expressing prejudice" when carrying out their official duties.

Following the Gulf War, the regime continued to promote an Islam
that did not delve into "differences in jurisprudence or sect" (*fiqhi aw
madhhabi*).[41] In 1995, Saddam issued a law that required a three-year
prison sentence for anyone who insulted the beliefs of another "religious
sect"; debased their rituals or interfered with the celebrations surrounding
those rituals; destroyed the place of worship of any religious sect; printed
or distributed "holy books for a religious sect that deliberately pervert
their text or change their meaning;" or finally, for anyone who insulted
a sanctified subject of a religious text. The new law was distributed to all
Party branches.[42] In 1997, the Iraqi Intelligence Service overhauled its
"Hostile Activities Directorate," adding sections specifically devoted to
neutralizing sectarianism.[43] The regime was particularly concerned with
Salafis and Wahhabis[44] who preached explicitly anti-Shi'i interpretations
of Islam.[45] These laws and administrative actions were clearly meant to
deal with problematic sectarian sentiments within the regime and among
the general population. To some extent, they were also an admission that
such sentiments existed. In other words, the regime clearly recognized
that there was a gap between its intentions (as defined by senior Ba'thist
officials) and the actions of its representatives on the ground. This was an
admission that violated Ba'thist axioms rejecting the existence of sectarian
divides in Arab society, and it was something that Saddam had been unwilling to acknowledge openly in previous periods.

Ba'thists also maintained their taboo against depicting the opposition to their rule as "Shi'i." Instead, Shi'is who opposed the regime were
described either as ethnic Persians, as religious radicals, or as lower
classes who rejected modernity. The regime's most common term for Shi'i
dissidents was "*shu'ubii*," which described adherents of a medieval, mostly

Persian sect that accepted Islam but resented Arab dominance of the religion. In the modern period, Arab nationalists adopted the term to describe their opponents. The regime's documents also describe Shi'is who rejected its interpretation of Islam as "sectarian," "extremist," or those who "practice politics under the guise of religion." Shi'is were also described as "backwards," "poor," and people who perform "obsolete" practices. However, although these term were sometimes used as euphemisms for Shi'is by sectarian Sunni officials not able to express their views openly, they were not simply code words for Shi'is. In fact, some terms that are normally understood to be tinged with sectarian undertones were used by the regime to describe both Sunnis and Shi'is. For example, Saddam also used the term *shu'ubii* to describe Sunni Islamists.[46] Conversely, the term *takfiri* is normally associated with Sunni extremists who excommunicate other Muslims, but the regime also used it to describe Shi'i Islamists who considered the Ba'thist regime to be un-Islamic.[47]

This ambiguity makes clear that despite some blatantly anti-Shi'i views—such as those expressed in the *al-Thawra* articles after the uprisings in the south—the regime did not view its policies as those of a Sunni regime. In fact, it saw itself in exactly the opposite terms. It worked to repress both Sunni and Shi'i sectarianism and tried to carve out a place for itself between different tendencies that it represented as errant and extremist. Thus, the regime attempted to eliminate Salafism among Sunnis at the same time as attacking Shi'i sectarianism. Moreover, in the 1990s, the regime did not treat Shi'is simply as Shi'is. The Ba'thists differentiated between those who had helped the regime in 1991 and those who did not.[48] To add further nuance, the regime distinguished between those who took part in the uprising against the regime and those who simply looted, as well as between those who fled to Iran to escape the violence and then returned, and those who did not return.[49] Interestingly, the regime also implicated some Sunnis in the uprisings. These Sunnis suffered the same grim fate as their Shi'i counterparts.[50] As such, even in the aftermath of the 1991 uprising, the regime's policies were intended to treat Shi'is as individuals and as members of families and tribes rather than as a sect.

It should be noted, however, that this increased attention Saddam afforded to sectarianism did not temper the regime's anti-Iranian views or the tenuous line it drew between acceptable Shiʻism and unacceptable "Persian" or sectarian practices. As in the past, the regime's hope to transcend sectarian divisions was plagued by Sunni biases that undercut its attempt to present its policies as a type of ecumenism. The Baʻthists claimed that although they opposed Persian influences in Iraq, they had no problem with Shiʻism. However, they considered certain mainstream Shiʻi practices, such as marching on foot during the month of Muharram, as abominable "Persian" innovations. As such, policies that the regime intended to be anti-Persian or anti-Islamist were perceived by most Shiʻis as sectarian.

Further Sunni biases can be found elsewhere in the regime's practices. For example, although lessons on Islam Iraqi schoolbooks during the 1990s paid a great deal of respect to Shiʻi figures such as Imam ʻAli and his sons, they never openly contradicted Sunni beliefs. By contrast, the books venerated the so-called Rightly Guided Caliphs, whom Sunnis consider legitimate, but the first three of whom are illegitimate usurpers in the Shiʻi tradition.[51] This type of bias was also evident in training material for Baʻth Party cells.[52]

As such, the Baʻth Party promoted a generic Arab nationalist Islam that was often by default more Sunni than Shiʻi. However, it is incorrect to assert that regime became more sectarian in the wake of the Gulf Crisis. These biases had always existed. If anything, the regime more actively clamped down on open expressions of sectarianism in the 1990s as a divisive and potentially destabilizing force.

CONCLUSION

Although the transformation that occurred in the regime's relationship to the Iraqi religious landscape following the Gulf Crisis was not ideological in nature, it did have a lasting impact on religion and politics in Iraq. The threats to the regime that emerged in this period, especially from

Wahhabis, would be a central concern for the Ba'thists throughout the last decade of their rule. Similarly, adjustments that the regime made in its policies toward sectarianism would guide it over the next decade. The regime channeled it strategies to address these and other religious issues through institutions, which outside actors had assisted to develop, but that it now completely controlled. These institutions would become the foundation of what Saddam termed his national "Faith Campaign," lasting from 1993 until the fall of the regime.

PART III

The Faith Campaign
1993–2003

A Transformed Religious Landscape

The 1991 war significantly transformed Iraqi state–society relations. Most dramatically, the regime largely lost control over the Kurdish regions in the north. Within the Arab regions, state–society relations were also dramatically altered. Of particular interest to this book, the regime related to the religious landscape in the Arab regions still under its control differently than it had in earlier decades. Over the past few years, the regime's internal archives forced scholars or Iraq to rethink state-society relations in Iraq. Along the same line, the relationship between religion and state in Iraq during the 1990s also needs to be reexamined.

By the 1990s, the Ba'thists were able to reap the fruits of their efforts to construct an Iraqi religious leadership that was loyal to their regime. The regime never gained absolute control over every religious leader, and religiously motivated resistance to Saddam continued to bubble under the surface. However, after two decades in power, the Ba'thists had enough control over the religious landscape to implement their policies effectively. They had filled a critical mass of mosques with co-opted—or at minimum, compliant—religious leaders, and almost all religious institutions were now firmly rooted in the regime's authoritarian system. This cadre of trusted religious leaders would play an indispensable role in Iraqi policies toward religion during the 1990s and early 2000s.

However, before outlining how a co-opted religious landscape functioned and its effect on the regime's policies, it is important to re-emphasize how the regime constructed such a landscape. First and fore-most, it was not the result of a shift in rhetoric or symbols. It was not created with new interpretations of religion, nor by speeches or propa-ganda. As previous chapters have made clear, it was created by having the right people, institutions, and bureaucracy in place. Creating this system was a long, arduous process, carried out by countless officials, to co-opt, coerce, and create religious landscape that would be capable of contributing to the Ba'thists' political goals.

The result of this process was a shift in the manner that the regime re-lated to the religious landscape. Whereas previously the regime was dis-trustful and therefore cautious when employing the religious landscape to achieve political goals, by the 1990s, the regime felt much more comfort-able with its level of control over Iraqi religious leaders and therefore it was much less restrained in instrumentalizing religion in its public policies. Following the Gulf War, the regime lost much of its financial resources and traditional forms of power due to harsh international sanctions. However, it was able to compensate for these fiscal constraints by relying on the large cohort of trusted religious leaders that it had coerced, co-opted, and created since the late-1970s. These religious leaders performed some of the functions previously carried out by the state. In other words, the re-gime responded to the fiscal constraints of the 1990s by replacing certain costly state apparatuses with loyal elements within the religious landscape.

Saddam's deputy, Izzat Ibrahim al-Duri, organized trusted religious scholars to participate in what the regime termed "voluntary popular religious supervision." The primary goal of this project was for the reli-gious scholars to "treat condemnable phenomena in society." The program specifically combated theft, bribery, extortion, and other social ills. The regime also expected these religious leaders to instill a sense of "integ-rity" and "duty" in state employees as well as foster respect for the regime's leadership among the general population. In that sense, the regime turned to religious leaders to perform functions that teachers, police, and state-run media had carried out in the past.

However, these religious scholars were not independent from the regime. The regime organized them into committees to "create a system for supervising" the people. These committees were designed to "benefit from the existing popular structures and the [security] services that specialize in monitoring [the population]." They also worked closely with the Ministries of Endowments and Religious Affairs, Justice, Interior, Labor, and Society. In other words, these religious leaders were loyal to the regime and deeply enmeshed in its authoritarian structures.[1] The main benefit that this so-called voluntary popular religious supervision provided was, as Saddam's Presidential Office made clear, it did not cost any money. The religious leaders who implemented this plan had been indoctrinated into the Ba'thist system and saw their participation as a duty of patriotic religious leaders in Iraq.[2] Such strategies allowed the state to withdraw services from some areas while mitigating the regime's loss of control over Iraqi society.

The relationship between the state's withdrawal in some areas and the empowering of an entrenched cadre of co-opted religious leaders has been completely overlooked in the secondary literature on 1990s Iraq. The historiography of Iraq in this period tends to portray the Iraqi Ba'th Party (and thus the regime itself) as in uncontrolled retreat. Because the Iraqi Ba'thists were isolated internationally and weakened by sanctions, the secondary literature on Iraq has depicted them as unable able to control large segments of the Iraqi population. As a result, many analysts claimed, the regime began to permit—or was unable to prevent—the opening of "autonomous social spaces" as well as discussions of topics once considered taboo.[3] Importantly, this narrative of the regime's loss of control often focuses on mosques and other religious establishments. The secondary literature on Iraq depicts the religious landscape as beginning to function independently from the regime.[4] Some have even argued that in the 1990s, "grassroots religious leaders" began to emerge in Iraq's new mosques and the Saddam University for Islamic Studies. Thus, the mosques were out of the regime's control and "inside their [the mosques'] walls, people could feel free."[5] Other academic accounts of the period portray an opening of religious discourse in Iraq, a new found freedom for Iraqi religious leaders, and even an openness to once taboo ideas such as Islamism.[6]

The regime's internal documents challenge this narrative. Certainly, there was a groundswell of religious observance in Iraq in this period, as there was throughout the Middle East. The Faith Campaign was at least partially a reaction to this increased religiosity, but there is no evidence in the archives to suggest that the regime acquiesced to newly independent religious leaders, or that such an acquiescence explains the Faith Campaign. Throughout the 1990s, the regime maintained detailed records on the political loyalty of every Iraqi religious leader in every mosque. The national surveys the Ba'thists used to track such data will be discussed in more detail in the following chapters, but for now it is worth mentioning that by 1995, the regime considered only 70 out of 1,501 religious leaders in the Iraq to be problematic. As Aaron Faust has argued, these numbers demonstrate that the Ba'thists "succeeded in filling religious posts throughout the country with loyalists and purging Islamists, both Shi'i and Sunni."[7]

In addition to the regime's records, independent sources have noted that by the end of Saddam's rule, some of the most ardent religious opposition began to work with the regime. For example, Muhsin abd al-Hamid was one of the last leaders of the Iraqi Muslim Brotherhood to avoid exile, prison, or death. He remained in Iraq throughout Saddam's presidency. However, he was eventually arrested and tortured in the mid-1990s. It is unclear how or why he was released from prison, but by the end of Saddam's rule, he was actively contributing to regime-sponsored propaganda against other Islamic leaders.[8]

Clearly, some religious leaders in the country disagreed with Ba'thist policies on religion, and some of these leaders were able to slip through the cracks of the regime's authoritarian system. For example, the Salafi scholar Subhi al-Samarrai held positions in the regime's religious institutions during the Faith Campaign. However, al-Samarrai and others like him were forced to hide their true beliefs from the Ba'thists. Following al-Samarrai's death, one of his closest students wrote that he had studied Salafi texts with him in the 1990s but that he did so in secret because "at that time those books were forbidden. Those who possessed them were imprisoned by Saddam's regime and were exposed to danger."[9] In another instance, Ibrahim al-Badri, who would later gain fame as the leader of Islamic State under the name Abu Bakr al-Baghdadi, managed to obtain degrees in Islamic studies in Baghdad despite having hardline salafi and, according to some, even jihadist tendencies.[10] However, the future leader of the Islamic State had two uncles who served in the Iraqi security services, and his family was closely connected to the regime. This probably allowed him to pass the security checks when he applied to study Islam at regime-controlled universities even if he possessed problematic ideological inclinations.[11]

Proponents of salafism (let alone salafi-jihadists) could not openly practice their version of Islam in Saddam's Iraq. Iraqis certainly were not "free" inside the walls of mosques. Those with problematic views who survived did so through a combination of secrecy and regime connections. However, they clearly existed below the surface in Saddam's Iraq—a fact that would become very important following the regime's demise in 2003, when the security apparatuses that were designed to suppress them suddenly evaporated.

This depiction of the regime strength in relation to Iraq's religious landscape in the 1990s complements recent scholarship on Iraq that has used the regime records to challenge previous assertions about the Ba'thist regime's demise during this period. For example, Joseph Sassoon argues, "we now know from the archives that the Ba'th Party did not weaken in the 1990s: no committee was ever set up without a representative of the party secretariat, and membership increased by roughly 38% between 1991 and 1996."[12] Sassoon explains earlier misperceptions by distinguishing the Iraqi state from the Ba'th Party. He claims that the state weakened and that outside observers mistook this for the weakening of the ruling Party. It is undeniable that the state lost many of its economic resources in the 1990s. It could no longer (or at least chose not to) fund basic services, let alone the large economic development projects of earlier decades. This weakened the regime's position considerably, as it could not offer as many incentives to Iraqi society.

However, one should not assume—as has been the case in much of the historiography up until this point—that these diminished financial resources led to the regime's inability to control the Iraqi population. If the Ba'thist regime was weakened in that it lost the ability to provide lavish incentives and new development projects, it often made up for it in other ways. Fear, of course, played a role. Yet, fear was only the most overt component of a system that relied on entrenched loyalists who occupied almost all positions of authority. This was especially true in the religious landscape where trusted religious leaders—not independent or Islamist religious leaders—formed the foundation of Iraqi policies during the 1990s.

THE FAITH CAMPAIGN'S ROOTS IN BA'THIST AUTHORITARIANISM

The religious landscape that the Ba'thist regime had created during the 1970s and 1980s proved remarkably durable. The Gulf War in 1991 destroyed much of Iraq's infrastructure and depleted its finances, but it did not replace the hundreds of religious leaders that the regime had coerced, co-opted, and created over the past decades. Previous chapters have highlighted Saddam's elimination of independent and hostile religious leaders. This process climaxed in the wake of the 1991 Gulf War when mass uprisings engulfed Iraq, especially, but not only, in the Shi'i south. The regime's cleansing of undesirable elements in Iraq's religious landscape during the uprising provided the Ba'thists with an opportunity to continue rebuilding Iraqi Islam in accordance with their designs. Indeed, the regime intensified its policy of placing regime loyalists in almost every significant position of authority.

The Ba'thists' construction of a religious landscape that was willing to work toward the regime's goals also had significant repercussions for the regime's public policies and particularly the willingness of Saddam to employ Islam in the public sphere. In June 1993, Saddam announced a national "Faith Campaign" with great fanfare. Commemorating its launch, he delivered grandiose speeches amidst the pomp of expansive official ceremonies. The tightly controlled Iraqi press highlighted these events on the front pages of newspapers and in the broadcast news.[13] The inauguration of the Faith Campaign began a steady proliferation of regime-sponsored religion in Iraq. Some observers understood this as evidence that Saddam had shifted course, foregoing his Ba'thist roots and instead attempting to ride the rising tide of Islamism.[14] This claim also needs to be reconsidered.

In the 1990s, Ba'thized religious officials in Iraq continued to champion the same interpretation of religion that Saddam had articulated at the beginning of his presidency. Indeed, behind closed doors, the regime's outlook toward religion during the 1990s appeared remarkably similar to its outlook in the late 1970s and early 1980s. In both cases, Ba'thists highlighted that they were believers in God. They depicted Islam as the embodiment of Arabism, and they often blurred the lines between the two. Throughout Saddam's presidency, the Iraqi Ba'thists maintained the propensity and even the desire to employ these Ba'thist interpretations of religion politically—*as long as they could do so without jeopardizing the regime's security or legitimacy*. In the early 1980s, the regime's lack of control over Iraq's religious landscape meant that they could not do so. By the 1990s, however, the Ba'thist leadership felt comfortable that a critical mass of Iraqi religious leaders would propagate the "correct" message. The rising religiosity of Iraqis during this period certainly provided extra incentive to launch the Faith Campaign, but it ultimately resulted from a change in means, not in intent or ideology. Thus the point of the Faith Campaign was not to shift away from a Ba'thist understanding of religion but rather to accelerate the spread of this interpretation of religion throughout Iraqi society.

Its policies toward religious leaders were similar to the manner in which the regime treated other intellectuals. Eric Davis, for example, argues that the Ba'thists attempted to employ "organic intellectuals" to "promote a worldview designed to delegitimize and marginalize alternative and competing political frameworks by stigmatizing their core assumptions."[15]

Similarly, the regime expected Ba'thized religious leaders to play an "organic" role so as to "delegitimize and marginalize alterative and competing" religious interpretations—particularly those put forth by Islamists. Thus, Iraqi religious leaders presented Ba'thism, and Arab nationalism more generally, as "natural" and in line with "normal" interpretations of religion.

The regime's ability to shape Iraq's religious discourse in the 1990s was based on policies that Saddam had implemented a decade earlier. As outlined in previous chapters, Saddam had co-opted religious leaders who had previously opposed, or were indifferent to, his regime. These co-opted religious leaders supplemented, and to some extent conferred legitimacy on, a wave of new, fully Ba'thized Islamic scholars that the regime developed in the religious institutions it had established in the 1980s. These institutions were explicitly designed, in the language of the regime's plans, to "create an Islamic leadership" designed to "spread the proper [Ba'thist] Islamic understanding of the Arab spirit of Islam." As such, the regime used them to produce a "young active leadership" that would "agree with the ideas of the President Leader."[16]

This "young active leadership" was the necessary foundation of the regime's policies during the Faith Campaign. It was no coincidence, therefore, that Saddam's announcement of the Faith Campaign occurred the same week as the first cohort graduated from Saddam University for Islamic Studies.[17] Ba'thist policies during this period explicitly ordered that "the graduates of the religious colleges be placed [in the mosques and religious institutions]." The regime's documents also made the reasons for such policies unambiguous. In short, these graduates could be trusted "in light of the close evaluation [they have undergone] to assess their loyalty to the Party and the revolution." The policy of populating Iraq's religious institutions with regime loyalists was accompanied by its inverse, namely, that "absolutely no permission is to be given to sermon-givers who are not officially licensed to give sermons in mosques." To be officially licensed, one had to "obtain permission from the security services and the Party." This process was designed to establish the "intellectual integrity" (i.e., adherence to Ba'thist interpretations of Islam) of religious leaders and ensure that they had a "political background similar to other important [state] employees."[18] As will be demonstrated in the following chapters, the regime tirelessly enforced these policies until its demise in 2003.

Such policies clearly establish the link between the availability of Ba'thized religious scholars and the Faith Campaign's goal of spreading Islam. In that sense, the role of Saddam University for Islamic Studies and similar institutions should not be understated. Not only did they provide a cohort of scholars who had been through strict background checks and passed numerous ideological hurdles—these institutions were also a means of tracking students after they graduated. The university's administrators and security service personnel continued to monitor graduates and maintained lists of scholars that they trusted. When the regime needed Islamic leaders for a new project associated with the Faith Campaign, these institutions would send lists of former students to the Ba'th Party Secretariat, noting those who could be trusted—or in the regime's jargon, those who possessed "intellectual integrity"—and those who did not.

Of course, the students' mere presence in these schools meant that they had already cleared a rigorous background check. Therefore, it is not surprising that most of them were deemed trustworthy. However, the various institutes and universities would sometimes change their opinions about some students during the process of their studies. For example, one list of former students compiled in 1996 contained 957 names of students who had "intellectual integrity" and a separate list of 65 students who did not. The 65 students who did not pass muster were then prevented from holding any position in the religious landscape.[19]

CHANGES IN THE RELIGIOUS LANDSCAPE

These new institutions for Islamic studies transformed Iraq's religious landscape in several ways. Clearly, they altered the political ideology of the religious leadership in the country. However, the changes did not end there. Ba'thists often looked down on the "traditional" students who had previously pursued Islamic education at higher levels. In 1992, the president of Saddam University for Islamic Studies bemoaned the fact that 90% of the university's applicants came from students in the religious studies system rather than the secular state schools. He maintained that it was obvious to everyone that students from the religious system were inferior because they generally came from the poorest and most undeveloped sectors of society. In his opinion, they did not meet the standards of students in other fields. Thus, under the guise of increasing the quality of students, he limited the number of these traditional students to a maximum of 50% of the student body.[20] The remaining students needed to have graduated from the modern, secular state schools.[21]

As such, Saddam University for Islamic Studies was not intended to empower the traditional religious class. The traditional class of Islamic leaders relied on a network of religious schools and mosques often found in the countryside or in urban slums. They dressed in non-Western clothing and they continued to live according to tribal and religious customs. Conversely, the Ba'th Party's traditional center of support was in a newly urbanized middle class that had embraced a narrative of modernity but also rejected atheism.[22] As such, they were inclined to promote religious belief, but they often distrusted the traditionally minded students of religious schools. The regime hoped to replace traditional religious leaders by training a new type of religious student whom it deemed both more trustworthy and better able to meet the Ba'thists' political needs. The new graduates came from the Ba'th Party's traditional centers of support in the urbanized middle class but would have the religious pedigree that accompanied a degree from an Islamic university. Through such subtle shifts in policy, Ba'thists were able to dress their supporters in the garb of traditional religious leaders and insert them into the religious sphere.

In that sense, one finds different types of religious leaders heading the regime's Islamic institutions in the 1990s. In the 1980s, as detailed in earlier chapters, the regime often relied on Ba'thists who possessed modern-secular educations. These officials often held an academic specialization in Islam or Islamic history, but they were not traditionally trained Islamic scholars. Bashshar 'Awwad Ma'ruf epitomized this phenomenon. He had received a secular education in Iraq and Germany and was then appointed as the Secretary General of the Popular Islamic Conference in the early 1980s and was the inaugural president of Saddam University for Islamic Studies later in the decade. Tellingly, he wore a suit and no head covering. In contrast, by the mid-1990s, one finds people like Abd al-Razzaq al-Sa'adi and Abd al-Latif al-Humayyim—both of whom wore the garb of Islamic scholars and possessed more traditional Islamic educations—leading institutions such as the Popular Islamic Conference. By this period, the regime had Ba'thized large portions of Iraq's religious landscape as well as the educational institutions that produced religious leaders. Therefore, it could present the Iraqi people with Ba'thized Islamic leaders who looked the part and had the background one expected of a religious authority. Yet, although the garb of these leaders may have changed, the Ba'thist interpretations of Islam that they preached—as will be demonstrated in the following chapters—did not undergo a fundamental change.

It is not clear to what extent religious scholars in Iraq comprehended the system in which they found themselves; but by the 1990s, they could clearly no longer operate outside it. Certainly leaders such as Abd al-Razzaq al-Sa'adi and Abd al-Latif al-Humayyim understood the regime's goals and their roles in accomplishing them. But as Joel Migdal has argued, "social control" by a regime can range from "legitimation" and "participation" to simply "compliance."[23] The Ba'thists obviously preferred religious leaders in the first category, and the most prominent Ba'thist religious scholars clearly fell within it. However, other Islamic actors in Iraq were simply compliant. The regime's efforts to discover whether a religious leader was compliant were often intrusive and sometimes violent. These efforts included constant surveillance and harsh interrogations. Yet, once the regime felt comfortable that a religious leader was at minimum compliant—and was not a Salafi, Wahhabi, or Islamists—then it could take a softer approach. Thus, the process of establishing control over the religious landscape in the 1970s and 1980s was more violent than simply maintaining that control. This could easily be misinterpreted by religious leaders who were not privy to the regime's thinking. From their standpoint, the regime was more invasive in earlier periods and then had let up. In fact, the opposite was true. The deeper the regime penetrated the religious landscape, the less it needed to resort to violence.

The multiple layers of security sometimes also obfuscated communication both between the regime and Iraqi society, and within the regime itself. The additional restrictions that the regime imposed on all religious matters could sometimes become quite burdensome. For example, the president of Saddam University for Islamic Studies noted in 2001 that "our university applies special controls in making appointments." But he complained that the multistage security check that was at the center of these special controls took too long. It impeded the university from hiring necessary administrative staff in a timely manner.[24]

The security checks and secrecy surrounding all matters dealing with religion meant that one part of the regime sometimes had no idea what the others parts were doing. This confusion often had severe consequences for religious scholars. In one case from 1997, a group of Sunni imams from al-Anbar Province had been banned from preaching and thus had been unemployed since 1995. In Iraq at that time, even those who worked suffered greatly. To lose one's job was to be condemned to destitution.[25] The imams petitioned Saddam to reverse the verdict. As a result of the petition, the regime conducted an investigation. One imam was subsequently informed that he had never in fact been banned from preaching. This was news to him. He had been unemployed for two years without knowing why or that he could reapply for another position. He was caught in the authoritarian system that had given him the impression that he was forbidden to work in the religious sphere.[26]

In a Kafkaesque case from 2001, a local Ba'thist official decided to ensure personally that a local imam's sermons were in accordance with the regime's anti-Wahhabi campaign. Therefore, he instructed the imam to use certain, very specific language. This put the imam in a precarious situation, as he already had orders from the Ministry of Endowments and Religious Affairs to use different language. The imam told the Ba'thist that he already condemned the Wahhabi movement in his sermons in accordance with the Ministry's guidance. But then the Ba'thist insisted that he must use specific expressions about the Wahhabi movement. The imam answered that he "did not have instruction from the Ministry of Endowments to use the expressions that he [the Ba'thist official] stated" and that "the book from the Ministry for religious guidance does not designate these expressions, which if used, could possibly reflect negatively on the imam and on security and stability." The imam insisted that he did not have the authority to deviate from the Ministry's instructions.

The Ministry of Endowments and Religious Affairs maintained tight control over the content of sermons, and had the imam deviated, he would probably have been arrested by the security services. Thus, he was caught between two authorities, which were instructing him to do two different things. To obey one was to disobey the other. The imam decided to heed the orders of the Ministry of Endowments and Religious Affairs, as he was probably accustomed to doing so and knew the punishment for disobeying. The Ba'thist did not accept the imam's reasoning. He arrested him and "forcibly" took him to the Party's security department, where the imam was formally accused of not cooperating with Party apparatuses. The imam protested and even provided the instructions from the Ministry of Endowments and Religious Affairs. It was of no use. He was eventually released, but was prohibited from being an imam.[27]

As these examples indicate, the system that the regime constructed to control Iraq's religious landscape may not have been bureaucratically efficient or transparent, but it was pervasive. Unlike in earlier periods, religious leaders could not operate outside the system during the last decade of Saddam's rule.

CONCLUSION

Unsurprisingly, given some of the dysfunction mentioned in this chapter, not all Ba'thist intentions were met in the religious sphere. As chapter 9 will outline, this was especially true in its dealings with the Shi'is. Yet as chapter 9 will also demonstrate, the regime's failures on some issues did not undermine its creation and maintenance of a trusted cadre of religious leaders or damage the relationship of this cadre to the regime during the Faith Campaign of the 1990s. Indeed, these religious leaders were the foundation of Iraq's religious policies in both Sunni and Shi'i regions of Iraq. It remained so throughout the last decade of Ba'thist rule. It was the essential component on which all other policies toward religion rested.

The Regime and the Shi'is
in the 1990s

ecause Shi'is were the largest sect in Iraq, Shi'i Islamic institutions were a critical component of the Iraqi religious landscape. It is, therefore, vital to understand how the regime interacted with Shi'i religious leaders and institutions in the 1990s. As this chapter will make clear, the Ba'thists were able to exercise a great deal of control over the Shi'i religious landscape despite the rising sectarianism in the country. These points are important for understanding how the regime instrumentalized Islam during the Faith Campaign. They are also significant for post-2003 Iraq. As will be discussed in later chapters, Western strategists based their plan for occupying Iraq on the assumption that the regime had lost control over and had no support among Iraqi Shi'is. As this chapter will show, these assumptions did not reflect the reality on the ground in Iraq.

THE SHI'IS AND THE REGIME DURING
THE FAITH CAMPAIGN

Not everything in Iraq functioned according to Ba'thist intentions. Importantly, the regime had designed institutions such as the Saddam

University for Islamic Studies to be non-sectarian. The Baʿthists hoped to construct a generic, Arab nationalist Islam that would unite the Sunnis and the Shiʿis. However, students at these institutions were almost exclusively Sunnis. Sunnis were already overrepresented among the regime's top-ranking religious officials. The fact that the new Islamic university and other similar institutions were producing almost exclusively Sunni scholars only furthered that trend, and it frustrated the Baʿthist plans to unite all Arab Muslims in Iraq under a single interpretation of Islam.

Moreover, whatever the regime's intent, many Shiʿis interpreted its crackdown on the uprisings in southern Iraq following the 1991 Gulf War as a sectarian act. The trauma of those events had a profound effect on Iraqi society. And although many Iraqi Shiʿis remained members of the Baʿth Party at all levels, the events of 1991 bred discontent among many other Shiʿis. Furthermore, some pro-regime Sunnis viewed the uprisings as a Shiʿi betrayal. These trends fed on each other and led to a rising tide of sectarianism in the country.

Despite these developments, the regime's records from the 1990s clearly reflect its preference for seeing the world through a non-sectarian lens. The regime's internal records rarely discuss events or people as either Sunni or Shiʿi. Overtly anti-Shiʿi language is conspicuously absent in the Baʿth Party's archive during this period—as it was in the 1970s and 1980s. Sectarian Sunnis, who undoubtedly existed in the Party, clearly understood that they could not denounce Shiʿism directly. As in earlier periods, they found ways to employ coded language and metaphors. They sometimes used harsh but not overtly sectarian language to describe Shiʿi institutions. Some Baʿthist reports derided Shiʿi mosques and religious leaders as adhering to "backward" or "obsolete" concepts and accused them of playing "a role in intellectual and psychological sabotage."[1] Such harsh language avoided explicit sectarianism, but it is clear that the authors had little love for the people, institutions, or traditions they described. Thus, some Sunni Baʿthists clearly either misunderstood or did not always agree with official Baʿthist doctrine on Shiʿism. And if one reads between the lines of Baʿthist reports, it is clear that despite its immense efforts, the regime struggled to quell such sectarian views among both Sunnis and

Shi'is. The regime's documents never explicitly state it, but the series of anti-sectarian policies that the Ba'thists enacted in the 1990s[2] would only have been necessary if sectarianism had become a problem. Thus, when one of Saddam's closest advisors (and cousin) Ali Hassan al-Majid ordered Ba'thists to monitor and control Shi'is ceremonies "without expressing prejudice toward any Islamic ritual," it was clear both that the regime had a policy of suppressing anti-Shi'i discourses among Ba'thists and that such discourses were prevalent enough—even within the Ba'th Party—that high-ranking regime officials felt the need to address them.[3] Nevertheless, although imperfect, the regime's attempt to suppress sectarianism clearly helped to hold the country together under quite austere conditions in the 1990s and early 2000s.

The flaws in Ba'thist policies toward Shi'is did not prevent the regime from working closely with the new generation of Shi'i religious leaders or from integrating them into the regime's authoritarian structures. The regime's policies in the 1980s had allowed it to gain a foothold within the Shi'i religious establishment and to implement a system of control. Throughout the 1970s and 1980s, the regime had mapped the religious landscape of southern Iraq and marginalized many of its opponents. Then, the 1991 uprising provided an opportunity for the Ba'thists to eliminate countless more Shi'i religious leaders who they considered problematic. A 1992 United Nations report highlighted not only the decimation of the Shi'i establishment during the 1980s but also its dire situation in 1991. The report claimed that following the uprising, "virtually all" of Iraq's Shi'i clergy were "under arrest" or had "disappeared."[4] When Iraq's Foreign Minister, Tariq 'Aziz, was asked about the location of these men, he replied, "if they have been executed, I'm not going to apologize for this."[5]

By design, the religious leadership that survived these cataclysmic events included fewer scholars who were ideologically opposed to the regime. Furthermore, the regime's brutal response to the uprising instilled a sense of terror among the Shi'is that would last until 2003. As a result, one finds Shi'i religious leaders working closely with the regime and the security services throughout the 1990s and early 2000s.[6]

TERROR AND ACQUIESCENCE

Although the regime never again carried out repressive operations against the Shi'i religious leadership on the scale that it had in 1991, the regime's security services continued to act with uncompromising violence against any form of opposition in the Shi'i regions of Iraq. At times, the regime took extensive and unprecedented measures to shape Iraq's social, and, indeed, physical landscape to crush dissent. For example, following the Gulf War, the Ba'thists drained the difficult to control marshes along the Iraq-Iran boarder. These marshes often sheltered Iraqi opposition and allowed for clandestine transit to and from Iran. With no concern for the ensuing ecological disaster or the destruction of the local Marsh Arab's ancient culture, the regime drained the wetlands, imposed an economic blockade, and continued to conduct deadly raids into the area. Much of the region became uninhabitable, and many of its residents fled to Iran.[7]

In the latter years of the decade, the regime also executed several senior Shi'i clerics in the traditional centers of Shi'i learning. Two Ayatollahs were assassinated in 1998. Then a year later, the regime killed one of Iraq's senior most Shi'i authorities, Muhammad Sadiq al-Sadr, as well as two of his sons.[8]

The regime's violent actions should not be minimized; and indeed, violence played a larger role in the regime's policies toward the Shi'is than it did toward the Sunnis. Yet, this violence must be understood in the context of the regime's changing relationship to the Shi'i religious landscape. Violence was but one tool of many at the regime's disposal, and it was not the Ba'thists' preferred course of action.

In post-2003 Iraq, it has become taboo for Shi'i Iraqis to discuss support from their community for Saddam's regime. However, as Patrick Cockburn has noted, in rare moments of candor, some Shi'is will admit that one could not openly oppose the regime even in Shi'i strongholds because "in many houses though not in all, there was a brother and a sister who was a Ba'thist."[9] The Ba'thists' were particularly skillful at infiltrating the Najaf *hawza*, which for most of the 1990s was primarily managed by two senior Shi'i religious scholars—Ayatollah Ali al-Sistani and Ayatollah Muhamad

Sadiq al-Sadr. One non-Ba'thists student later described the regime's success in penetrating the *hawza* during the 1990s: "The government sent a hundred to a hundred and fifty young security and intelligence officers to be students and teachers" in the *hawza*. Moreover, he explained, "some of those who had important jobs in [Muhamad Sadiq] al-Sadr's office became students only after the uprising of 1991 and after al-Sadr himself became important. So many new and strange people were entering the *hawza* that we knew they were from the intelligence agencies." Al-Sadr had several methods to determine who was a truly committed student and who was a regime agent. For example, he would ask students to take off their turbans, unravel and then re-wrap them. Only the committed students knew how to do so; the Ba'thists did not.[10]

Nevertheless, al-Sadr and the other senior Shi'i scholars were fighting a losing battle. The Ba'thists had been inundating the *hawza* with their agents since the 1980s. The regime's strength and persistence proved too much for independent religious scholars to resist. For every scholar who resisted the regime, there was one or two more who had succumbed to the regime's combination of carrots and sticks. Indeed, the regime worked closely with Shi'i religious scholars at all levels.

Examining the way that Shi'i religious scholars learned to live within the regime's authoritarian system and even to use it to their advantage is telling. In one instance, worshipers in a Shi'i mosque did not like their sermon-giver. They complained that his beard was unkempt and that he wore a shirt and pants instead of the garb of a religious leader. They did not want to pray behind him, and, as a result, the Ministry of Endowments and Religious Affairs dismissed him. However, when the new sermon-giver arrived with the order from the Ministry, the old sermon-giver refused to accept it. A long argument ensued. The old sermon-giver had clearly been working with the regime's security services and decided to take matters into his own hands. He dug up some damaging information on the new sermon-giver and presented it to the security services with the intent of regaining his position. The new sermon-giver was indeed dismissed from the position. The old sermon-giver's case was presented in front of a board to decide whether he could return to his old position.

Unfortunately, the results are not given.[11] Yet, it is clear that the sermon-giver had experience in working with the regime's security apparatuses because he knew how to use them to his advantage.

Other religious leaders utilized the system in subtler ways. For example, when religious scholars wanted a new seminary or library, they learned to justify their requests in term of the Ba'thists' broader political struggles against Iran, Israel, or the West. They learned to glorify Saddam. They learned what was forbidden and which subjects should not be discussed. And finally, they learned to use these to their benefit, and to the detriment of their rivals. Thus, the Ba'thists were able to employ these religious leaders to influence Islamic discourse in the country.

By the mid-1990s, the Ba'thists could count on the support of even the most senior Shi'i authorities.[12] Such control was evident in the final years of the regime. In 2002, the regime secured fatwas from the most senior Shi'i scholars—the maraja'—in Najaf denouncing the impending American invasion. The regime asked Ayatollah Sistani two questions: what is the obligation of Muslims toward the American attack? And, what is the judgement for those who assist in the assault on Iraq? Sistani began the first reply by citing two Qur'anic verses: "Fight in the way of Allah those who fight you but do not transgress" (Q 2:190); and, "It is permitted for those who fight because they suffered injustice and surely God is able to assist them" (Q 22:39). He then made clear that an invasion would be an injustice worth fighting. In responding to the second question, Sistani ruled that it was not permissible to aid a foreign country's invasion of Iraq. Anyone who aided the invasion was guilty of "major sins and of violating taboos," and that shame would follow in this life and the next. Sistani then quoted the Shi'i Imam al-Sadiq. "There will be no mercy on the day of judgment if you hurt a Muslim." Sistani reasoned that if this applied to injuring one Muslim, it would be even greater for attacking a Muslim people. The other senior scholars in Najaf were even more emphatic in their support for the regime and their denunciation of an invasion. They specifically denounced America, asserting that its supporters "want to return to the crusades." They claimed that an American attack on Iraq would be an attack on "an Islamic land and Muslims," and they denounced what they referred to as "this evil attack." They issued fatwas stating that it was incumbent on all Muslims to unite to succeed in the battle, and they warned anyone who would help the American that God will curse them in this life and the next. Some of these senior Shi'i scholars claimed that defending Muslims against the infidels was "an Islamic legal obligation" for all Muslims whether Sunni or Shi'i.[13] As will be demonstrated next and in the following chapters, the Ba'thists used these scholars not only to issue fatwas but also to monitor and control less cooperative elements in the Shi'i religious landscape.

THE AUTHORITARIAN CONTEXT OF THE REGIME'S POLICIES TOWARD THE SHI'IS

Because the regime maintained considerable control over Shi'i scholars and institutions in the 1990s, it was free to act differently than it had in previous decades. The assassination of Muhammad Sadiq al-Sadr in 1999 is telling in that regard.

The regime's relationship with al-Sadr remains unclear, and outside observers have been divided over whether or not he was cooperating with the Ba'thists, especially during his rise to prominence in the early 1990s. The Ba'thists actively manipulated public perceptions, making it difficult for outsiders to understand the true relationship between the regime and the religious landscape. Unfortunately, the regime's internal records do not clear up these debates. In public during the early-to-mid 1990s, the regime appeared to promote Muhammad Sadiq al-Sadr as an Arab alternative to Iranian born scholars. The regime even forced the late Ayatollah al-Khu'i's son, Taqi, to support al-Sadr's candidacy.[14] There is no evidence that al-Sadr was a party to these plans. In fact, he claimed that the regime had feigned support for him to undermine his reputation. He argued that the Ba'thists knew "anyone they oppose will ascend socially and people will think well of him, while anyone they endorse and praise, or at least look away from him, will descend socially and people will think ill of him." Therefore, al-Sadr insisted, the regime publicly attacked certain scholars so that their reputation would improve, and it praised others whom the Ba'thists actually opposed.[15] After surveying the regime's internal records, Abbas Kadhim argued that this dynamic led to a widespread misconception about the relationship between Shi'i scholars and the state. Nevertheless, the role that the regime played in al-Sadr's rise to power remains unclear.[16]

The Ba'thist archives do contain evidence for the regime's intentional manipulation of public perception about its relationship with Shi'i religious leaders. Shi'i Ayatollahs who were willing to support the regime also worked with the Ministry of Endowments and Religious Affairs to conceal their cooperation. For example, in 1997, representatives from the Ministry asked a senior Ayatollah for two fatwas. The Ayatollah responded that he could issue one but not the other. His reasoning for not issuing the second fatwa was that he had recently published a fatwa on the subject, and if he were to reverse his stance, everyone would know that the regime had influenced him to do so. This would strip the fatwa of any authority and would undermine the standing of a senior Ayatollah who was willing to assist the regime. The Ba'thists accepted this as an appropriate precaution and only requested that he issue one fatwa.[17] Behind closed doors, senior regime officials openly acknowledged this phenomenon. They recognized that if their support for a Shi'i religious leader was discovered, it would lead to his delegitimization. As Saddam's deputy, Izzat Ibrahim al-Duri, put it, a Shi'i religious leader would be "burnt as soon as he was recognized as a collaborator with the state and this will be the fate of anyone who works with the state."[18]

It is possible that al-Sadr had a similarly amenable relationship with the regime behind closed doors in the early 1990s and that the regime supported him and his followers' rise in prominence during that period. However, by the end of the decade, the regime's documents make clear that whatever relationship had once existed between the two sides was becoming severely strained. In 1997, regime officials asked al-Sadr for the same two fatwas as other Ayatollahs; but unlike his counterparts, al-Sadr was very rude to them, dismissing their concerns and refusing to help. Thus it is clear that by the late 1990s, he opposed the regime—even behind closed doors—and that his relationship with the ruling Ba'th Party was rocky.[19]

Considering the animosity between al-Sadr and the regime in the late 1990s, it is not surprising that the regime wished to eliminate him. However, the broader context needs to be taken into account as well. The regime had worked hard to entrench itself in the Shi'i religious landscape, and other senior Ayatollahs in southern Iraq had succumbed to its authoritarian measures. Thus, al-Sadr could be removed from the *hawza* without destroying it as an institution; and, just as importantly, the regime could use these co-opted Shi'i scholars to prevent violent reactions that could potentially result from al-Sadr's death.[20]

Following al-Sadr's assassination in 1999, the regime was able to activate its networks of co-opted Shi'i religious leaders to create doubts over Ba'thist culpability in his death. Even a decade after the fall of Saddam's regime, some prominent Shi'is as well as some Western analysts were still unsure if the regime was to blame or if some rival Shi'i faction had carried out the assassination. Most notably—and all too conveniently for the Ba'thists—some Shi'is and Western analysts continue to blame Iran or the regime's nemesis, Muhammad Baqr al-Hakim, for al-Sadr's death.[21]

The Ba'thists were particularly adept at employing their influence in the main Shi'i mosques to deflect criticism. In addition to hinting at the Hakim family's culpability, several prominent Shi'i scholars blamed Israel for the assassination during their sermons. A commonly repeated story was that al-Sadr had predicted his own martyrdom and that he knew Israel would be behind it. Some quietist scholars simply encouraged an end to strife or encouraged unity. Others explicitly finished their sermons with a call for "long life and victory" for Saddam.[22]

In mosques with less cooperative sermon-givers, the regime employed a network of spies and informants to quickly and quietly crush any potential unrest.[23] And when resistance to the regime did manifest among the religious leadership, the regime could rely on other senior scholars to counter it. For example, after al-Sadr's assassination, other senior Shi'i scholars informed the regime when and where his son, Muqtada, planned to hold prayers in remembrance of his father. As such, the regime crushed these potentially dangerous events before they even began.[24] In some cases, violence did break out. For example, in the days after the assassination, one finds reports of demonstrators marching toward local Ba'th Party headquarters. In such instances, the Ba'thists opened fire on the marches, killing some, injuring many, and quickly dispersing the crowds.[25] This combination of violence and cunning allowed the regime to prevent potential disturbances from escalating into a real threat.[26]

SHI'I COMMEMORATIONS IN THE 1990S

Another important indicator of the regime's control over southern Iraq was its ability to maintain calm during the Shi'i holy month of Muharram. This does not imply the absence of disobedience. The archives contain numerous reports on, and arrests of, Shi'i Iraqis who attempted to perform the pilgrimages of Muharram by marching on foot—something that Saddam wished to eliminate.[27] Some Shi'i Iraqis continued to perform the pilgrimages on foot as means of political protest. Others claimed that they misinterpreted the regime's policies. One Shi'i later recalled that after Saddam declared the Faith Campaign in 1993, he thought that open signs of piety such as making a pilgrimage on foot would be welcomed.[28]

Yet the regime continued to view any form of mass assembly, including religious pilgrimages, as a potential threat. The regime devised coercive and sometimes elaborate measures to counter these pilgrimages. The Shi'i who had misinterpreted the Faith Campaign to be an invitation to make a pilgrimage on foot was quickly arrested. He spent half a year in the security office of the Ba'th Party's Karbala Headquarters where he was brutally tortured.[29] The regime also employed more subtle means to suppress the pilgrimages. Saddam's cousin, Ali Hassan al-Majid, seems to have taken particular pleasure in concocting such plans. In one instance, he ordered a detachment of Party members to watch roads that marchers had illegally used in the past. Members of the Party would approach the groups who tried to march on foot and explain that the practice did not constitute true Islam but rather a "reprehensible Persian innovation which benefits the enemies." While doing so, the Ba'thists would make a list of the marchers' names. Another Ba'thist who owned a taxi would be called to return them to their homes. The marchers would be unaware that the taxi driver was a Ba'thist who worked for the regime. The driver would discretely write down the marchers' addresses. Finally, the report stipulated that "the driver of the car should listen to them and create a report about their reactions [to being stopped by the Party]." In doing so, the Ba'thists hoped to discover "who among them [were] truly dedicated to the great country of Iraq."[30] For those who failed to meet expectations, the repercussions could be harsh.

In the mid-1990s, the Muharram ceremonies were further complicated by Saddam's decision to allow Iranians to begin making pilgrimages to Iraq's holy cities. The decision was intended as a goodwill gesture, but it brought the danger of Iranian agents potentially inciting Iraqis to rise up against the Ba'thists. Iraq's Directorate of Military Intelligence (*al-istikhbarat al-'askariyya*) responded by creating a detailed security plan designed to counter the threat and even to recruit Iranian spies. The regime coordinated its operations through two secret intelligence centers— one in Najaf and one in Karbala. Iraqi Military Intelligence used these centers "to build relations with the owners of all shops, restaurants, cafes, and hotels near the shrines of the Imams." Regime agents worked with the hotel owners in the two cities "in order to slip our elements in with [the Iranians] to analyze and target the beneficial elements for our work and prepare them for recruitment." Then, the regime's agents would use "rewards, interests, public benefit, threatening and blackmail" to recruit spies. Iraqi Military Intelligence also established "secret coordination with the Ministry of Religious Endowments" to install its agents "as tourist and religious guides for groups [making the pilgrimage]."[31]

Through such tactics, the regime largely prevented potentially problematic Muharram ceremonies from ballooning into a real threat. As Aaron Faust has noted, "party reports about the Shi'i Muharram activities show that the regime succeeded in keeping them under control and even benefiting from them at times. By 1989, the practices had almost ceased completely and although they saw a brief uptick in 1996 and a few other points in the late 1990s, they otherwise never again seriously threatened the regime as they did in the 1970s."[32]

Interestingly, the regime's policies toward the Shiʿis during the 1990s demonstrated a remarkable ideological consistency with its policies in earlier decades.[33] In fact, with the exception of a few months following the Gulf Crisis, the regime's strategy toward Shiʿi institutions and religious leaders remained stable throughout Saddam's presidency. Throughout the 1990s, the regime worked to limit Shiʿi marches, to identify and neutralize potentially threating elements in southern Iraq, and to educate the people and Party members on the Baʿth Party's positive view of Islam. As it had done since the early 1980s, the regime continued to emphasize the need to "intensify awareness and cultural indoctrination of the Party apparatuses on the topics of religion, heritage, and the religious-political phenomenon."[34] This indoctrination also continued to emphasize traditional Baʿthist principles. There were no signs of a turn toward Islamism. For example, Party plans during the month of Muharram often include instructions to exploit people's nationalist sentiments and use them to gain cooperation against the Persians and harmful political parties.[35] The Party held special "lectures on religion, heritage, and the [deplorable] religious-political phenomenon for all the students of the colleges and institutes of the country as well as lessons on patriotic (*wataniyya*) culture, and nationalism (*qawmiyya*) in the universities."[36] This nationalistic, anti-Islamist language was identical to that of earlier Party plans the regime had developed throughout Saddam's presidency.

The main difference in the regime's records between the 1980s and the 1990s was not the regime's policies but its perception of success in implementing those policies. In the 1980s, the regime had begun to co-opt Shiʿi religious leaders, but it was a difficult and often violent process. Regime reports from the early to mid-1980s express some reservation about the Shiʿi religious leadership and whether it could be trusted; but throughout the 1980s, the regime's ability to implement its policies during the Muharram commemorations increased. By the 1990s, the regime regularly worked with Shiʿi religious leaders and appeared confident that these Shiʿi authorities would support Baʿthist plans. Again, one sees this subtly reflected in the archival documents. For example, Party plans during Muharram in the 1990s state that Ba'thists would work with the Shi'i men of religion "as we have been doing."[37] Party officials also seemed confident that Shi'i religious leaders would instill "a refusal to surrender and strengthen the patience and steadfastness of the citizens."[38] In doing so, the regime hoped that Iraqis could better deal with the punishing economic situation that accompanied international sanctions following the 1991 Gulf War.

The Ba'thists themselves tracked changes to official policies concerning the month of Muharram. From the late 1980s through the 1990s, only minor adjustments were implemented.[39] Following the 1991 uprisings, the Ba'th Party created emergency plans for its local offices. These were designed to prevent or, if need be, suppress similar events in the future. Local Party officials enacted the plans for one or two days around the 'Ashura on the 10th day of Muharram. The plans consisted of a heightened state of readiness, increased patrols, and so forth.[40] However, these emergency plans did not represent a change in the regime's attitude toward the Muharram festivals. Rather, they were meant to reinforce existing procedures.

CONCLUSION

Although the Ba'thists' approach toward Shi'i religious leaders did not differ with regard to ideology in the 1990s, the regime's records demonstrate that its relationship to the Shi'i religious landscape had altered significantly. Through two decades of authoritarian rule—culminating in the extreme violence of 1991—the regime had worked to eliminate hostile elements in the Shi'i religious establishment and to co-opt Shi'i scholars at all levels. By the 1990s, these policies had a clear effect. The Shi'is became part of the regime's authoritarian system in Iraq. Thus, in addition to relying on senior Shi'i scholars to assist in achieving the regime's political goals, the Ba'thists were able to prevent the type of sectarian insurrection that typified southern Iraq in the early 1980s. Resentment toward the regime, and toward Sunnis in general, certainly existed within the Shi'i religious landscape in the 1990s; but the regime's repressive system was able to prevent this resentment from transforming into the violent tit for tat escalation that led to civil war in post-2003 Iraq. Outside analysts largely misinterpreted the regime's relationship with Shi'i scholars and institutions during this period. Therefore, as later chapters will show, they were not prepared for what occurred in southern Iraq after the fall of Saddam's regime.

Mechanisms of Control

I n addition to creating a critical mass of trusted religious leaders in Iraq, the regime also constructed a means to monitor and control it. This was no easy task. As in its other strategies, the regime employed a combination of violence, manipulation, and cunning to maintain its control over Iraq's religious landscape in the 1990s and early 2000s. First and foremost, the regime used its security apparatuses to monitor religious leaders and punish those who fell short of Ba'thist expectations. But the security forces were only one of many means that the regime used to manage the religious landscape during the Faith Campaign. As important were the ever-increasing institutionalization and bureaucratization of the religious landscape. Finally, the regime also controlled religious leaders and religious discourse in Iraq by increasingly controlling the spaces in which these leaders and their discourses operated—namely, the mosques and other places of worship in Iraq. This chapter will address these topics; and in doing so, it will provide an outline of the regime's security architecture and mechanisms of control over Iraq's religious landscape during the Faith Campaign of the 1990s and early 2000s. Later, chapter 11 will demonstrate how this control was essential for the proliferation of state-sponsored religion in Iraq.

RELIGION AND STATE SECURITY APPARATUSES
IN THE 1990S

In the 1990s, international sanctions devastated Iraq's traditional, uniformed security forces in the military and police. However, Saddam's control over Iraq was not rooted in these traditional forces. While the Army crumbled under international sanctions, the overall size of Iraqi security forces—and the role they played in controlling Iraqi society—increased considerably in the 1990s. The regime relied on paramilitary and Ba'th Party militias as well as a ballooning cadre of covert security agents. Unlike a professional Army or police force, these security personnel were largely hidden from public view. They did not wear uniforms and their identities were kept secret.

With limited resources at its disposal, the regime also needed to decide where it would focus its efforts. Following the overthrow of the Iraqi regime in 2003, Saddam's cousin, Ali Hassan al-Majid, told his interrogators that in the 1990s, the regime had concentrated more on controlling the domestic population rather than on external threats.[1] Other senior Iraqi officers in the military and security services confirmed this assertion. A declassified US government report on the interrogations states that Iraqis "had to contend with at least five major security organizations: the Special Security Office, the Iraqi Intelligence Service, the Directorate of General Security, the General Directorate of Military Intelligence and various 'security service' offices within the Republican Guard's bureaucracy." The report continues: "Moreover, the number of security personnel in each of these organizations increased dramatically after 1991. In many cases, new spies were sent to units to report on the spies already there, even those from their own organization."[2]

Within this domestic focus, the regime's security services were particularly interested in the religious sphere. Thus, Saddam restructured them to deal with religious issues more effectively. The Special Security Organization (*jihaz al-'amn al-khass*) was a particularly formidable organization in that regard. Created by Saddam in the early 1980s, its mission was to control the other security services and the Ba'th Party itself.[3] In other words, it spied on the spies and controlled those tasked with controlling Iraq. During the 1990s, the organization paid particularly close attention to religious matters. In the summer of 1993, just as Saddam announced the Faith Campaign, the Special Security Organization (SSO) formulated a plan to "Double the activities of the Party organizations to seize the initiative in the religious sphere [especially] in the religious colleges, institutes, and schools." It kept detailed "inventories" on all Party members who operated in what it termed the religious sphere. The SSO paid close attention to Ba'thists who worked as Qur'an readers, imams, and servants in the mosques to make sure, in its words, that they were "serving the march of the Party and [Ba'thist] revolution."[4]

The SSO was particularly concerned with preventing Islamists from influencing these Ba'thists or other officers in the various security services. For example, one finds reports highlighting the SSO's concern that "hostile activities in mosques and places of worship" were negatively influencing Party members.[5] The regime worked quickly to counter such threats.

Other regime intelligence agencies dealt with similar threats in their own areas of responsibility. For example, one finds reports from Iraqi Military Intelligence (*al-istikhbarat al-'askariyya*) on Iraqi soldiers who participated in religious ceremonies with suspected Wahhabis.[6] The regime security apparatuses worked with the local Party branches to eliminate various Islamist movements and replace them with what the regime termed "Islam and Arabism" (i.e., Ba'thized religious leaders preaching Ba'thist interpretations of Islam).[7]

The regime possessed a highly developed doctrine for dealing with the opposition in general, and hostile religious groups in particular. Members of the security services received in-depth instruction on methods to "strategically infiltrate" the opposition and to develop "quality sources" among opposition members. Having permeated these circles, Ba'thist agents learned, as one training manual put it, various tactics to "widen differences between Iraqi opposition members in order to create doubts and a more frustrating situation among their members as well as to incapacitate them by using highly effective and secret intelligence techniques."[8]

When these more subtle tactics failed, the regime was not above employing violence. As such, throughout the 1990s, one finds reports of the regime's security services executing both Sunni and Shi'i religious leaders. In 1994, for example, the regime targeted the Sunni religious leadership in a wave of arrests and executions throughout the Sunni Arab districts of Fallujah, Ramadi, Mosul, and Baghdad.[9] A year later, in 1995, the Iraqi general-turned-Islamist Muhammad Mazlum al-Dulaymi attempted to assassinate Saddam. The Dulaym tribe is the largest Sunni Arab tribe, and it was closely linked to the regime. Hence, the confrontation that resulted from the attempted assassination sent shockwaves through the Sunni Arab establishment. Several religious leaders were arrested. Most analyses at the time portrayed this as a tribal conflict.[10] That depiction is only partially true. Muhammad Mazlum al-Dulaymi was extremely religious and eventually developed Islamist sympathies. It was these religious beliefs that led to the attempt on Saddam's life.[11] Afterword, Saddam's crackdown on the would-be assassin's family sparked a broader tribal uprising. Thus, the conflict was originally over religion rather than tribal affiliation. Nevertheless, the event clearly signaled to the regime how problematic religious views could lead to large-scale destabilization and even threaten Ba'thist rule. The regime also maintained a campaign of what the United Nations termed the "systematic suppression" of the Shi'i religious leadership.[12] It is clear, then, that the regime responded violently to any hint of resistance.

The security system was not perfect. It was sometimes undermined by corruption and the influence of personal relationships. In one example, the head of a local Ba'th Party division (*firqa*) accused a subordinate Ba'thist of engaging in abnormal religious ceremonies and having a negative influence on the youth in his area. He reported this to the Party Secretariat in Baghdad. The Secretariat reported this information to the SSO. The SSO conducted an investigation and found the accused Ba'thist was innocent. It noted that the accused had a bad relationship with the head of the Party division, and that the division head had assaulted him the previous January. The SSO reported this to the Party Secretariat and stated that it had worked out an agreement between the two Party officials.

The Party Secretariat informed the headquarters of the Party branch (which was above a division in the Party hierarchy) of the SSO's findings. However, the secretary-general of the branch responded that "there is no truth to the accusations of SSO. The head of the Party division has no relationship to the accused either in the past or present, and no assault took place last January because the two do not even live in the same area." Then the Party branch reported that the member in question was indeed practicing abnormal religious ceremonies. The Party secretariat reported this back to the SSO, but no further information is given.[13] This incident makes clear that someone was either covering for someone else or that personal relationships had interfered with Party practices. In a web of corruption and lies, it is impossible, even today, to reconstruct what actually occurred.

However, the security services took proactive steps to mitigate these problems. For example, in homogeneous areas where a single sect or tribe existed, the SSO would bring in outsiders to work on religious issues. In doing so, it hoped to mitigate tribal or sectarian loyalty and prevent any potential collaboration against the regime.[14] SSO agents would also "infiltrate" the Party leadership in potentially problematic areas of the country.[15] This would help to break up potentially dangerous networks between the security services, the Ba'th Party, and the religious landscape.

Throughout the 1990s, the regime fine-tuned the organization of its security services to meet the threat posed by Islamists and other religious trends. It created special branches to monitor the Muslim Brotherhood, Wahhabi networks, and various Shi'i Islamists.[16] In the early 1990s, the regime tasked its oldest internal security service, referred to simply as General Security (*al-amn al-'amm*), with developing a department that would "specialize in religious issues and pursue the activities of men of religion."[17] In 1997, the Iraqi Intelligence Service (*jihaz al-mukhabarat*) overhauled its "Hostile Activity Directorate." This directorate was responsible for countering Iraq's domestic opposition. The 1997 reform added sections specifically devoted to "religious parties" and to neutralizing sectarianism. It also increased the operational budget for missions that countered these religious parties by 60%.[18]

Furthermore, the SSO worked with the Party and the Ministry of Culture and Information to create counter-propaganda targeting various Islamic movements. For example, the regime published a book entitled "The True Wahhabi Movement and its Roots" and distributed it to all Party branches. As of September 1993, it had circulated 10,000 copies.[19] Elsewhere, the Iraqi state archives preserved a similar (possibly the same?) book, entitled "The Birth of the Wahhabi Movement and Its Historic Roots." This book was in circulation in 2002. Such studies were inundated with conspiracies and offered only a superficial rendition of religious thought, creed, or theology. "The Birth of the Wahhabi Movement and Its Historic Roots" was written by a Colonel in the Iraqi Intelligence Service. He was not a religious leader. The book attempted to delegitimize Wahhabism by linking it to Western imperialism, and—in the most damning insult that the Ba'thist could muster—by claiming that its leaders were Jewish. Indeed, the book claimed Muhammad bin Saud—the 18th-century founder of the first Saudi State—was "of Jewish descent." It also asserted that Muhammad ibn abd al-Wahhab—the 18th-century founder of Wahhabism—came from a line of secret Jews who maintained "one fake Muslim name, and one original Jewish name." Thus, although it was commonly believed that ibn abd al-Wahhab's grandfather was named "Sulayman," his real name according to the book was "Schulman."[20]

As the sources discussed in this section demonstrate, the regime was never able to eliminate religious opposition. Indeed, the proliferation of activities especially against Islamists suggests that the regime was engaged in constant conflict with them. Moreover, Party officials and security services often identified and worked to restrict "unauthorized" mosques and sermon-givers who "practice religious extremism."[21] Regime officials also regularly encountered anti-Ba'thist propaganda and illegal radio broadcasts by Shi'i Islamists.[22] The Da'wa Party and other organized Shi'i opposition movements continued to be a menace.[23] Furthermore, as in the 1980s, insurgent attacks were not uncommon. One finds examples of plain-clothed insurgents, sometimes dressed as women, suddenly opening fire on members of the Ba'th Party or the security services.[24]

Nevertheless, these sources also make clear that the Baʿthists never abandoned this fight. They did not, as many assumed, recede into the background or cede the field to independent or Islamist religious actors. As will be shown in later chapters, this fact is important for understanding post-2003 Iraq when the regime's collapse brought an end to its active suppression of various Islamic and Islamist actors in the country.

FORMALIZATION OF COMMITTEES AND CONTROL

Contrary to the theory that the regime ceded religious affairs to independent or grass roots Islamic leaders in the 1990s, the Baʿth Party's records demonstrate a pattern of increasing control over both Sunni and Shiʿi religious leaders. Even with a pliable religious landscape largely in place, the regime did not feel comfortable employing it without significant oversight. Most notably, it formalized official religious committees at the provincial level. The Baʿthists had formed religious committees at the local level in the early 1980s. The regime used them to regulate sermons and other activities at mosques throughout the country. During the 1980s, these committees were often ad hoc. As such, the regime tasked low-ranking local officials with convening them. It seems that these local officials would only involve higher authorities if they encountered a problem.

The local committees continued to meet in the 1990s. Their primary role remained to oversee the appointment of local religious leaders. The regime also required that these committees work with the Ministry of Endowments and Religious Affairs to approve all religious sermons.[25] In 1995, the regime formalized these committees at the provincial level as well. The Baʿth Party Secretariat instructed the Party branches to form standing committees consisting of the secretary general of the Party branch (which in most cases was in charge of a province), the chief security manager of the province, and the manager of religious endowments for the province. Thus, decisions related to religion would now involve much higher ranking officials than had been the case with the local committees. The provincial committees assessed men of religion in regular meetings and kept the national Party Secretariat updated on all developments.[26]

The regime considered both the local and provincial committees to be politically sensitive and essential to its security. The committees carefully assessed all religious leaders in their areas of responsibility, recording their political outlooks, if they had any problematic incidents in their past, and whether anyone in their family was suspected of disloyalty to the regime. Tellingly, the forms that the committees used in these assessments were similar to those used in background checks for all sensitive government positions.[27]

In 1997, the regime modified the mandate of the committees. According to the 1995 directive, the provincial standing committees were not required to meet with the men of religion in their areas. They simply had to conduct assessments. They could complete these assessments using the records of the security services, the Party, and the Ministry of Endowments and Religious Affairs. The 1997 directive modified this mandate, stating that because of the importance of the issue of religion, the committees now needed to hold symposiums with the men of religion in their area every three months.[28]

Throughout the 1980s, the Ba'thists had developed a cadre of Party members who specialized in religious matters. These specially trained Ba'thists facilitated the efforts of religious committees, both at the provincial level and within the Ministry of Endowments and Religious Affairs. Therefore, the officials who worked in religious institutions often overlapped with those who served on regime committees tasked with monitoring those institutions.[29] Interestingly, officials on these committees were sometimes female. Hence, female Ba'thists were tasked with overseeing male religious leaders and deciding the appropriateness of their sermons.[30]

As with other sectors of Iraqi society, the regime not only spied on the population but also spied on its spies. Thus, the regime developed various methods for monitoring these religious committees and those who served on them. When the Party branches nominated a Ba'thist to serve on a religious committee, the branch was required to fill out the "form for special information" on him or her. This was the same form used to conduct background investigations for all sensitive postings within the regime.[31] The regime conducted these investigations on all committee members, even senior Ba'thists such as the head of a Party division (*firqa*), who would have already held considerable responsibility.[32] To further control these committees, the regime also limited the period of time that one could serve on them.[33]

A STRATEGY OF MAINTAINING RATHER THAN GAINING CONTROL

These religious committees were tasked with the "normal" functioning of religious affairs such as approving routine sermons and appointing local religious leaders. However, they did not possess unfettered control over these issues. In some cases, the security services presented these committees with a fait accompli. For example, when members of the security services suspected a sermon-giver of having ties to Islamists or other opposition groups, they would remove him. Often the security services would immediately replace the sermon-giver with someone else.[34] Consequently, the security services had considerable influence in shaping Iraq's religious landscape.

The security services' quick replacement of religious leaders in the mosques marked an important shift in the regime's strategy for controlling religious discourse in the country. In the early 1980s, it should be recalled, the regime was primarily concerned with cleansing the religious landscape of hostile religious leaders. It did this by placing strict limitations on who could work as a sermon-giver. These policies left numerous mosques without any leadership. When Iraqis asked the Ba'thists to ease their restrictions so that each mosque would have a sermon-giver, the regime refused. During that period, the regime trusted very few religious leaders. The regime simply did not know who they were or what they believed. In such a context, an empty mosque was not very problematic. A mosque without a sermon-giver was vulnerable to exploitation by opposition members, but so was a mosque with an unvetted—and possibly hostile—sermon-giver. The risk was basically the same.

In the 1990s, the cost–benefit analysis of the regime's actions had completely transformed. After a decade of working to bring Iraq's religious landscape under its control, most religious leaders operated within the regime's authoritarian system. Therefore, in the 1990s, the Ba'thists' strategy was not to gain control but rather to maintain it. Under such conditions, the regime had a considerable incentive to ensure that every mosque had an official sermon-giver. If a mosque was left without a sermon-giver, it could be exploited by the opposition. However, unlike in the 1980s, this would be a net loss for the regime.

Unsurprisingly, the Ba'thists devoted considerable time and resources to mitigating this threat. The regime considered mosques to be particularly vulnerable during periods of transition. Therefore, in the 1990s—and unlike in the 1980s—if a sermon-giver was arrested or transferred to another mosque, the security services would always emphasize the need for an immediate replacement so as "not to give the opportunity for suspicious elements to exploit the mosque."[35] Along these lines, in the 1990s and early 2000s, the regime not only wished to assign an official sermon-giver to each mosque but also to make sure that he was continuously present at the mosque—again, to ensure that unauthorized individuals could not stand up and deliver unvetted sermons. Thus, one often finds instances of the security services removing a sermon-giver because "he is not present at the mosque except one or two days a week and his absence has given birth to a state of competition between the those attending the mosque to pray as to who should lead the prayers."[36] In one instance, a local Ba'thist official claimed that he met regularly with a wide range of imams and sermon-givers "for the purpose of cooperating and coordinating on the matter of fighting this malignant [Wahhabi] movement." He had successfully met all men of religion in his region with the exception of one, who was not present at the mosque when the Ba'thist official called on him. Because of his absence, the Ba'thist official ordered the imam to be arrested; and even when he was released, he was banned from working as an imam.[37] For a regime that wished to completely control religious discourse, an empty mosque that could be exploited by unvetted religious leaders was unacceptable.

FORMALIZED SURVEILLANCE

The regime's focus on maintaining control over the religious landscape in the 1990s led to intensified and increasingly institutionalized surveillance of religious leaders. During this period, regime officials spoke of "ongoing and rotating assessments of every man of religion and sermon-giver to ensure that all of them are supporters of the march of the Party and the revolution."[38]

In addition to these regular assessments, the regime conducted a national "inventory" (*jard*) of religious leaders in 1992, 1995, and 1998.[39] In these inventories, the Party Secretariat asked each branch to survey the religious leaders in its territory. The branches were to provide clear judgments of each religious leader's ideas and what he discussed both during his sermons and in his conversations with those who attended the prayers. The regime often provided documents for the local branches to fill out. The religious leaders were classified as either Ba'thists, Independent Nationalists (*watani mustaqill*), or Not Cooperative/No Good. Their sermons were judged in accordance with Soundness of Creed (i.e., that they adhered to Ba'thist interpretations of Islam and that they were not Islamists, Wahhabis, or Salafists), Agreement with the Party and the Revolution on political/policy matters, and that they mention Saddam.[40] The Party Secretariat asked the branches to make special note of "men of religion from religious trends (*salafiya*, *wahabbiya*, and Muslim Brotherhood)."[41] The Ba'thists kept close track of Shi'i Islamists as well. In some cases, they were also interested in Sufis and the owners of alms houses (sing: *takiyah*).[42]

As is evident from the preceding, the target of these inventories was Iraq's Muslim majority. However, in some limited cases, the regime took similar inventories of Christians. These normally occurred in response to a specific threat. For example, in 1996, the regime felt that "sectarian" elements of the Christian community in the north were working with the "American-Zionist Intelligence Service." Thus, it ordered the Party branches to conduct an inventory of the Christians in their areas and to determine if they had family members in the north or outside the country. If so, the branches were ordered to carefully monitor their movements.[43]

The regime not only used these inventories to track potential threats, it also identified individuals who might be useful. The Party branches noted any influential religious leader who was a Baʻthist or who could potentially be helpful. For example, the Party Secretariat specifically asked for the names of students in the Najaf *hawza* who were Baʻthists or who had a Baʻthist family member. The names of these individuals were forwarded to the Directorate of General Security to ensure that they were being utilized to the fullest extent possible.[44]

A great deal can be learned from these inventories. First, it is clear that throughout the 1990s, the regime was never as concerned with religious knowledge as much as it was with political loyalty. Religious leaders were never categorized by their piety, level of knowledge, or the quality of their sermons. The regime was only interested in whether they were politically hostile. Another clear trend that emerges from these inventories is one of overwhelming regime control. Even in what were thought to be Shiʻi strongholds and bastions of independence,[45] it was quite rare for a religious leader to openly dissent from the regime's official positions. As mentioned previously, Aaron Faust calculated that in 1995, only 70 out of 1,501 religious leaders in the Iraq had any negative notation next to their names. Of course, one must account for the possibility that regime officials, for one reason or another, did not always wish to report the truth.[46] Yet, it should also be emphasized that the regime had an ever-deepening system of monitoring not only the citizenry but also the Party and security services themselves. Attempting to present false information to the Party Secretariat was, therefore, a precarious task. Moreover, the Baʻthists conducting these inventories were not shy about reporting negative information. Therefore, it can be assumed that the inventories offer an imperfect, but possible, representation of the religious landscape.

The negative notations that religious leaders received next to their names in the inventories were wide-ranging. They provide a glimpse into the regime's outlook. As such, they are worth recounting in detail. Of course, it was always bad to be labeled an Islamist. The inventories had various names for this. Sometimes they specified that a religious leader was a member of the Muslim Brotherhood, or a follower of Sadr. There were also numerous examples of Wahhabis and Salafis—terms that the regime used interchangeably—and even members of Turkmen Islamic parties. Sometimes the labels were less specific. For instance, some religious leaders were listed as puritanical (*mutazammit*), or extremist.[47] Others labels were even more ambiguous. Sometimes "supporters" of the Party were said to "suspect" somebody of being an Islamist. Some religious leaders were said to be "shaky" or "inconsistent" in their view of the Party.[48] The regime also worried about religious practices that contained what the regime considered to be either Islamist or sectarian elements. Thus, one finds reports about religious ceremonies that were not practiced in "their proper way."[49]

Often, regime officials included additional derogatory information, for example, specifying not only that religious leaders were Muslim Brothers but that they had studied in Saudi Arabia. One sermon-giver was reported to be "spiteful" of the Ba'th Party and had called for an Islamic state. Others were said to be sectarian, or to have created discord (*fitnah*).[50] The regime officials conducting these inventories also noted former sermon-givers in the area who had problematic histories, even if they were no longer actively preaching. One Islamic scholar was said to have been a sermon-giver previously, but the regime arrested him "due to excess in one of his sermons."[51] Another was said to have fled with the Afghan Mujahidin.[52] Thus, even though no specific threat remained, the Ba'thists were on the lookout for others who shared these hostile ideas.

Having a family member who was suspected of opposing the regime could also get one into trouble. The inventories noted that although a man held a positive view of the Party, his son had been killed due to involvement in acts of "sabotage and treachery." If someone had a family member associated with Islamists, such as the Da'wa Party, he would be suspect.[53]

In many of these cases, the results of the inventories were sent directly to the security services so that they could deal with the religious leaders who failed to meet the regime's standards.[54]

As mentioned previously, these inventories were also useful in identifying religious leaders who supported the Party. This information was valuable to the regime, especially if the religious leaders were influential. The regime did not have any derogatory information on the vast majority of religious leaders. Supporters of the Ba'th Party were also quite common, but most men of religion were listed as "independent" or "independent nationalists." Of these independents, the regime often attempted to identify potential supporters. The most common positive notation was simply that he was "good." Another popular description was that "his speech and sermons are consistent with the principles of the Party." These descriptions seem to imply that the sermon-giver was at least not causing trouble. Other widely used notations implied more active support. For example, the inventories stated that numerous religious leaders "cooperate with the Party." Interestingly, just as one's family could be held against him, having family members who supported the regime was viewed positively.[55]

These descriptions go on for hundreds of pages and cover thousands of Islamic leaders. This small sample should make clear that the regime never moved toward Islamism or even cared much for piety. Contrary to the idea that the regime shifted toward Islamism after the Gulf War, these inventories demonstrate—both in their scope and their content—that the regime continued to distrust anything that even slightly resembled religious fundamentalism or political Islam. Loyalty to the Ba'th Party and the regime were the only measures that mattered in Saddam's Iraq, even in the 1990s.

BEYOND SURVEILLANCE

The inventories that the regime conducted in the 1990s provided a glut of information on Iraq's religious landscape. They helped the Ba'thists to identify problematic regions, but mass inventories were an imperfect system of surveillance. Sermon-givers were acutely aware that the regime was monitoring them. They learned to adhere to Ba'thist prescriptions in their public sermons. On one hand, this was a significant victory for the regime. Suppressing certain ideas by preventing them from entering public discourse was one of Saddam's most important goals. Yet, on the other hand, those same sermon-givers who adhered to Ba'thist stipulations in public sermons could lead their followers astray in private. Such details were difficult to discern in a project as large and resource-intensive as the national inventories. Unlike other, more limited operations dealing with religion, the scale of the inventories required mass participation from Ba'thists. Thus, the regime could not limit its operations to those Ba'thists who were specially trained to deal with religious matters.

In some cases, the Ba'thists tasked with monitoring sermons were completely inept. For example, Salafis are often defined not only by their beliefs but also by their appearance. Most notably, they grow long beards and wear a short version of the *dishdashah* (the one-piece, often white robe traditionally worn by Arab men). However, as one salafi-leaning sermon-giver would later recount, "everyone knew who they [the Ba'thists] were because they were the ones wearing short dishdashahs but on their faces they had only mustaches."[56]

The regime employed several tactics to mitigate this problem. Most prominently, it was always on the lookout for ways to infiltrate various circles within the religious opposition. In one case, a junior Ba'thist reported to his superiors that he had spoken with a Wahhabi and that the Wahhabi had given him some books and expressed his beliefs. Higher ranking Ba'thists instructed their junior colleague to follow-up with the Wahhabi on the matters they had discussed and to win his trust. Then they put him under the supervision of the Directorate of General Security in the hope that he could infiltrate Wahhabi circles as a regime spy. The regime even offered the young Ba'thist a monthly salary for his work.[57] One finds similar examples among the Shi'is. The archives have preserved cases of Ba'thists who made a point of frequenting mosques in poor Shi'i districts of Baghdad. One report stated that "through these visits" a Ba'thist "was able to establish positive relations with a number of worshipers who have negative influence." From the information that the Ba'thist gathered, he was able to publish a report on "hostile religious tendencies."[58]

These more aggressive efforts were often able to overcome the limitations inherent in the large and unwieldy nationwide inventories. For example, in 1998, a provincial standing committee for religious affairs convened to consider the reappointment of sermon-givers. One case was particularly telling. At first the sermon-giver in question seemed like a strong candidate for reappointment. Initial reports described him as a Ba'thist. The regime had conducted regular reviews of his sermons throughout the 1990s and had not uncovered any derogatory information. Agents who had visited his mosque reported that he mentioned Saddam in his sermons, that he maintained a sound creed, and that his stance toward the Party was as it should be. Moreover, his family was described as "very good."[59] However, before approving his reappointment, the committee checked to see if there were any other reports on him. As it turns out, there were. A Ba'thist agent had gone undercover in 1996. He had won the sermon-giver's trust and managed to speak with him in private. In doing so, he discovered that when the sermon-giver was away from the prying eyes of the regime, he expressed sectarian views and even declared those he disagreed with to be apostates.[60] In typical Ba'thist fashion, the report suggested that the sermon-giver was "infected with a mental illness that causes him to be unnatural and to lose evenhandedness."[61] His reappointment was denied.

BUILDING NEW MOSQUES

Thus far, this chapter has focused on the regime's attempt to influence religious discourse in Iraq through controlling religious leaders. In addition to managing people, however, the regime also made a concerted effort to control the space in which religious discourse took place—most prominently, the mosques. As mentioned in earlier sections, the regime's strategy was to place all existing mosques under the management of the Ministry of Endowments and Religious Affairs. However, Saddam also sponsored a large campaign to build new mosques. He was the benefactor of numerous mosques and shrines in the 1980s, but the bulk of Iraq's new mosques were constructed during the Faith Campaign of the 1990s. These projects had an enormous effect on the religious landscape of Iraq. In the mid-20th century, the ratio of mosques to Iraqis was roughly one for every 37,000. By the 1990s, that ratio had increased to one mosque for every 3,500 Iraqis.[62] Though the regime directly financed the building of some grand mosques,[63] many of these mosques were built by "ordinary" Iraqis.

Saddam depicted the flurry of mosque building as proof of his commitment to Islam. He often said that any citizen could build a mosque in his area of residence. The regime even held conferences and symposiums during the Faith Campaign to highlight its efforts in this regard.[64] The Western press also noted the proliferation of mosques, calling it "The most visible part of the [faith] campaign."[65] Often Western media coverage simply regurgitated the regime's hyperbole. The New York Times, for example, reported that "Mosque building . . . has become Mr. Hussein's grand obsession." The Times also repeated Iraqi assertions that this project was "on a scale that no Arab leader has undertaken since the days of the great Abbasid caliphs."[66] Saddam depicted this "obsession" as a benevolent act meant to spread and strengthen the practice of religion in the country. However, the regime's records reveal that despite Saddam's assertions to the contrary, the freedom to build mosques in Iraq was a mirage. The construction of new mosques was tightly controlled. Indeed, controlling who could build mosques was an important means for the regime to exert control over the religious landscape and to stifle any independent manifestations of religion. In that sense, the proliferation of mosques was simply another brick in the regime's authoritarian system.

The relationship between the Faith Campaign and the proliferation of mosques is perhaps best illustrated by the fact that the Faith Campaign was sometimes invoked not to build mosques but rather to destroy them. For example, in 1996, the regime discovered a number of unsanctioned mosques in a poor Shi'i district of Baghdad. Officials in the Ba'th Party and the security services averred that the opposition was likely "exploiting" them for political ends. The Party Secretariat ordered local Ba'thists to bring all of the mosques under the management

of the Ministry of Endowments and Religious Affairs, and also to "limit
the number" of mosques in the area. This limiting of mosques was to be
done "in accordance with [the guidance of] the leadership of the Struggler
Comrade Leader Saddam Hussein (may God preserve and guide him)
for the Faith Campaign." Hence, in this example, the regime invoked the
Faith Campaign to suppress religious expression and destroy mosques.
Accordingly, the campaign is better understood as a tool of power rather
than a strategy to spread religion for its own sake.[67]

Despite Saddam's supposedly magnanimous declarations, the regime
maintained tight control over who could build mosques and where they
could build them. The Ba'thists swiftly dealt with anyone who attempted
to build a mosque without permission.[68] These controls were not only
applied to constructing new mosques. If one wished to tear down, rebuild,
or even to rename a mosque, the regime's approval was required.[69] Iraqis
seeking permission to build a mosque underwent an intense background
check similar to that of applicants to sensitive positions within the regime.
This process was the same for both Sunnis and Shi'is. It normally took
about a month, though in some cases, where contradictory information
emerged, it could last significantly longer.[70]

To build, rebuild, or rename a mosque, one needed to file a request with the
local representatives of the Ministry of Endowments and Religious Affairs.
One had to provide not only the proposed name and location of the mosque
but also the details of one's political background and finances. Ministry
officials then forwarded this information to the Ba'th Party Secretariat. The
Secretariat would assign the local Party branches and the security services
to conduct a thorough investigation. Following the investigations, all the
information would be sent back to the Party Secretariat, which would decide whether to approve the request. The Party would forward its decision
to the Ministry of Endowments and Religious Affairs, which would inform
the applicant. Consequently, someone applying to build a mosque would
only interact with the Ministry of Endowments and Religious Affairs. In
an attempt to project a civil façade onto its authoritarian structures, the
regime was careful not to give any indication that the Party or the security
services were involved in the decision.

The regime would deny permission to build a mosque for numerous reasons. Sometimes officials would simply decide that "the area does not need another mosque." Therefore, they would reject the application.[71] More often, ideological considerations existed. If the regime's investigations revealed that someone was an Islamist or was suspected of having ties to Islamists, the application would be denied.[72] As with other assessments of political loyalty, one could come up short due to the actions or sympathies of ones relatives. For example, one Iraqi was denied permission to build a mosque because of his two sons. One son had fled to Saudi Arabia during the 1991 uprising and only returned as a result of a general amnesty. The other remained a fugitive.[73]

The regime disapproved applications to build mosques for less nefarious reasons as well. One investigation revealed that an applicant "did not donate to the building of schools." He was therefore not sufficiently committed to assisting the regime and his application was denied.[74] One's influence was also taken into consideration. However, influence cut both ways. Someone who possessed considerable influence could be either a greater threat or, conversely, a greater asset. Accordingly, the regime enthusiastically approved applications of Iraqis who possessed "large influence in the area" if they were deemed "cooperative" and "no negative information" had surfaced during the investigations.[75]

When reviewing an application to build a mosque, the regime considered the applicant's finances to be as important as his ideology. The system that the regime had implemented was designed to control the mosques through ensuring that their owners were loyal to Saddam and the Ba'thist regime. If one did not possess the financial resources to build and maintain the mosque, the regime feared that others, who had not been through the extensive vetting process, would step in to help. The regime considered that situation to be problematic because these unvetted individuals would undoubtedly influence the mosque, and thus religious discourse in Iraq.

As such, the regime inquired about the applicant's finances in all investigations connected to building mosques. The local Ba'thists and security services were required to include this information—whether positive or negative—in the report they sent back to the Party Secretariat. The regime denied applicants who lacked the financial resources to carry out the project even if no other derogatory information about them emerged in the investigations. Sometimes, the regime made this decision even if the applicant felt that he could afford the mosque. For example, one otherwise unproblematic Iraqi was retired. In his retirement, he wished to build and run a local mosque. He owned a house that was split into two sections. He lived in one half and leased the other to make money. The investigators felt that the property would not provide enough to maintain a mosque, and subsequently the Party Secretariat denied his request.[76]

The regime was especially careful not to grant permission for mosques that had financing from someone outside the country and who was, therefore, outside of its control. One report describes a man who was said to have "good morals," which in Ba'thist discourse meant that he was loyal to Saddam and the regime. However, during their investigation, local Ba'thists had learned that "one of his relatives is an expatriate outside Iraq, and that he will assist him in building the mosque." That was unacceptable, and the application was rejected without further thought.[77]

Some Iraqis attempted to circumvent the problem of financing through communal fundraising. This was also problematic for the Ba'thists because they would have had difficulty tracking the financiers. Furthermore, it would be unclear whom to hold responsible if the mosque was used for hostile activity. Thus, one finds rejections that stated someone wished to "rely on fundraising, and that is not permitted at the current time."[78]

Communal funding of a mosque was also problematic in that the regime relied on Iraq's political economy to ensure that mosques did not fall into the wrong hands. During the 1990s, crippling international sanctions had devastated the Iraqi economy. There were ubiquitous reports of ordinary Iraqis "selling their gold and furniture," and of poor families who were "giving children to orphanages." Some Iraqis were even reported to be "selling their internal organs for hard currency."[79] Yet, as others have pointed out, those with connections to the regime were able not only to maintain their status but to flourish. In fact, a new class emerged for whom "money [was] no object."[80] Anyone who possessed enough resources to finance a mosque was usually tied to the regime. As a result, requiring that one must finance the project individually—rather than communally—was simply another means of ensuring that the mosque would not fall into the wrong hands.

The cases mentioned thus far refer to Sunni and Shi'i Muslims who wished to build mosques. It should be noted, however, that Christians who wished to build churches and other religious structures went through the same process. Comparing and contrasting the experiences of Iraqi Christians with that of their Muslim counterparts reveals a great deal about the nature of the regime in religious matters. First, and most strikingly, the mechanics of the process for a Christian to build a church were exactly the same as for a Muslim to build a mosque. A request was made with the Ministry of Endowments and Religious Affairs. The ministry forwarded the application to the Ba'th Party Secretariat. The Secretariat would then oversee an investigation and conclude whether or not to approve the project. In the regime's records, one even finds the files on churches intermixed with the files on mosques. Thus, officially, the regime did not distinguish between churches and mosques. However, sifting through the regime's files, it quickly becomes apparent that the regime rarely approved Christian requests to build churches.[81] Sometimes the regime's official response differed in tone among the various Christian communities. Requests from the Assyrian community, which had a history of nationalist agitation, or the Protestants with their strong ties to the West, were rejected rather bluntly. The Ba'thists gave the Armenians, who posed no political threat in Iraq, a gentler response—namely, that the church they had was sufficient, and therefore the regime would like to "delay" granting permission for a new one.[82] No matter the nicety of the language, the answer was still "no."

These instances depict a clear bias in the regime's attitude toward Christians. However, these rejections are also telling in what they do not say. Not a single file on the requests to build churches mentions Islam or Muslims. Instead, the regime continued to rely on the principles of Ba'thism, which downplayed religious differences. If the regime had turned to Islam or Islamism as some academic treatments of Iraq suggest, one would expect that this would be a clear case in which to observe the transition. The regime could have easily referred to the Christians as a protected religious minority (*dhimmi*), which, in traditional understandings of

Islamic law, would not be permitted to build new churches. Or, more mildly, the regime could have simply claimed that it did not wish to harm the sentiments of local Muslims. Yet both the local Ba'thist investigators and the Party Secretariat provided strictly secular justifications for their rejections. Most commonly they stated that the existing church was adequate and that there was no need for a new one, or that there were already enough churches in the area. As mentioned previously, the regime often employed the same language and reasoning when rejecting a Muslim's request to build a mosque.[83] The regime continued to use this logic and language even into the final year of Saddam's rule.[84] Thus, although there is clear evidence of de facto bias in the regime's actions, there is no sign of de jure discrimination against Christians or official Islamization of the regime's policies.

CONCLUSION

Instrumentalizing religion required that the Ba'thists empower religious leaders to some extent. Previous chapters have discussed how the regime developed a cadre of religious leaders that the regime trusted. This chapter has shown that the regime only trusted these religious leaders to a certain extent. In Iraq during the 1990s, the regime forced them to operate within layered networks of security architecture. A spiraling bureaucracy of committees, Party bureaus, and security services controlled who could work in the religious landscape as well as what they could say. The Ba'thists managed the construction of mosques and the appointment of religious scholars. This system took years to build and put in place. It was a vital component of Saddam's strategy of instrumentalizing religion without empowering people or ideas that threatened the regime's security. Chapter 11 will demonstrate how the regime's religious policies during the Faith Campaign were embedded in the security architecture that was outlined in this chapter. Then the final part of this book will discuss what occurred in 2003, when this system, with all of its checks and controls, was suddenly shattered.

Putting the System to Work

As previous chapters have alluded, and as this chapter will make explicit, the Ba'thist Islam that Saddam wished to promote in Iraq deviated significantly from "traditional" interpretations of the religion. Consequently, if the regime wished to propagate its Ba'thist interpretations of Islam, it first needed to neutralize traditional religious leaders who might contradict Ba'thist assertions. The regime also needed to create institutions and bureaucracies to monitor Iraq's religious leaders and, therefore, to control religious discourse. The resulting authoritarian system had a dramatic impact on the way that the regime instrumentalized Islam. As such, to understand the regime's discourse on religion during the Faith Campaign, it is necessary to situate it within the context of authoritarian state–society relations. Previous chapters have laid out the regime's system of control. It is now appropriate to discuss the regime's attempts to spread Ba'thist interpretations of religion. This chapter will outline the content of Ba'thist ideas on religion in the 1990s and early 2000s. In doing so, it will demonstrate that the nuance and ambiguity of this content required strict regime oversight and necessitated that the regime employ it in very specific ways. Thus, as this chapter will make clear, the propagation of Ba'thist ideas on religion were necessarily rooted in authoritarian

structures. Understanding how the regime manipulated Islam in this period will also be important to understanding the evolution of religious
discourse in Iraq after the regime fell in 2003.

AUTHORITARIANISM AND RELIGIOUS DISCOURSE
DURING THE FAITH CAMPAIGN

Throughout the 1990s, the Iraqi regime propagated religious—especially
Islamic—symbols as part of Saddam's so-called Faith Campaign. Saddam
built the "Mother of all Battles Mosque," which had minarets shaped as
Scud Missiles around its perimeter and then more four minarets shaped
like the barrel of an AK-47 machine gun closer to the mosque's dome. The
outer minarets were 37 meters high and the four inner minarets stood
at 28 meters. Together the numbers involved (4-28-37) denote Saddam's
birthday. Inside the mosque, Saddam placed an ornate Qur'an written in
his own blood.[1] The symbolism of these and similar projects was clear. Not
only did they depict Saddam as a champion of Islam, they also aimed to
create a personality cult in which religious belief was tied to support for
him and his regime.

These more extravagant measures were paired with other less bom-
bastic, but equally important, religious programs. The Popular Islamic
Conferences that Saddam had begun in the early 1980s continued
throughout the 1990s and into the 2000s. The regime also inaugurated
radio stations dedicated to broadcasting Qur'anic recitation.[2] Saddam
began to require some civil servants such as judges to take courses and
even pass an exam on the Qur'an.[3] In schoolbooks on Islam, girls are
shown wearing hijabs.[4] It is not surprising, then, that many Western press
reports as well as the academic literature on Iraq depict Iraq as becoming
a quasi-Islamic state during this period.[5]

As tempting as a narrative depicting Saddam's turn toward Islamism
might be, the regime's internal documents tell a different story. In fact,
these internal files are absolutely essential to understandings the regime's
ideology in this period. Saddam was not above misleading potential

supporters about his views when it was in his interest to do so. For example, Saddam relied heavily on the leader of the Nation of Islam in the United States, Louis Farrakhan, to present the Iraqi regime's views to Americans. Accordingly, the regime appointed Farrakhan both as the American representative to the Popular Islamic Conference Organization and as a member of its board in Baghdad.[6] Despite Saddam's public support for Farrakhan, Saddam did not share his views. In fact, when one of Saddam's advisors mentioned Farrakhan in a private discussion, Saddam replied "By God, I do not like them. I do not like those who engage in politics under the guise of religion. I don't trust them."[7] In this case and many others, public appearances were misleading.

Fortunately the regime's internal documents help to clarify which positions Saddam took for tactical reasons in specific circumstances, and which views on religion represented more foundational stances on which the regime based its actual policies. In March 1996, during the heart of the Faith Campaign, Saddam made a landmark thirty-three page speech to parliament. This speech is significant in that several months after it was delivered, Saddam ordered it to be distributed to the Party leadership in every province and to the national offices. It was to be read aloud to every Party member and to be made the basis of the regime's policies toward religion.[8] Thus, it is a reliable indicator of the regime's actual views rather than its tactical posturing.

The ideas Saddam expressed in this speech as well as in his other religious rhetoric needs to be properly contextualized within Arab nationalists' perceptions of their differences with Islamists. Arab nationalists saw themselves as distinct from Islamists due to their position on the Arabness versus the universality of early Islam, as well as over the precedence one gives to Arab or Islamic unity. "Precedence" is the key word. The ideas were not mutually exclusive. A great illustration of the Arab nationalist position on these topics can be seen in the writings of Abd al-Rahman al-Bazzaz, who was one of Iraq's most prominent Arab nationalist intellectuals, activists, and politicians in mid-20th century. Like Saddam, al-Bazzaz admired the pre-Islamic past and depicted Arabs and Muslims as heirs to the great ancient civilizations of the Middle East. Yet, this did not negate his devotion to Islam. In 1952, he justified Arab nationalism by arguing, "We base ourselves on the wisdom of the [Qur'an] itself, on the true laws of the Prophet, and on the actions of the early caliphs who represent it best. It is these which represent true Islam, not the false and obscure concepts which have gradually become common in the Islamic world."[9] However, as a committed Arab nationalist, al-Bazzaz's Islam was an Arab religion. He clarified that clear Qur'anic verses "confirm that Islam is the religion of the Arabs before being a universal religion."[10] And although he insisted that Islam was important, he maintained that "to say this is not to imply a call for Pan-Islamism. To say that Islam does not contradict the Arab national spirit is one thing, and to make propaganda for Pan-Islamism is another." Al-Bazzaz was not completely against Pan-Islamism in theory. He noted that "the call to unite Arabs . . . is the practical step which must precede the call for Pan-Islamism." However, he then clarified: "It is strange, however, to find that some of those who call themselves supporters of Pan-Islamism in the Arab countries are the most violent opponents of Pan-Arabism."[11] As al-Bazzaz's arguments highlight, debates between Arab nationalists and Islamists were not about the theoretical legitimacy of Pan-Islamic unity but whether it had precedence over Pan-Arab unity. Most Arab nationalists also insisted that within a theoretical Pan-Islamic unity, non-Arab Muslims would need to recognize the preeminence of the Arabs and their leadership of the broader Islamic community. Other Arab nationalists in Iraq in the mid-20th century had very similar debates with Pan-Islamists and came to very similar conclusions as al-Bazzaz.[12] Even Michel Aflaq argued that although Islam was essentially Arab in character, it was still applicable to all nations.[13] In other words, Islam was an Arab religion for the Arab people, but if others wished to follow it, the Arab nationalists would not object.

If one is to understand Saddam's arguments, they need to be contextualized within these ideological debates. In his landmark 1996 speech, Saddam made his position clear on these points. First, Islam was an unmistakably Arab religion. To make his point, Saddam discussed how some of the Prophet's companions had used Ethiopia as a temporary base while they were waiting for the right conditions to move to Medina.

Yet, they insisted on making their capital among the Arabs in Medina. Thus, Saddam argued, the priority was for Arab lands and the Arab people (*umma*). Ethiopia could not be used "in exchange" for Arab land. "Medina, not Ethiopia became the base for liberating Mecca." He then gave several other examples of how the early caliphs' identity was primarily Arab.

On the debate over whether to give precedence to Arab or Muslim unity, Saddam was also quite clear. He attacked "two-faced" men of religion who denied the need for Arab unity and replaced it with a call for Islamic unity.[14] Saddam rejected this outright, stating "it is not permissible to be fooled by this ruse." He then argued that those who gave precedence to Islamic unity in place of Arab unity were expressing a "tendentious call, even if it covers itself with religion."[15] He noted that the regime saw itself as ideologically closest to the "new generation" of "Nasserists in Egypt and Yemen whose call was based on the sincere foundation . . . of nationalism."[16]

In this and many other cases, the regime's internal documents confirm that whereas Saddam promoted religion in Iraq, he never adopted Islamism. Joseph Sassoon has gone as far as to argue that "the documents, in numerous instances, clearly indicate that [. . .] the regime publicly launched a faith campaign but simultaneously, behind the scenes, continued to be anti-religious and to repress any sign of real religiosity."[17] If by "real religiosity" Sassoon intends traditional interpretations of Islam, or Islamism, then he is correct. Yet this chapter will attempt to show that the situation in Iraq was more complex than a simple dichotomy between religious and anti-religious policies would suggest. Much of the confusion on both sides of this debate stems from a Ba'thist discourse on religion that was intentionally ambiguous. This intentional ambiguity and the role it played will be detailed following. But first it is necessary to outline briefly why theories of either Islamization and or anti-religiousness do not sufficiently explain Ba'thist religious policies in Iraq during this period.

Sassoon is certainly correct in claiming that theories about Islamization of the regime are unfounded. Islam never overtook other political identities—most importantly, Arab nationalism. In many of the regime's records where one would expect to find Islam, it is absent. Some of these

cases have been mentioned in previous chapters, but religion is absent
in other important areas as well. For example, one of the basic tools that
the regime used to understand and control the population was school
registers. The Ba'thists used a number of categories to classify students
in these registers: political affiliation, party rank, reputation of student,
ethnic nationality, and so forth. In the 1990s, these categories expanded
considerably. They began to include the number of martyrs in the student's
family, whether members of the student's family participated in the 1991
uprising, if the student was a member of one of the state militias, and so
forth. However, religion was not among the classifications. It simply was
not as important to the regime as ethnic and political identities.[18] This is
also apparent in the regime's cultural indoctrination plans from the period. They emphasize Arabism and often fail even to mention Islam or religion.[19] Furthermore, the regime maintained laws that clearly emphasized
an Arab rather than an Islamic identity. For example, in 1997, Saddam
signed a law[20] that granted "Iraqi nationality" to anyone who had reached
the age of majority, had two Arab parents, and continued to live in the
Arab homeland (*watan*). The law does not mention religion, and no
similar law referring to Islam existed.[21] Moreover, as Sassoon has noted,
senior regime officials spoke disparagingly of traditional forms of religion,
were openly hostile to Islamism, and feared that fervent religious observa-
tion could lead to, or be a sign of, Islamist opposition. For example, they
closely monitored anyone who regularly attended mosque, especially if
they came during non-prayer times.[22]

Nevertheless, these details do not tell the complete story. Regime
officials may not have espoused traditional interpretations of religion
or Islamism, but they were not against religion when it was interpreted
to their liking. This may not have been acceptable in the minds of many
believers, but neither was it hostility to religion full stop. In fact, the regime continued to propagate Ba'thist interpretations of religion both in
public and in private. Thus, the regime was not completely anti-religious,
even behind closed doors. The dichotomy between public religiosity and
private antagonism toward religion is further undermined by the fact that
the regime's public rhetoric and symbols were not entirely in line with

traditional interpretations of Islam or Islamism. For example, the Baʿthists continued publicly venerating pre-Islamic civilizations that would have been an affront to many pious Muslims. In 2003, when the Americans invaded Iraq, they faced elite Republican Guard Divisions named after pre-Islamic pagans such as Nebuchadnezzar and Hammurabi. The regime also continued to sponsor cultural events that glorified pre-Islamic culture, especially poetry. During this period, Saddam even linked his cult of personality to a pre-Islamic pagan god from the Epic of Gilgamesh.[23] For Saddam, such deference toward pre-Islamic civilizations did not negate his respect for Islam. In fact, as mentioned previously, Arab nationalists in Iraq, such as Abd al-Rahman al-Bazzaz, had a long history of combining veneration for Islam and pre-Islamic empires. As al-Bazzaz argued, "There is no contradiction at all between our sincere Muslim feeling and our holding precious the ancient Arab civilizations of the Yemen, such as the civilization of the Maʾinites, the Himyarites, and the Sabaeans, or the civilization of the Amalekites and of the Nabateans, and the Arab civilization which preceded these, the civilizations of the Assyrians and of the Babylonians."[24] Saddam appears to have shared these sentiments. In contrast, it is difficult to imagine an Islamist or "Islamized" state that would prominently employ such pagan symbols.

As discussed in previous chapters, the regime was also keen to transcend sectarian differences among the population. This necessitated restricting traditional Sunni and Shiʿi views of their own superiority or of the failings of their rivals. Such policies often appeared anti-religious to those not indoctrinated into Baʿthist thinking, but they were in accordance with Baʿthist assumptions about true Islam as a non-sectarian religion that could unite all Arabs.

Accordingly, the regime neither became "Islamist" nor completely hid its views behind closed doors. Instead, on one hand, the Baʿthists attempted to formulate a nuanced interpretation of religion that supported Baʿthist assumptions about the centrality of Arabism and the legitimacy of Saddam's rule. On the other hand, however, the regime remained hostile to any form of religious independence and especially Islamism in Iraq.

Analyses of Iraqi policies that question whether the regime remained secular or turned to Islam generally fail to identify the continuation of the Ba'thists' religious policies from previous decades. By focusing strictly on ideology, they neglect to consider the role that the regime's authoritarian system played in the public manifestation of official ideologies. For example, Amatzia Baram, one of the most forceful proponents of the Islamization narrative, quotes Saddam's boast in 2002 that "All the judges have learned the Prophet's Tradition and the Blessed Qur'an." For Baram, this statement was a clear sign that the regime had transformed from "militant secularism" in the late 1970s to "Islamism."[25] However, this interpretation ignores the fact that clear precedents existed for such a statement. For example, in a 1979 speech to Iraqi judges, Saddam had stressed that it was important for them to study and understand Islam. He also emphasized his previously articulated stance that "we do not stand neutral between faith and atheism. We support faith as we always have and will always do so."[26]

Accordingly, Saddam's insistence that knowledge of Islam was important for judges was not new. The main difference between the Faith Campaign and earlier periods was that the regime began to require judges to take courses on Islam. However, this should be attributed to changes in the regime's relationship to Iraq's religious landscape rather than changing ideology. In 1979, the regime could not force judges to take courses on religion because it did not trust Iraqi religious leaders to teach such courses. By the 1990s, the regime had an abundance of trustworthy religious leaders under its control. Therefore, during the Faith Campaign, the Ba'thists were confident that the judges would learn interpretations of the religion that legitimized Saddam's rule and undermined Islamism, salafism, and other hostile religious movements.

A similar dynamic was at work in the regime's promotion of courses on the Qur'an. During the Faith Campaign, the regime inaugurated a number of courses for Ba'th Party members and for Iraqi youth to study the Qur'an. Since the late 1970s, the regime had stated its desire to spread Ba'thist interpretations of Islam as widely as possible and to emphasize "the importance it puts on religion, men of religion, and holy places."[27]

However, in the 1970s and early 1980s, the regime struggled to find rep-utable religious leaders who would carry this message to the people. By contrast, the regime's internal plans for courses on the Qur'an during the Faith Campaign of the 1990s highlight the role of trusted religious leaders who could teach the lessons in a manner that would enhance, rather than detract, from the regime's legitimacy. As the regime's records demonstrate, "All the imams and sermon-givers who acted as lecturers in these courses were screened by the division leaders in the Party." These screenings were designed to ensure that "there could be no negative influenced during these courses."[28] After the Party divisions had screened trusted religious leaders in their areas, they forwarded their names to the Party Secretariat, which conducted another investigation. The Secretariat then sent lists to local Ba'thists of approved religious leaders who could act as lecturers in the courses. The regime also closely controlled which mosques could be used for the lessons and assigned specially designated Ba'thist officials to oversee them.[29] The regime tasked these officials with ensuring that the courses adhered to "proper guidance" and that they would "guarantee in-tellectual integrity for the students."[30] In their reports to the regime lead-ership, the Ba'thists who monitored the courses give a decent sense of the regime's priorities. The Ba'thist officials reported whether the lecturers praised Saddam and Iraq, spread patriotism, and explained the challenges of facing colonialism and "American-Zionist imperialism."[31] These ideas were not new. They certainly would not have been controversial in earlier periods. However, only in the 1990s did the regime feel comfortable that religious leaders would adhere strictly to these ideas, and only in the 1990s did the regime have the institutional capabilities to monitor such courses on a large scale.

A similar dynamic can also be seen in other regime-sponsored courses on Islam. Some of these went beyond the simple lessons on the Qur'an and also taught broader theories of Islam and politics. For example, in the late 1990s, Saddam began to require Ba'thist Party members to take courses on Islam. However, only now with the opening of the Ba'th Party archives have the curriculums of these courses become available to outsiders. These curriculums reveal that the regime held true to its earlier teachings on Islam until the end. The regime's internal documents state that the lessons on Islam were intended to "deepen the awareness for the Party apparatuses on the essence of Islam as it is understood by the Ba'th." The Ba'th Party is described as a "nationalist (*qawmiyya*) movement" that stands in contrast to Pan-Islamic movements.[32] As in the past, the courses suggested that the Iraqi Ba'thists wished to create "the new Arab man." The regime's records clearly state that the courses were designed to rely on the intellectual heritage of the Party and to employ the writings of the "Founding Leader," Michel Aflaq. Thus, it is not surprising that of the top five works listed in the curriculum for Party members, four were by Aflaq, and dated from the mid-20th century. Numbers one, three, four, and five on the list were Aflaq essays: "In Memory of the Arab Prophet" (1943), "Our View of Religion" (1956), "The Issue of Religion in the Arab Ba'th" (1956), and "The Ba'th and Heritage." The number two work on the list (and the only non-Aflaq piece in the top five) was Saddam's 1977 speech, "A View on Religion and Heritage." The plan also instructs Ba'thists to study the chapter titled "The Religious Issue" in the Central Report for the Ba'th Party's Ninth Regional Conference held in 1982.[33] This document cautioned against the Islamization of politics within the Ba'th Party and instructed Party officials not to use religion as a means to judge others or as the basis of Party policies. It pointed Ba'thists to earlier Party treatises to the same effect. Thus, as this curriculum demonstrates, the ideas in that report continued to form the foundation of the regime's view of Islam.

Clearly, the ideas being taught in these courses were not new, but only after shaping Iraq's religious landscape and establishing a system to monitor it could the regime aggressively promote such ideas.

AMBIGUITY OF RELIGIOUS RHETORIC
IN THE FAITH CAMPAIGN

A close reading of foreign press reports from the period of the Faith Campaign demonstrates that the regime struggled to articulate its interpretation of Islam convincingly. The Western press ran articles supposedly revealing that the Iraqi regime was espousing an "apocalyptic Islamic vision" in an attempt to win over the Iraqi population. Yet the Ba'thists recoiled at such descriptions. They insisted that the regime's policies were an "attempt to defuse the threat of Islamic militancy rather than encourage it."[34]

The nuances of the regime's religious policies in Iraq were muddled by Saddam's willingness to work with and even support foreign Islamist militants with whom he shared enemies. Thus, whereas Saddam provided no quarter to Iraqi Islamists, he often aided their foreign counterparts as part of a strategy to foment opposition in adversarial states. However, Saddam's support for such groups—which included everyone from the most moderate Islamists to Osama bin Laden[35]—was not dependent on shared ideology. Rather, the regime based its policies on a pragmatic assessment of whether these groups would support Saddam's goals. It should be noted that such policies were not limited to the regime's dealings with Islamists; rather, they were part of a broader strategic approach that distinguished between domestic and foreign affairs. For example, the Iraqi Ba'thists brutally repressed the Iraqi Communist Party, but they allied with sympathetic communist movements abroad.[36]

Saddam outlined his strategy explicitly in his definitive 1996 speech.[37] As discussed previously, Saddam attacked Islamist and traditional religious leaders in the speech. He supported proponents of Arab nationalism such as the new generation of Nasserists. Despite these ideological inclinations, Saddam stated that he did not assess men of religion or Islamic activists solely by whether they were Ba'thists or they agreed with the regime's ideology. The regime, he insisted, would work with those who have supported it. Indeed, he allied with some Islamic activists outside Iraq who did not view the Ba'thist regime kindly but supported Saddam during Iraq's wars. Saddam insisted, "it is permissible to work with them, and it is not shameful."[38] Nevertheless, as the case of Louis Farrakhan mentioned earlier demonstrates, Saddam was often unequivocal about his distaste for some of his foreign partners.

In addition to decoupling the regime's foreign and domestic policies, any analysis of the Iraqi Ba'thists' religious ideology during the Faith

Campaign also needs to deal with the regime's intentional ambiguity. This issue is, by design, much more difficult to untangle. For example, the concept of "faith" was obviously central to the Faith Campaign, but how exactly did the regime define the term? A course book for Ba'th Party members juxtaposed "faith" and "atheism," claiming that "the Ba'th is on the side of faith and against atheism." This would suggest that faith had some religious significance. Yet, the same course book stated, "religion is not a principle equal to faith." So faith was clearly distinguishable from religion and indeed superior to it. However, this still did not provide a definition of faith. When the book finally defined the concept, it stated the following: "Faith, which means having faith in the Party's principles." As such, the concept of faith had very little to do with traditional religious belief. Nevertheless, the regime would often quote statements by Saddam such as "the basis of our effort is faith and therefore, faith played a significant role within the Ba'th Party's ideology and life."[39] What role did "faith" play in such a statement? How should it have been understood? It remains unclear. However, when the regime felt the need to present Ba'thism as religiously legitimate, this ambiguity allowed it to do so.

Another important term that the Ba'thist often left ambiguous was "*umma*." The Arabic term *umma* simply refers to a group of people. It is often used to describe the global community of Muslims, but this has never been its only definition. Arab nationalists—and Ba'thists in particular—often spoke of an "Arab *umma*," and thus employed the term as synonymous with nation. Iraqi rhetoric would regularly play on the term's opacity as well as its religious undertones. Regime officials spoke about unity of the *umma* without specifying what exactly they meant. Or, even more ambiguously, they sometimes referred to the "Arab and Islamic *umma*," which again left unclear whether the *umma* was a community of Arabs or of Muslims. Nonetheless, the regime was able to use these ambiguities to present standard, and long-established, Ba'thist rhetoric as compatible with religious terminology and to conceal the gap between traditional interpretations of Islam and Ba'thism.

Clear examples of this phenomenon were widespread in the regime's public rhetoric. In particular, the religious textbooks used in Iraqi public schools during the 1990s were a testament to the regime's manipulation of language. A fourth-grade textbook stated "Islam is our heritage, we are Arabs. It is our creed, we are Muslims. Today we complain about the partition that rips apart our *umma*."[40] What was the definition of *umma* in this statement? Did it consist of Arabs or Muslims? It is unclear. In another typical example, a fifth-grade textbook explained that because religion taught unity, it could help to restore "our raped land." Of course, unity was also a central concept in Ba'thism. In traditional manifestations of Ba'thism, however, unity was always understood as unity of the Arab *umma*. The fifth-grade textbook, however, was unclear. It called for the students to strive for the "unity that existed in Medina so that we can act with one hand, one voice, and one will, and work for the good of our religion and our *umma*."[41] This seemingly straightforward statement needs to be unpacked. On one hand, Medina was a holy city in the history of Islam. Yet, on the other hand, every Muslim who lived in Medina during the period of the Prophet was an Arab and the Ba'thists normally claimed that that story of Medina described Arab history. Thus, it is difficult to determine exactly how unity of the *umma* should be defined in the textbook. It could have easily described either a Muslim or an Arab unity.

Manipulations of language in the textbooks were not limited to the term *umma*; rather, they were ubiquitous throughout the books. Another telling example dealt with theories of the state in Islam. One year of the high school religious curriculum was devoted to this subject. The textbook for the course discussed classical theories of Islam. As such, it defined the caliph (and sometimes, in deference to Shi'ism, the Imam[42]) as "the head of the state in Islam." In English, this seems fairly straightforward, but in Arabic it had different connotations. In Arabic, the word *ra'is* is used both for "head" and for "president." Thus, in another reading, the text defined the caliph as "the president of the state." Such subtleties had clear implications for Saddam's legitimacy as the president of Iraq. For example, the textbook used this careful manipulation to assert that "The Prophet established a state in Medina and he practiced certain matters that only the president (*ra'is*) of a state can practice today." These included "declaring war, making peace, making treaties, [and] leading the executive and judicial apparatuses." In short, the president was completely responsible for all "internal matters and international politics." Furthermore, it was incumbent on Muslims to be obedient to the president.[43] This play on words managed, fairly successfully, to insert the modern concept of a secular republican presidency into classical Islamic discourse. Of course, no such concept had existed in the mediaeval Islamic world.

Interestingly, this manipulation of language was carried out by Ba'thist censors rather than the author of the text. Everywhere that the term *ra'is* appears in the book,[44] one can detect an ever-so-slight box around the word—as if someone cut out the original word with a razor. Often the word *ra'is* also appears in a different font, or is slightly unaligned with the rest of the sentence. Clearly the author had used a different term, but a censor had later inserted *ra'is* in its place.

Other manipulations of the text are also evident. In each case, the censors' intent was to depict Saddam as a legitimate ruler. In some cases, the alterations went as far as to present Saddam in a semi-divine manner. For example, the author of the text provided verses from the Qur'an and below them, sayings of the Prophet Muhammad. The censors then added quotes by Saddam, carefully inserting them under the Qur'anic verses and the Prophet's sayings.[45]

The Ba'thists manipulated other traditionally religious terms and concepts outside of the schoolbooks. Often, they would empty these concepts of their classical meanings and then employ them with a new Ba'thist definition. For example, the term "martyr" typically refers to someone who died in the cause of Islam. However, as Dina Rizk Khoury has pointed out, "For the Ba'th Party, a martyr was an individual—civilian or military—who had died in the service of the party and in the cause of the Arab nation as defined by the Ba'th."[46] Similarly, apostasy usually refers to someone who has turned away from their religion. Yet, the Ba'thists employed the term "apostate" to describe Iraqi prisoners of war in Iran who "had betrayed their sacred duty to their nation."[47]

Similar ambiguities were evident in other regime policies. For example, in the 1990s, much was made of Saddam's decision to amputate the hands of thieves and deserters from the military. This policy seemed to resemble some interpretations of Islamic law. Saddam paired the amputation of hands with a policy of branding and cutting off ears—neither of which have a basis in Islamic law. As such, the motivations for such punishments were unclear. The presidential decree that established these penalties did not mention Islam or Islamic law, and they gave no indication that they were based on religious motivations.[48] Some Iraqis understood them as derived from Islamic law and others viewed them in secular terms, as a means to fight crime and prevent desertion.[49] In a private discussion, Saddam discussed the reasons for implementing such policies. At first, he stated simply that the criminals who were subject to these new penalties lacked a strong sense of "nationalism" (*wataniyya*). In fact, when Saddam initially explained the penalties, he did not mention—or even elude to— the Qur'an, God, Islam, or any other religion. He presented his motivation for enforcing the new laws in completely secular terms. The only explanation that he gave was that the punishments were an effective means of preventing crime and desertion: "Cutting off his hand sometimes has a more psychological effect than death, in my opinion. The effect that accompanies the fugitive is stronger than expulsion or execution."[50] Later in the same conversation, the subject comes up again in the context of doctors offering cosmetic surgery to help people hide the wounds. In this instance Saddam, clearly annoyed, stated that the punishments were articulated by the Prophet and the Qur'an. Saddam had left such justifications out of his initial statements on the matter. It appears that they were not his primary motivation because although his new policies required the amputation of ears and hands as well as branding, when he later referred to the Qur'an and the Prophet, he only discussed the amputation of hands. In this latter portion of the conversation, he conveniently left out ears and branding, as there was no Islamic justification for these parts of the policy.[51] Thus, although imposing Islamic law did not seem to be the motivation for his decisions and cannot fully explain them, he was not against employing it rhetorically when he felt it was useful.

Whatever Saddam's motivations, he must have understood that the nature of the punishments meant that they could be interpreted as stemming from Islam. It is therefore unlikely that he would have permitted them if he had been reluctant to introduce Islam into the public sphere. Yet, by this point, his perception of control over the religious sphere in Iraq meant that he did not view public manifestations of Islam as a threat. Consequently, one could argue that the existence of a trusted cadre of religious leaders in Iraq allowed for policies that were not religious in their motivation but could be misconstrued as such.

There were equally ambiguous motivations for other policies that resembled traditional interpretations of Islamic law. The Ba'thists never banned alcohol, but when they restricted it in some areas, they gave social and economic explanations concerning conspicuous consumption in a period of severe austerity under the international sanctions. At the time, reports suggested that the restrictions were enacted "to appease an impoverished middle class resentful of the speculators and professional criminals who alone have the money to drink . . . in Baghdad's nightclubs, restaurants and bars." Moreover, the restrictions on alcohol were put in place at the same time as the regime banned 300 imports it deemed as luxuries. The regime wished "to concentrate on bringing in essential foods rather than luxuries for the rich."[52] A similar example could be found in the regime's attempt to limit usurious loans, which are traditionally forbidden in Islamic law. However, the Ba'thists had forbidden these loans in their original constitution published in 1947. Article 35 of the document clearly states that "Usurious loans are prohibited between citizens."[53] This constitution was adopted by the Party in Syria in the mid-20th century. Its proposed policies can hardly be attributed to an Islamization program in Iraq in the 1990s. And its ban on usury was designed to foster unity and ameliorate class divisions, not to impose religious law.

That these high-profile instances do not appear to have been motivated by Islamic law does not mean that the regime never referred to Islamic law. In the Ba'th Party files, which outline in detail how the regime carried out and justified its policies, one is hard pressed to find references to Islamic law—even in cases where it would have been convenient to do so. Contrary to the desires of their Islamist rivals, the Iraqi Ba'thists never made Islamic law a foundation for public policies. However, there were cases during the Faith Campaign in which the regime publicly referred or eluded to

Islamic law to legitimize its actions. Thus, Islamic law was sometimes part of the regime's rhetoric, but not its practices. This was not a new tactic. The Iraqi Ba'thists had done so repeatedly throughout their rule.[54] Saddam was not above referring to Islamic law to legitimize his most important policies. For example, at the first Popular Islamic Conference in 1983, Saddam referenced religious law as a motivation, arguing that he would accept the decision of religious leaders at the conference on how to end the Iran-Iraq War even before he knew what that decision was. To justify this statement, he argued that consensus (*ijma'*) among Muslims, which is one of the sources for Islamic law, superseded secular considerations and that this Islamic legal concept would be the basis for one of his regime's most vital political decisions. In doing so, he suggested that Islamic law overrode secular law: "I may apologize to the Iraqi people, the scholars of international law, and those involved in politics and legislature, for they may criticize Saddam Hussein[55] and say how can a head of state agree in advance to something he has not yet read or seen or known. I would say to this criticism that when such a gathering of good men who have come from all parts of the globe, representing Muslims, are in consensus on an opinion, it must be the right one."[56] The purpose of such a statement was clear to all the Islamic scholars in attendance—Saddam would adhere to Islamic law, and he challenged the Iranians to do the same. Thus, the Iraqi regime's references and allusions to Islamic law as a binding set of rules were not new in the Faith Campaign. As mentioned previously, these public references to Islamic law were almost never referenced in the regime's internal documents. That fact did not eliminate the Islamic undertones of such policies, but it contradicts the notion that they could be attributed to purely "religious" motivations.

ARABISM AND RELIGION IN BA'THIST DISCOURSE

The ultimate goal of the regime's contortions in its Islamic rhetoric was to conceal the gap between traditional interpretation of Islam and Ba'thist theories of Arab nationalism. To some extent, the regime's discourse was also meant to chip away at the barriers between religious faith and faith in the Ba'thist regime. However, this conflation of Islam and Ba'thism was not new. Michel Aflaq had argued against the "separation of nationalism (*qawmiyya*) and religion." He averred that, "indeed the Arabs are distinct from other nations in that their national awakening is akin to a religious message."[57] The Ba'thists' official slogan, from the early years of the Party, was "An eternal message for a single Arab *umma*." In Arabic, this slogan carried strong Islamic undercurrents. The Ba'thists' "eternal message" (*risala khalida*) was clearly linked to the Prophet Muhammad's revelation. In Arabic, Muhammad is described as "the messenger" (*al-rasul*), and his revelation is referred to as a "message" (*risala*). As already mentioned, the term *umma* also carried religious connotations. Thus, Ba'thist rhetoric had appropriated religious content from the very beginning.

Saddam's mixing of Arab nationalist and religious symbols during the Faith Campaign was a continuation of this tradition. As other Ba'thists had done before him, Saddam depicted Arab nationalism and Islam as essentially the same thing. During the 1990s, he discussed the "false theories" articulated by religious activists who argued that Arabs "must choose between Arabism and Islam." Saddam disputed these "false theories," insisting that "the Ba'th Party's view" was that "Islam is a substitute for Arabism or vice versa."[58] It is impossible to deny the resemblance of such a statement to Aflaq's thought on the same issue in the mid-20th century. As Sylvia Haim pointed out in the 1960s, "For Aflaq, Islam *is* Arab nationalism."[59] As such, when the regime's propaganda discussed Islam and Islamic history, it was not always clear whether they were making nationalistic or religious arguments.

This ambiguity was also evident during regime-sponsored celebrations of what many Muslims consider to be religious occasions. For example, on the Prophet's birthday, the regime approved slogans that unmistakably reflected Ba'thist interpretations of Islam and Muhammad's role in history. The slogans included "The Prophet's birthday is a new revival and the renewal of creating Arabism," and "The Great Messenger is the symbol of the history of Arabs, their civilization, and their eternal message"; and they quoted Michel Aflaq's famous statement, "Muhammad was every

Arab and every Arab today is Muhammad."[60] To attempt to parse out what exactly the Ba'thist meant in each instance misses the point. It is not possible to state that in one instance they intended secular Arabism and in another they intended Islamic religiosity, because from the very beginning, the symbols and rhetoric of the regime, and Ba'thism more generally, were ambiguous by design.

The regime's blending of Arabism and Islam was sometimes put into practice in ways that must have seemed strange and unusual for unindoctrinated observers. For example, reducing Islam to a form of Arabism meant that all Arabs—even Arab Christians—were closely connected to Islam and Islamic history. As such, Arab Christians could at times speak officially as pseudo-Muslims on behalf of the regime. It has already been mentioned that the ideas of the Syrian Christian, Michel Aflaq, formed the basis of Ba'thist courses on Islam and appeared in official slogans for celebrating the Prophet Muhammad's birthday. Furthermore, in the late 1970s, Tariq 'Aziz, a high-ranking Christian Ba'thist, asserted, "The Ba'th has always respected Islam and looked upon it as the spirit of the Arab nation."[61] 'Aziz continued to make similar statements throughout Saddam's presidency. In 1999, he represented the regime at Iraq's Popular Islamic Conference. He began his lengthy address to the attendees: "Brothers: May God's peace, mercy, and blessings be upon you. It is a pleasure for me to participate in this conference. I would like to address some of our Arab and Islamic concerns."[62] Such words coming from a Christian at an Islamic conference would seem absurd if one did not properly grasp Ba'thist interpretations of the religion.

AUTHORITARIAN ROOTS OF RELIGIOUS RHETORIC
IN THE FAITH CAMPAIGN

The content of Ba'thist Islam had an effect on the manner in which the regime could instrumentalize it. Ba'thist interpretations of Islam deviated significantly from traditional discourses on the religion. Accordingly, the regime required religious scholars to break dramatically with the past. Yet, the regime wished to present Ba'thist rule as Islamically legitimate and in line with standard interpretations of the religion. Therefore, the Ba'thists attempted to conceal the radical nature of their interpretations of Islam through the use of closely controlled ambiguities that blended traditional Islamic discourse with widely recognized Ba'thist rhetoric on Arab nationalism. Such a strategy required certain concepts to be left undefined. If a religious leader delved too deeply into Islamic history, or attempted to define a term such as *umma*, the illusion of compatibility between Ba'thism and traditional interpretations of Islam would be lost. Consequently, the regime needed religious leaders who understood and were willing to remain within the tight parameters of acceptable Ba'thist idiom. Thus, the rhetoric and symbols of Ba'thist Islam could only be instrumentalized after considerable efforts to shape an obedient religious landscape.

The regime's instrumentalization of Islam also relied on the institutional and bureaucratic capabilities it had built to monitor its message. Even with a cadre of committed religious leaders, the regime's message was sometimes misconstrued. As an independent analyst wrote near the end of Saddam's rule, "all literature of the Muslim Brotherhood was banned in Iraq." This was true at Saddam University for Islamic Studies, "even for reference purposes." However, some works by Muslim Brothers or their sympathizers sometimes slipped in through the cracks in the system.[63] Sometimes this was due to the disconnection between the regime's foreign and domestic policies toward Islamists. To the regime's dismay, the non-Iraqi Islamists that it sometimes supported would at times attempt to exploit their good relationship with the regime to spread Islamist literature inside Iraq.[64] Others, such as salafis, had to keep their beliefs and activities secret, but they continued to exist in Iraq.

Similar issues were present within the Iraqi Ba'th Party itself. The regime constantly suppressed overtly sectarian discourses and actions both in society as well as among the Ba'th Party and security services. However, these actions would not have been necessary if sectarian ideas had not been a problem among the Party's rank and file. Some lower ranking Ba'thists and members of the security services appear to have misinterpreted the regime's policies on Islam. They heard the regime promoting its Faith

Campaign and they assumed that it was synonymous with, or at least closely related to, more traditional interpretations of the religion. As such, the regime's instrumentalization of Islam needed to be much more than rhetoric or symbols. To prevent its religious symbols and rhetoric from spiraling out of control, the regime's instrumentalization of its particular version of Islam required an entire system to monitor and control the message. For example, censors who reviewed the content of courses on Islam given to Party members would periodically catch lessons that "treated a subject far from the culture of the Party and the guidance received in the past . . ." and that "carried negative aspects for the present and future."[65] Wendell Stevenson demonstrated what happened to those who violated Ba'thist taboos on religion in her profile of an Iraqi general for her book, *The Weight of a Mustard Seed*. The general became increasingly religious in the 1990s and appears to have had some salafi sympathies. In the end, the regime executed him for those beliefs.[66]

CONCLUSION

As previous chapters have shown, the regime's system of control over religious actors and their discourses was an imperfect system. The regime was not able to control every corner of the Iraqi religious landscape, and some people or ideas that it felt were nefarious slipped through the cracks of its authoritarian structures. Nevertheless, the system that the regime put in place succeeded in driving such nefarious religious trends underground and out of the public sphere. Thus, the regime was able to promote Islam enthusiastically, but at the same time to mostly keep it within certain ideological parameters. As will be discussed in the final two chapters, the 2003 war destroyed the regime's system and thus unleashed the forces that it was designed to control.

PART IV

The Invasion of Iraq and the Emergence of Religious Insurgencies

American Misconceptions about
Iraq and the 2003 Invasion

O n March 20, 2003, an American-led coalition invaded Iraq, putting an end to Ba'thist rule in the country. Almost as soon as the American-led forces overthrew Saddam's regime, intense debates began as to why they did so and why the war was going so wrong. The most common explanations usually entailed some combination of failed intelligence on Saddam's support for terrorism and possession of weapons of mass destruction, as well as American promotion of democracy. At times, the fear of another September 11 style attack and the history of animosity between Saddam and members of the Bush administration have also been invoked. Much ink has been spilled on these matters—including major US Senate investigations on Iraq's (lack of) weapons of mass destruction and links to terrorism.[1]

Each of the aforementioned issues clearly played some role in the Bush administration's decision to go to war. But these explanations for the mistakes and misjudgments that led to the invasion of Iraq do not necessarily provide reasons for the emergence of violent insurgencies in the country following 2003. Thus, they do not explain what is arguably the most important failure of the war. Had no links with terrorism or weapons of mass destruction been found, but had Iraq quickly transformed into a peaceful, pro-Western, liberal democracy, the conversations about the war would be quite different from those we hold today. In some quarters, it would have been hailed as stunning success.

Of course, that did not occur. Violent insurgencies—most of which were religiously motivated—emerged in the wake of the invasion and ripped the country apart. These insurgencies need to be explained. Thus far, this book has outlined the religious policies that Saddam enacted and their place in the ruling strategy of his regime. The book will now argue that these issues had direct effects both on the manner in which the invasion was carried out and the political strife that enveloped the country following Saddam's downfall.

The regime's strategy of Ba'thification created misperceptions about Iraqi state–society relations, particularly with regard to the regime's control over Iraq's religious landscape. Like their academic counterparts, US military planners and the George W. Bush administration failed to recognize the role that the regime had played in policing the boundaries of Islamic discourse in Iraq. Therefore, they assumed that the regime had lost control over the religious landscape. American war planners likened the Ba'thist regime to a "balloon" that only needed to be popped.[2] An American Army colonel who was in charge of planning the ground invasion later lamented, "there was an expectation from the start that the Iraqi regime was a house of cards and all it would take was one stiff wind and it would fall."[3] As the investigative journalist Bob Woodward reported, senior Bush administrations officials at the Pentagon, including Secretary of Defense Donald Rumsfeld, "seemed to think Iraq was a crystal goblet and that all they had to do was tap it and it would crack."[4] These metaphors depicted Iraq as a hollowed-out state that had lost control over its population and could therefore be easily removed without damaging Iraqi society. Its removal would also have little effect on Iraqi religious leaders, whom American analysts assumed were already operating independently and would continue to do so. However, this conception of the relationship between religion and state in Iraq significantly underestimated the robustness of the Ba'thist regime. It failed to account for the role that the Ba'thists played in suppressing religious extremists and sectarian ideas that had the potential to tear the country apart. Accordingly, analysts also failed to contemplate what would happen once the regime no longer suppressed these religious actors and their ideas.

Only now, with access to Iraq's internal archives, can one fully appreciate what occurred during and after Saddam's downfall. This chapter will first outline how the regime's strategy of Ba'thification led to American misperceptions about the relationship between the regime and the Iraqi religious landscape under Saddam. Then, it will show how this misperception laid the groundwork for the religious insurgencies that followed. Chapter 13 will discuss the rise of religious insurgencies in post-2003 Iraq.

ILLUSIONS OF INDEPENDENCE

The fact that Iraqis, and especially Iraqi religious leaders, had learned to operate within the regime's authoritarian system significantly impacted the manner in which outsiders interpreted the relationship between the regime and the Iraqi religious landscape during the latter years of Saddam's presidency. If the regime's sources are reliable, the regime's strategy of Ba'thification largely succeeded in creating a cadre of religious leaders who were controlled by the regime. However, the results of Ba'thification are by their very nature concealed from outside observers. The regime's strategy was designed to mask direct Ba'thist influence by presenting elements of the Iraqi population under the regime's control as independent representatives of civil society. As this process occurred, the regime's increasing dominance over the religious sphere could sometimes give the false appearance that religious leaders were becoming more independent.

Evidence for this phenomenon is clear in the regime's records. By the 1990s, the Ba'thists had managed to wear down many prominent religious scholars who had resisted their overtures in the 1980s. The regime's methods of co-optation and coercion have been discussed in previous chapters and are by this point well known. They included torture, exile, and of course, execution. When necessary, the regime was not above applying these methods to the family members of dissident religious leaders as well. Therefore, fleeing the country was not always an attractive option. After enduring a decade of Saddam's rule, and with its end nowhere in sight, many formerly independent preachers, imams, and even Ayatollahs appear to have simply given up their opposition. Some began to work for the regime actively.

Once a religious leader had proven that he was trustworthy, the Ba'thists permitted him to travel and speak publicly. In some cases, this could give the impression that the regime was loosening its restrictions.[5] In fact, the opposite was true. Iraqi religious scholars were permitted to speak because the regime trusted them to spread Ba'thist propaganda or otherwise support the regime. As Abbas Kadhim has noted, "pro-regime religious figures enjoyed a more generous margin of freedom to express their strong views, albeit in a calculated way."[6] Thus, a religious scholar's ability to speak publicly was not necessarily evidence that the regime had lost control over him. On the contrary, it often meant that the regime had gained control over him.

The regime's archives have preserved several examples of this phenomenon among both Sunni and Shi'i scholars.[7] The case of one senior Shi'i cleric is telling. He had been a known supporter of Muhammad Baqir al-Sadr in the 1970s, and the regime arrested him after it assassinated al-Sadr in 1980. Later in the decade, he was arrested again and brutally tortured. Yet, in the late 1990s, he was able to speak publicly and travel outside the country. He even participated in religious delegations traveling to Western countries. The Ba'thists would never have permitted him to do so in the 1980s. Without any further information, an outside analyst might assume that the regime had loosened its restrictions on him. However, the archives reveal another explanation. By the mid-1990s, he had been completely co-opted and was actively working for the regime. When he traveled abroad, he did so as an agent of the regime. He was not—as both he the Ba'thists maintained—an independent member of a religious delegation. Instead, he acted as a spy, reporting back to the regime on sensitive issues and sometimes even condemning his counterparts for disloyalty.

In one instance, he traveled to an important Western state. The purpose of the trip was to demonstrate to Western audiences—and Christian religious leaders—that Iraqis were suffering from what he termed an "American-Zionist attack." After returning to Iraq, he met with regime officials. He claimed that the trip was successful. He was able to explain Iraq's position to various Christian clergy, to the press, and to other officials. However, he insisted that the Iraqi ambassador in this particular state was not playing "any role in explaining the suffering of the Iraqi people." Moreover, the ambassador was not at all interested in assisting the delegation's "patriotic mission."

The Director General of the Office of the Party Secretariat in Baghdad was appalled. He sent a memo to Saddam explaining what had occurred. He insisted that the ambassador be removed from this sensitive post due to his obvious lack of "good morals."[8] The archives did not preserve the ambassador's fate, but clearly the cleric put him in a precarious situation.

It is important to note that this was not a case of passive acquiescence to regime policies, or simply a lack of resistance. The senior Shi'i cleric could have remained quiet about his experience. After a decade of torture and imprisonment, he was in an impossible position. Following the fall of the regime, he discussed how Iraqi intelligence officers would show up at his house in the middle of the night and take him away for questioning. At the same time, the regime also wooed him with various incentives. These incentives were dependent on his providing such important details. Apparently the strategy worked. This created an illusion of independence for the cleric. From the outside, his ability to travel and speak publicly seemed to indicate that the regime had lost control; but in reality, these abilities were evidence that he had succumbed to Saddam's carrots and sticks.

This was not an isolated case. In post-2003 Iraq, almost no senior religious leader wishes to be associated with Saddam's brutal regime. However, many of those who now claim to have been dissidents were in fact actively supporting the regime (though the cleric's case is also representative in the sense that religious leaders were often imprisoned or tortured before finally coming around). If the regime needed a religious fatwa, it could count on receiving one signed by the most senior scholars.[9] And when resistance to the regime did manifest among the religious leadership, the regime could rely on other senior scholars to counter it.[10] As discussed in earlier chapters, senior regime officials openly acknowledged this phenomenon behind closed doors.[11] Therefore, when the regime co-opted scholars, especially among the Shi'is, it often worked to conceal its relationship with them.

Both the regime and the religious scholars saw a benefit in hiding their cooperation to preserve the appearance of independence for the latter.[12] From the regime's point of view, this approached was beneficial for at least two reasons. First, it allowed the Ba'thists to co-opt religious leaders more effectively. Second, and perhaps even more importantly, the regime's policy of concealing its relationship with religious leaders created the illusion that independent religious actors were supporting the regime's initiatives.

Thus, instead of destroying social institutions, the Ba'thists infiltrated them, and then transformed them into an instrument of their regime's authoritarian system. The Ba'thists did so while continuing to present them as independent elements of civil society. Therefore, as this phenomenon increased throughout the 1990s and early 2000s, it created the illusion that the regime had lost control. In the end, some scholars supported the regime openly, and some did so secretly, but almost everyone was compromised. Those who rebuffed the regime generally did not survive or were forced into exile. American policymakers and strategists clearly missed this fact as they planned to invade Iraq in 2003.

It would be easy to attribute American missteps in planning for the Iraq war to the ideologically driven analysis of the Bush administration. However, doing so fails to take into account a number of factors. First, as just shown, the Iraqi system was designed to mislead both its own population and outside observers about its control over its population. Second, the view of the Iraqi regime as hollow and crumbling was the dominant view of American policymakers prior to Bush taking office, and of independent academics experts.

For example, in 1999, over a year before Bush took office, American military planners held an interagency exercise called Desert Crossing on removing Saddam's regime. One of their key assumptions was, "Under today's conditions, observers believe that many of the services that still exist are sustained at the local level, as Baghdad can no longer provide services to many areas."[13] In other words, the centralized regime was losing control. This assumption mirrored trends in academia—both before and after the invasion—that portrayed Iraq's Ba'thist regime as receding in power throughout the last decade of its rule. They argued that the Ba'thists were isolated internationally and weakened by sanctions. Thus, they were no longer able to exercise control over large segments of the population.[14] Academic accounts of the period portray an opening of religious discourse in Iraq and a new-found freedom for Iraqi religious leaders.[15]

These portrayals likened Saddam's regime to a shell that surrounded but did not penetrate into Iraqi society. In such depictions, the shell could easily be removed, leaving social institutions intact. Scholars, such as Kanan Makiya, brought this conventional academic understanding of Iraq to the Bush administration.[16] In fact, Makiya famously told the Bush administration during the build-up to the war that American soldiers would be greeted with "sweets and flowers."[17] Another influential historian, Bernard Lewis, offered his analysis to Vice President Dick Cheney specifically and to the Bush administration in general during the build-up toward war. He described Iraq as the "already crumbling tyranny of Saddam Hussein."[18] Thus, independent analysts were not immune to the regime's deceptions about its level of control. And the idea that Saddam's regime was less robust than it turned out to be was not solely the failing of the Bush administration.

Where the Bush administration and its war-planners appear to have fallen short was their confidence in their assessment. Their predecessors in President Bill Clinton's administration were much more cautious when making judgements about Saddam's Iraq. As one of Clinton's top Middle East advisors, Martin Indyk, recalled, "We had very little intelligence about what was exactly going on in Iraq."[19] This uneasiness is evident in pre-Bush-administration records. The after action report for the 1999 interagency exercise, Desert Crossing, is fairly straightforward on this point: "The United States lacks sufficient information on individuals and groups within Iraq to plan for, or respond to, Saddam's departure. . . . the United States does not have a clear understanding of their policies and agendas."[20] This reticence is repeated throughout the document, and at time the lack of insight about Iraq is demonstrated unintentionally. For example, at one point, the Desert Crossing report describes the Iraqi *mukhabarat* as "domestic intelligence services)."[21] However, the *mukhabarat*, also known as the Iraqi Intelligence Service, was not strictly a domestic intelligence agency. It had some functions in Iraq, such as monitoring opposition and hostile groups, but it was very much an international intelligence agency similar to the American CIA, the British MI6, or the Soviet KGB. Even if this was an oversight, the fact that it could occur tells us a good deal about how well American officials knew Iraq. Though the KGB, like the Iraqi *mukhabarat*, conducted domestic operations, it is doubtful that a similar report on the USSR would have made such a simple mistake as characterizing the KGB as the Soviet Union's "domestic intelligence services." American analysis seem to have been so poorly versed in Iraq affairs that simple oversights like this one could slip through the review and editing process. Nevertheless, Bush administration officials built elaborate plans based on this very uneven knowledge of Iraq.

EFFECTS ON THE INVASION

American misperceptions about the robustness of the Iraqi regime and its control over Iraq's religious landscape clearly affected plans for the invasion and foiled many of the Bush administrations goals. The first signs that something was amiss occurred during the initial weeks of the American-led invasion. In the words of two prominent historians of the war, the pre-war assumptions about the nature of the regime left the invading forces "utterly unprepared for the mission." One US military officer would later recall, "No assessment ever accounted for the threat we faced."[22] The invading forces often encountered fierce resistance from Saddam's militias and security forces. Tellingly, they received no aid from the population, even in Shi'i regions with high levels of disdain for Saddam. Clearly, many Iraqis disliked the regime, and some Shi'is later recounted that if there had been "any sign of weakness by the government," there would have been an "uprising."[23] This may not have been a pro-American uprising in support of the invasion, but if Iraqis had indeed seen an opening, many of them would have attempted to throw off the regime's yoke. Yet, in 2003, there was no sign of weakness, and there was no uprising. The Iraqi Shi'is were simply too afraid. Patrick Cockburn, who was in Iraq during the invasion, reported that "security services were everywhere on the alert." Even the opposition, such as the Sadrists, by their own account, did not challenge the regime in any meaningful way.[24] On the ground, the regime was much stronger than outside observers had anticipated. The regime's power, however, was not based on a highly visible army and uniformed police. Instead, the Ba'thists relied on civilian-clothed paramilitary militias and Ba'thized elements of Iraqi society that were loyal to—or at least too afraid to act against—Saddam. Most analysts, both in academia and the US government, seem to have underestimated these alternative sources of power.

The American military had to adjust its policies mid-battle to account for its mistaken assumptions about the ability of Saddam's regime to control the population. To take just one example, the Bush administration had removed numerous sensitive sites from its "hit list" prior to the invasion. American officials believed the Iraqi regime did not exercise any meaningful control over them and, therefore, they would not pose any threat to US forces. This again was a mistake, and the Americans were forced to change their rules of engagement halfway through the operation.[25]

Importantly, many of these "sensitive" sites were mosques and other religious establishments. Though both academics and military planners believed the religious landscape had begun to function independently from the regime, neither the events of 2003 nor the regime's internal records support these theories. In fact, mosques and other religious institutions were centers of regime-sponsored resistance during the 2003 invasion. Perhaps most surprisingly, the regime's control was not limited to Sunni institutions. The regime's records demonstrate that the Ba'thists were quite

comfortable operating in Shi'i areas as well. The Ba'thists felt they could
rely on the support of the venerable Shi'i seminaries (the *hawza*) in Najaf,
and in southern Iraqi towns US Army officers reported that the Shi'i religious leaders based in the mosques were aiding the Ba'thist regime's
fighters against the invading Americans.[26] During the build-up to the
American invasion, Iraqi contingency plans stressed that in the event the
regime was no longer able to maintain direct control, the Party apparatuses
resisting the invaders should use the mosques and other religious places,
including the Najaf *hawza*, to spread their messages.[27] Ba'thist operatives
were also instructed to "recruit dependable sources and direct them to
the mosques."[28] Interestingly, the regime also instructed Ba'thists to assassinate religious leaders in the mosques. It is unclear which religious
leaders they should kill, but because the regime's plans assumed it would
receive support of religious establishments, one can assume that the regime planned to assassinate unreliable religious leaders while allying with
those it trusted.[29] Despite such ambiguities, the Ba'thists clearly felt that
religious institutions were bastions of regime support rather than centers
of independence and opposition.

Misperceptions about the former regime's relationship to the Iraqi religious landscape continued to plague the American-led coalition even
after the Ba'thist regime had been overthrown. Because the Bush administration saw the regime as weaker than it actually was, it assumed that
religious leaders were self-policing and operating in a type of equilibrium
outside of state power. Thus, the removal of the regime should not have
radically affected them. For war planners, this was especially true among
the Shi'is in southern Iraq, whom American officials saw as natural allies.
As George Packer has argued, Shi'i power "was the key to the whole ne-
oconservative vision for Iraq."[30] Senior officials in the Bush administration felt that " . . . traditional Iraqi Shiism (as opposed to the theocratic,
totalitarian kind that has taken Iran captive) could lead the way toward
reorienting the Arab world toward America and Israel."[31] If the regime had
indeed lost control in the 1990s, then the logical conclusion would have
been that the quietist interpretation of Shi'ism that dominated southern
Iraq in the final years of Saddam's rule represented the natural order.

As this book has shown, this simply was not the case. Iraq's senior Shiʻi scholars were not as independent as some analysts thought. The regime had shaped and demarcated the Shiʻi religious landscape in accordance with its political goals. Perhaps the best demonstration of the regime's ability to coerce the Shiʻi religious leaders came several months prior to the invasion when the Baʻthists forced the most senior Shiʻi scholars—the *marajaʻ*—in Najaf to issue blatantly pro-regime fatwas that denounced the invading forces and defended Saddam's regime as a legitimate Muslim state. As mentioned previously,[32] Sistani himself ruled that it was impermissible to aid a foreign country's invasion of Iraq. He argued that doing so would make one guilty of "major sins and of violating taboos," which would follow the perpetrator in this life and the next; and he denounced anyone willing to work "with the foreigners to attack a Muslim country," including Iraq.[33] Such statements clearly demonstrated the regime's control. Sistani's reasoning in these fatwas was not controversial from an Islamic standpoint, but in earlier periods, scholars from Sistani's quietist school of Shiʻism would have avoided making such overtly political statements. By 2002, he and his colleagues had no choice. The Baʻthists were clearly in control.

Yet, war-planners did not appreciate the role that the Baʻthist regime played in creating a docile Shiʻi religious landscape in southern Iraq. Those misperceptions were baked into the plans for occupying Iraq. Thus, planners placed Shiʻi areas such as south-central Iraq under the control of multinational forces, which had separate, more restrictive rules of engagement. These forces, from states such as Spain and Italy, had been brought into the coalition for political reasons; and as two prominent historians of the war put it, they "had come to Iraq expecting to do little more than occupy checkpoints and conduct patrols."[34] They were not prepared to fight a religious insurgency; and because of misperceptions about the nature of the former Iraqi regime, and thus of the state of the Shiʻi religious landscape, no one thought they would have to.

This was a critical error. Without Saddam's repressive system in place, the Shiʻi religious landscape looked considerably different, and it was much more dangerous for occupying forces. The areas of south-central

Iraq that American planners considered to be docile became home to violent religious movements backed by hardline Shi'i clerics such as Muqtada al-Sadr, who had not been permitted to operate openly under Saddam. These hardline clerics were often openly sectarian, and they held more extreme views about religion and politics. This made them dangerous for any authority that wished to rule over a united Iraq. A similar phenomenon occurred among Sunnis.

L. Paul Bremer, who headed the occupation of Iraq following the invasion, noticed almost immediately that something had gone horribly wrong. In his memoir, he states that he received all sorts of briefings prior to arriving in Iraq, "but nobody had given me a sense of how utterly broken this country was."[35] He argued that "by the time he was driven out in April 2003, Saddam's Baathists had been in power three times longer than Hitler. The effects of his ruthless dictatorship were deeply woven into the moral and psychological fiber of Iraqi society."[36] Since he left Iraq, Bremer has been in open disagreement with some of the war's architects about the problems he faced. Bush administration officials such as former Deputy Secretary of Defense, Paul Wolfowitz, and former Undersecretary of Defense for Policy, Doug Feith, have argued that specific policies the United States implemented, rather than a larger misconception about what was possible in Iraq, were the root causes for the coalition's failure to secure the country. For example, they have argued that power should have been transferred to Iraqis much earlier. In a 2016 interview, Bremer countered, "the damage to civil society under Saddam was so profound that there was simply no credible, representative group of Iraqis capable of handling government in the immediate postwar period."[37] The idea that an independent, cohesive Iraqi civil society exited was based on a misconception about how the Ba'thists ruled the country. It was an illusion caused by Ba'thification.

Bremer's impression of what he faced in 2003 has been echoed by other occupation officials as well. Soon after the fall of Saddam, a young British coalition official named Rory Stewart became the acting governor of two Shi'i dominated provinces, Dhi Qar and Maysan, in southeastern Iraq. These territories included marshes that, during Saddam's rule, had been a refuge for anti-regime activists, refugees, and people who generally wished to avoid Ba'thist attention. In the 1990s, Saddam drained the marshes in an attempt to gain control over the region. In doing so, he destroyed the ancient way of life for the residents. Thus, as one might expect, this was one of the most hostile regions toward the former regime. If there were a place in Arab Iraq that American assumptions about Saddam's lack of control would hold, the marshes—or what was left of them—should have been it. Yet, as Stewart reported, when "Saddam Hussein had drained the marshes and scattered the inhabitants . . . the old structures of society had been shattered and replaced with the apparatus of the Baath party." It should be remembered that in the Desert Crossing exercise in the late 1990s, senior American analysts had argued that "the services that still exist are sustained at the local level, as Baghdad can no longer provide services to many areas."[38] But, even here, in this poor, disenfranchised, and remote corner of the country, Stewart relayed that prior to the fall of Saddam, "Everything began in Baghdad, passing through the hands of the president's corrupt family and his security service."[39] In other words, the regime remained highly centralized, and Saddam had not lost control.

Misperceptions about the independence of these areas and the existence of some sort of civil society contributed to the coalition's lack of planning for post-invasion Iraq. Independently functioning social institutions were supposed to be the bedrock on which the country would be built. But they simply did not exist.

CONCLUSION

The relationship between religion and state in Saddam's Iraq had significant repercussions for the country following the invasion. As mentioned previously, the US military operated under the assumptions of what it termed the "balloon theory." Other Bush administration officials saw Saddam's Iraq as a delicate "crystal goblet." In other words, the American invaders treated the regime as if it was a thin, fragile layer covering a largely independent Iraqi society. Their assumption was that this thin, fragile layer

could be shattered and that social institutions would remain largely intact. However, not everyone in the US government shared this understanding of state–society relations in Iraq. Some dissenting analysts feared
"the balloon might turn out to be a bowling ball."[40] And Bob Woodward
explained that the delicate crystal goblet "turned out to be a beer mug instead."[41] Such nonconformist views were not looked on kindly by parts of
the Bush administration, and they were unceremoniously brushed aside.
Yet, as this book has attempted to show, the dissenting views were largely
correct with respect to the Ba'thist regime's relationship to the Iraqi religious landscape. Iraq's religious sphere was more bowling ball than
balloon, more beer mug than crystal goblet. In both of these cases, the
alternative metaphors suggest that the Iraqi regime was stronger and more
solid than American analysts predicted. Its security forces and the social
institutions that it had co-opted controlled large parts of Iraqi society. The
regime kept dangerous ideas and the people who held them out of the
public and political spheres. When this system was shattered, people who
held such views were suddenly free to preach their ideas and to influence Iraqi politics. It was out of this situation that religious insurgencies
emerged in Iraq. And it is that topic this book now turns to in its final
chapter.

Emergence of Religious Insurgencies in Iraq

On April 9th, 2003, Baghdad fell to American forces; and then on May 1st, George W. Bush declared that major combat operations were over. The ensuing American-led occupation attempted to erase the previous regime by dissolving its institutions. It then banned senior Ba'thists from participation in any public sector employment. However, the attempt to install a new, pro-Western government was resisted by violent insurgencies. The resulting carnage that enveloped Iraq has killed untold numbers of Iraqis and lasted even beyond the American withdrawal from Iraq in 2011. In 2014, religious insurgencies threatened the viability of the state itself, as the so-called Islamic State captured and held large sections of northern and western Iraq. Thus, in many ways, the American-led invasion of Iraq in 2003 set off a series of events that thoroughly transformed the country.

However, these events should not be interpreted as completely unrelated with the past. Saddam's regime had ruled Iraq with an iron fist. It had permeated much of Iraqi society and culture, bending them to meet its political purposes. The sudden lack of the regime's forceful hand in

Iraq transformed the political, social, economic, and cultural context of the country. However, the past never simply disappears. The legacy of Saddam's Ba'thist regime created the circumstances out of which religious insurgencies emerged in Iraq following the 2003 invasion. And as this chapter will show, the emergence of insurgencies in post-2003 Iraq can only be understood fully if it is placed within that context.

The relationship between these insurgencies and the former regime's policies is complicated and sometimes even contradictory. On one hand, the regime had spent decades suppressing Islamism, religious extremism, and overt sectarianism. These were the hallmarks of the post-2003 religious insurgencies. Thus, one cannot draw a straight line connecting Saddam's religious policies with the religious ideologies that emerged among Islamists in Iraq following his downfall. On the other hand, the Faith Campaign did promote religion in Iraq and made it an important feature of political and social life in the country. It did so in a controlled manner with clearly defined boundaries that the Ba'thists rigorously enforced. Following 2003, the Ba'thists were no longer able to enforce those boundaries. Iraqis continued to rely on religious institutions as they had under Saddam, but groups like the Sadrists, al-Qaida, and eventually the Islamic State were able to transform what it meant to be religious in Iraq. In some cases, an overlap existed between what the former regime said about religion and the ideologies espoused by Iraq's religious insurgencies. This was especially true concerning Western powers and the American occupation—which both radical Arab nationalists and Islamists fervently denounced. Islamist leaders capitalized on such convergences when they could; but unlike the Ba'thists, Islamist interpretations of their religion did not foster unity in the country. In some cases, their ideas about religion were specifically designed to rip the country apart along sectarian lines. This phenomenon manifested differently among Iraq's various sects and among different ideological streams within those sects. But in each case, ideas that the former regime had suppressed were unleashed in the aftermath of the 2003 invasion.

The ignorance of the occupying forces about Saddam's Iraq led them to make numerous missteps and to exacerbate the unrest. When the invading

Americans became occupiers, one of their first acts was to dismantle the presidential office, the Ba'th Party, and the security services. Religion in Iraq had been handled directly by these institutions since 1979. These institutions had penetrated deeply into the Iraqi religious landscape and formed layers of security, enabling the Ba'thists to monitor religious activity closely. As the regime promoted religion in the public sphere, the role of these institutions had become essential to keeping Iraqi religious discourse in check. Without them, the system that the regime employed to stifle dangerous interpretations of religion quickly crumbled.

The fact that religion had become ubiquitous in the Iraqi public sphere was not something the US military could reverse. However, following 2003, no one policed what sort of guidance Iraqis received from their religious leaders. Thus, the American occupation unwittingly uncorked the potential for extremist and sectarian interpretations of Islam that had been simmering—in some places boiling—under the surface of the Iraqi religious landscape but had been suppressed quite effectively by the regime until that point, were suddenly given the opportunity to organize around already politicized religious institutions.[1]

THE EMERGENCE OF SHI'I INSURGENCIES

Iraq's Shi'is had stronger religious institutions than their Sunni counterparts. Many of these institutions survived the Ba'thist regime and continued to function following 2003. However, the Shi'i religious landscape was dramatically transformed following the fall of Saddam. The former regime had enforced certain boundaries about what it meant to be an Arab Shi'i, and those Shi'is who could not abide by the regime's dictates were either forced out of the public sphere or into exile. Once the regime's authoritarian structures were removed, the forces they were designed to suppress came roaring back into Iraqi political and religious life. This had dire consequences for the social, political, and religious life in southern Iraq following 2003. As Rory Stewart, the British coalition official who worked in southern Iraq during the initial years of the occupation, argued, the "U.S.-led invasion had destroyed the old regime. Those who had been in charge fled, afraid of retribution, taking or buying whatever files had not been destroyed by the bombing and looting." In the void that followed, the traditional tribal forces who had once ruled the area tried to reclaim power but were unsuccessful. In their place, as Stewart recalled, "Islamic militia groups began to gather weapons and occupy buildings."[2]

Shi'i scholars who had been exiled—mostly living in Iran—returned to southern Iraq following the invasion. Many of these scholars were in exile precisely because the former regime had considered their interpretations of Islam unacceptable—either due to their Islamist sympathies or to the sectarian lens through which they viewed Iraqi politics. The leader of the Iranian-backed Supreme Council for the Islamic Revolution in Iraq, Ayatollah Muhamad Baqr al-Hakim, returned to Najaf shortly after the Ba'thists lost control of it. The Badr Brigade, a militia consisting of Iraqi Shi'is who lived in Iran and were commanded by Iranian officers from the Islamic Revolutionary Guard Corps, followed him into Iraq. Many of these Iraqis had suffered long years in exile. When they left Iraq, their families were punished. The Ba'thists had killed five of Muhammad Baqr al-Hakim's brothers and a dozen members of his extended family. These Shi'is often blamed not only the regime for such atrocities but also what they considered to be its base of support among Sunni Arabs. They were not interested in post-conflict power sharing or Muslim ecumenism. Further, when these exiles returned, they were often viewed with suspicion or were unwanted by the Shi'i leaders who had remained in Iraq during Saddam's rule. Thus, they further exacerbated an already unstable religious landscape in southern Iraq that had been rocked by the war.

Shi'i scholars who had been repressed by the former regime, but stayed in Iraq throughout the Ba'thist period, were also emerging from the shadows. Rashid al-Khayyun, who authored one of the most thorough Arabic language histories of political Islam in Iraq, has argued, "Until the morning of April 9, 2003, the day that the Ba'thist state fell, the Sadrist trend (*al-tayar al-sadri*) . . . was not known in any articles, books, or in the press."[3] Although al-Khayyun states that there was a Sadrist movement in London that participated in an anti-regime conference in 2002, he claims that it never mentioned the name Muqtada al-Sadr. In fact, Al-Khayyun could not tell if Muqtada was known in Iraq prior to the Ba'thists' fall.[4] However, the former regime's internal documents make clear that it was well aware of the Sadrist trend and of Muqtada al-Sadr. The reason that al-Khayyun could not find references to him was because the regime had prevented him from playing a role in public life.

The regime repressed the Sadrists for a number of reasons. Most importantly, Sadrists rejected the legitimacy of Ba'thist rule and refused to stay within the dictates of Ba'thist interpretations of Islam. They called for an Islamic state, and they saw their struggle through the lenses of religion and sectarianism instead of Arabism and national unity. The Ba'thists recognized these ideas as dangerous to a stable Iraq and argued that it would be impossible to rule over the country if they gained traction. Yet, following the 2003 invasion, the Sadrists, led by Muqtada, reasserted themselves on the Iraqi Shi'i religious landscape.

The Sadrists and the Ba'thists disagreed fervently on most matters of religion and ideology, but the political context of post-2003 Iraq differed significantly from that of the Saddam era. Prior to 2003, the Sadrists' primary goal was to overthrow what it considered to be an irreligious Ba'thist regime. Once the American-led coalition removed Saddam, the main impediment to achieving the Sadrists' goals became the occupation. Thus, the Sadrists and the Ba'thists, who were fierce enemies prior to 2003, shared a common foe following the invasion.

Under those circumstances, the Sadrists benefited in some ways from the former regime's policies. The Ba'thists had encouraged a religious discourse that was violently anti-imperialist in general and anti-American in particular. Iraqi Shi'is were accustomed to such language. It would not have appeared out of the ordinary or deviant. The Sadrists were able to tap into this discourse and thus to assert themselves as a natural element of the religious landscape. Yet this overlap between the Sadrists and the Ba'thists caught the American occupying forces by surprise.

L. Paul Bremer, who led the occupation through it first tumultuous year, claimed to be surprised and very concerned to learn that Muqtada al-Sadr made "vitriolic" attacks "on Iraqis cooperating with the Coalition and had listed 124 people by name, calling them traitors and stating that 'hitting these people is a patriotic duty.'"[5]

Like Bremer, the rest of the American-led coalition was completely un-prepared for Sadr and his actions, but that was out of ignorance. Even the highest Shi'i authorities had released religious rulings, which, although almost certainly coerced, nevertheless made clear that an American oc-cupation of Iraq would be illegitimate and that Iraqi Muslims were for-bidden to cooperate with potential occupying forces. They had claimed that an American attack on Iraq would be an attack on "an Islamic land and Muslims," and they warned anyone who wished to help the Americans that God will curse them in this life and the next.[6]

This language and reasoning was similar to that which Sadr employed after Saddam's downfall. Thus, the anti-American discourse that Sadr promoted was not out of the ordinary. And in that sense, people like Sadr, who despised Saddam, benefited from his legacy. This phenomenon becomes even more evident when one considers that the regime had given prominence to religion and had indoctrinated Iraqis to take their lead from religious scholars (who, during the latter years of Saddam's rule, delivered Ba'thist approved messages). If people like Bremer had possessed a better understanding of the Shi'i religious landscape prior to 2003, they would have anticipated, rather than been caught off guard by, Sadr's language and the threat it posed to the American-led coalition.

The rise of the Sadrists and the return of Iranian-backed exiles disrupted the Shi'i religious landscape considerably. The conflict between rival Shi'i groups was often framed in terms of who could best champion the Shi'i community's interests of Iraq. Numerous splinter parties broke off in every ideological direction, some of whom became extremely vi-olent. When combined with rising sectarianism and radicalism among the Sunnis, internal Shi'i conflicts led some Shi'is toward increasingly sec-tarian and anti-Sunni political outlooks. Power struggles ensued between Sunnis and Shi'is as well as between the Shi'is themselves. Instead of a sanctimonious reunification of Shi'is who had been separated under the previous regime, chaos and infighting broke out. Some prominent Shi'i clerics, such as Abdul Majid al-Khoei and Muhammad Baqr al-Hakim, were assassinated almost as soon as they returned to Najaf. Some of these scholars were killed by Sunni extremist who were intentionally fomenting a sectarian civil war. Others were assassinated by rival Shi'i militias. Often it was unclear who was responsible for the killings. Either way, these high-profile assassinations led to suspicion and violence directed both at Sunnis and among rival Shi'i factions.

SUNNI ARABS BEFORE AND AFTER 2003

The experience of the Sunnis differed from that of their Shi'i counterparts for a number of reasons. Because the Ba'thist regime was ruled by Sunni Arabs, and Sunni religious institutions were more susceptible to regime cooptation, the regime had penetrated the Sunni religious landscape much more thoroughly than it had the Shi'i landscape. In addition to this, the government that emerged in Iraq following 2003 was dominated by Shi'is who were sometimes openly sectarian in their outlook. This led to a higher propensity for Sunnis not only to reject the American-led occupation but also the political system that was emerging to take its place.

The Sunni Arab religious movements formed to oppose the American-led occupation and the newly emerging political system in post-2003 Iraq. They had a diverse range of ideologies and interpretations of Islam. Among the Sunni Arabs, the regime had been quite successful in creating a cadre of religious leaders that it trusted to spread Ba'thist ideas linking between Arab nationalism and Islam. These Islamic scholars did not simply disappear with the fall of the regime in 2003. They continued to have influence, and—at least initially—to propagate an Islam with clear Arab nationalist undertones. Many of them placed Arab nationalism at the center of their Islamic message and viewed solidarity between Muslim and non-Muslim Arabs as an Islamic imperative. They emphasized "unity" and "resistance," which were key terms from the Ba'thist period. They also derided "sectarianism" and "division." They insisted that Arab religious scholars—whether Sunni or Shi'i—felt nothing but distain for Iranians, and they maintained that non-Arabs could not possibly influence "real

Arabs."[7] Thus, the fingerprints of Arab nationalism remained clear. Yet, although this inclination for non-sectarianism and unity among some religious scholars could potentially have been beneficial to an occupying power hoping to hold the country together, other impulses far outweighed the imperative of unity.

As occurred among the Shi'is, ideas about Islam operated differently in the Sunni religious landscape in the changed political context of post-Saddam Iraq. Under the Ba'thists, these religious leaders had been indoctrinated to fight colonialism and "American-Zionist imperialism."[8] Indeed, the forces of American imperialism were considered the ultimate evil in the latter years of Saddam's Iraq. In 2003, many Iraqi religious leaders saw the American invasion as a manifestation of that great evil. Thus, the same ideas that led religious leaders to support the status quo prior to 2003 caused them to reject it following the invasion. Nevertheless, the trends that Saddam had introduced during the Faith Campaign continued. Iraqis continued to attend mosques, to study the Qur'an, and to seek guidance from religious leaders. Yet, whereas these leaders promoted loyalty and quietism—at least publicly—under Saddam, after his fall, these same religious leaders goaded their followers to resist American occupation by all means possible.

For the Sunnis who had worked closely with the previous regime, the most important organization to emerge in the wake of the 2003 invasion was the Association of Muslim Scholars in Iraq.[9] The Association was formed just days after the fall of Baghdad. It was an attempt to unify Sunni religious scholars and to provide direction in the absence of the regime. Many of the scholars who formed the Association had been educated in Ba'thist institutions and had been monitored closely to ensure their loyalty to Saddam. Thus, it is not surprising that the Association framed the conflict against the invading American forces in nationalistic rather than religious terms. Initially, they preferred the term "resistance" over "jihad." They were also ardently anti-sectarian. Even as sectarianism metastasized in post-2003 Iraq, the Association wished to "encourage unity and end the division between the sects."[10] Despite this continuity with the past, in post-2003 Iraq, none of the checks that the former regime had employed to police these religious leaders were in place. Ideas and people that the former regime would have censured were allowed to operate freely and to draw religious discourse into directions that would have been forbidden under Saddam. For example, Harith al-Dhari, who emerged as the fire-brand leader of the Association, had fled Iraq in the 1990s. He maintained close ties to the Muslim Brotherhood and Saudi Arabia. These facts would have prevented his ability to act openly in Iraq under Saddam. Following the 2003 invasion, no such restrictions were enforced. Thus, like Muqtada al-Sadr among the Shiʻis, Harith al-Dhari had not been permitted to pro-mote his Islamist tinged ideas in Saddam's Iraq. However, in the context of post-2003, he preached an anti-American/anti-imperialist version of Islam that in some ways coalesced with ideas that the former regime had promoted. Those who had been influenced by Baʻthist indoctrination were fertile recruits to his organization.

The breakdown of boundaries on permissible religious discourse among the Sunnis was exacerbated as waves of exiled Iraqis as well as non-Iraqi foreign fighters poured into the country to fight the invading American forces. Many of these fighters were violent jihadis who held ex-tremist views about Islam and were openly sectarian. Some were sympa-thetic to groups such as al-Qaida. These fighters and their sympathizers in Iraq introduced their radical ideas into Iraq's religious sphere and further skewed its discourses.

SUNNI JIHADISTS

There were numerous militant strands of Sunni Islam that emerged in post-2003 Iraq. The most important of these was promoted by the organi-zation called *Tawhid wal-Jihad*. It later joined al-Qaida, becoming al-Qaida in Iraq. Over the years, tensions between jihadists in Iraq and the central leadership of al-Qaida led the organization to pull away, becoming the Islamic State in Iraq, then the Islamic State in Iraq and Syria, and finally, just the Islamic State. The group was founded by Abu Musab al-Zarqawi, a militant Islamist from Jordan. Zarqawi had fought in Afghanistan and had ties to Osama bin Laden's al-Qaida organization prior to moving to Iraqi Kurdistan just before the American invasion. Iraqi Kurdistan had broken away from Baghdad's control after the 1991 Gulf War, and the high mountains near the Iranian border offered Zarqawi and his fellow militants a refuge that was outside of the power of any state authority. This is an important point. The Bush administration knew that Zarqawi was operating in Iraqi Kurdistan, and some American officials tried to link him to Saddam's regime. However, post-war investigations show that the Iraqis saw Zarqawi as hostile, and Ba'thist intelligence operatives were doing their best to monitor him rather that to recruit him. While Saddam's regime was in power, Zarqawi remained pinned down in the isolated mountain districts of Kurdistan; but when the Ba'thists fell, Zarqawi was able to move into Iraq's Sunni Arab heartland where he began his religious insurgency. The CIA analyst responsible for tracking Zarqawi during that period has argued, "The terrorist the Bush administration had cited as a reason for attacking Saddam Hussein had in fact become empowered by the Iraq leader's defeat."[11]

By 2003, Zarqawi was a devoted jihadist. He was committed to building an Islamic state in Iraq, and he was uncompromising toward political and ideological rivals. He loathed the Shi'is, the American-led coalition, and even Sunni Arabs, particularly Ba'thists who did not "convert" to his version of salafi-jihadism. At times he linked these forces together into an indistinguishable evil force. For example, in early 2004, he argued that the Americans were "handing over control" to a Shi'i-led "bastard government" that would "bring back the time of (Saddam) Hussein and his cohorts."[12]

Other leaders of Zarqawi's organization shared his ideology. After Zarqawi was killed in 2006, he was succeeded by Abu Omar al-Baghdadi, who had been a committed salafi-jihadist since the 1980s and had fought in Afghanistan. The Ba'thists had pursued and attempted to neutralize him throughout the 1980s and 1990s.[13] Other leaders in Zarqawi's organization likewise adopted an uncompromising jihadi ideology either prior to Saddam's fall or soon after.[14]

When collation forces dismantled Saddam's repressive system, there was nothing to prevent these jihadists from operating in Sunni Arab regions of

Iraq. They emerged quickly as a formidable force and were able to recruit new converts to their cause. Some of these new followers were former Ba'thists who had worked in the military and security apparatuses of the former regime but were now unemployed due to the American policies that dissolved the Iraqi military and security services and then banned senior Ba'thists from obtaining any public sector employment. The fact that some former Ba'thists joined with jihadists should not be misconstrued to suggest that there was a link between Ba'thism and the ideology of the organization that became the Islamic State. As Craig Whiteside has argued, former members of Saddam's regime "publicly recanted" their Ba'thist past and "acknowledged their mistakes when joining."[15]

There are a number of reasons that these ex-Ba'thists recanted their former ideology and joined the jihadists. Many ex-Baathists joined or wished to join the new military and security services that were controlled first by the Americans and then by the Shi'i led government in Baghdad. All too often Sunni Arab Iraqis (many of whom were former Ba'thists) were forced out of such positions or they were never given the option to join in the first place. This rejection combined with other factors to drive some former Ba'thist toward jihadists groups. The success of various Sunni Islamists in opposing the American-led occupation, and then the sectarian, Shi'i-led government in Baghdad, also led some former Ba'thists to make a cynical power play and join such groups. Finally, there were some Ba'thists who had always been sectarian and disliked the Shi'is, and some Ba'thists who were sympathetic toward Islamism and Salafism. Though sectarianism or sympathies toward Islamism, salafism, and so forth were taboo prior to 2003, they certainly existed. Ba'thists who held such views secretly prior to 2003 would be natural recruits for groups such as ISIS post-2003 as long as those Ba'thists denounced their former ideology and "converted" to ISIS's version of Islam.

Some militant groups were more welcoming toward Ba'thists. *Jaysh Rijal al-Tariqa al-Naqshbandiyya* (the Army of the Men of the Naqshbandi Order) was founded by Ba'thists and emerged several years after the fall of Saddam's regime. The group blended traditional Arab nationalist ideology with a militant version of Sunni Sufism. At times there has been some limited cooperation between this group and the Islamic State, most significantly when the Islamic State seized Mosul and large swaths of northern Iraq in 2014. However, as Aymenn Jawad Al-Tamimi has argued, this was due to converging interests and an alliance "of convenience" rather than ideological affinity. The Islamic State eventually consolidated power at the expense of *Jaysh Rijal al-Tariqa al-Naqshbandiyya*, driving the latter organization into insignificance.[16]

The hardline jihadists were not only successful in recruiting followers but also in skewing religious discourse among Sunnis more generally. As Roel Meijer has argued, the more mainstream Association of Muslim Scholars in Iraq had to compete with others who professed different beliefs about Islam. And as he shows, "the Association was ultimately unable to withstand the lure of calling for a jihad and adopting a discourse that resembles that of the jihadi salafis in its praise of violence."[17] This evolution in discourse was at least partially due to a deliberate strategy that Zarqawi and his followers implemented after the fall of Saddam's regime. In February 2004, he fomented a sectarian civil war in Iraq by striking the Shi'is with "one blow after another until they enter battle." He hoped this would "reshuffle the cards . . . and whether they like it or not, many Sunni areas will stand with the mujahidin."[18] Such a strategy was precisely what Saddam had feared and was the reason that the Ba'thists had worked so hard to repress people like Zarqawi. Following the invasion and the destruction of Saddam's authoritarian system, very few checks on such ideas were left in place, and an evolution in religious discourse occurred in Iraq.

This evolution can be detected among some of Iraqis who would become the most militant Sunnis. In 2014, a senior commander in the Islamic State gave a wide-ranging interview. The man, who went by the name Abu Ahmed, described the evolution of his outlook since the fall of Saddam. Although by 2014 he had joined the Islamic State, which considered Shi'is to be non-Muslims who must either "convert" or face death, such extreme sectarianism was not as prevalent in the Sunni religious landscape immediately following Saddam's ouster.

Abu Ahmed argued that the conflict between Sunnis and Shi'is in Iraq did not begin over theological disputes. "There was a reason for opening this war," he claims, and "It was not because they are Shia." Instead, Abu Ahmed insisted, the origins of sectarian conflict in post-2003 Iraq lay in the fact that "The American army was facilitating the takeover of Iraq and giving the country to them [the Shi'is]. They were in cooperation with each other."[19] In other words, Abu Ahmed felt that the Shi'is collaborated with imperialist invaders, and that the fight against the Shi'is began as resistance to occupation. Nevertheless, since 2003, the views of many Sunnis have become increasingly uncompromising on a wide range of issues, including the legitimacy of Shi'is and Shi'ism. By 2014, a critical mass had joined the Islamic State and viewed Shi'is as deserving of death simply because they adhered to Shi'ism.

The transformation of religious discourse had occurred as militant Sunnis competed with each other. They were organized and to some extent radicalized in American-run military prisons. As Abu Ahmed states, "If there was no American prison in Iraq, there would be no IS [Islamic State] now."[20] This statement, although commonly heard, can be misleading. As mentioned previously, many of the core members of the organizations that would become the Islamic State held hardline salafi-Islamist or jihadi beliefs prior to the fall of Saddam's regime. Nevertheless, it is also clear that an evolution in religious discourse occurred among Sunni Arabs in Iraq following 2003. Along with jihadist strategies to foment sectarian civil war, the American prisons probably played some role in consolidating and organizing the insurgency.

Either way, the militant views that have spurred on religious insurgencies in Iraq since 2003 did not have their origins in Saddam's Iraq but rather in the aftermath of its downfall. In the absence of the Ba'thists' vast bureaucracy and Saddam's ever-watchful security apparatuses, there was no means of enforcing boundaries of acceptable religious interpretations or preventing spiraling extremism.

Following the overthrow of Saddam, the situation became even worse. Instead of providing a stable foundation for a new Iraq, religious actors took a leading role in the insurgency. This development took the Bush administration by surprise. American officials had expected to face resistance from what they termed "former regime elements," but not religiously motivated insurgencies. Yet, when George W. Bush convened a National Security Council meeting in February 2004, General John Abizaid, who headed US Central Command and was responsible for Iraq, argued that "the major threat was no longer coming from former members of Saddam's regime [. . .] but from hard-core Sunni terrorists affiliated with al-Qaeda, like Ansar al-Islam in northern Iraq and Abu Musab al-Zarqawi's Tawhid wal-Jihad in Anbar."[21] A similar phenomenon occurred in southern Iraq where Islamists such as Muqtada al-Sadr as well as Iranian-backed militias were fomenting unrest. These religious forces, which the invasion of Iraq had inadvertently unleashed, clashed with the occupying forces, the government of Iraq, and with each other. The resulting religious insurgencies tore the country apart, and as of this writing in 2017, continue to take lives daily.

CONCLUSION

As the previous two chapters have demonstrated, the occupying powers did not understand the potential of uncontrolled religious discourse in Iraq because they failed to understand the relationship between religion and state prior to 2003. Similar to much of the scholarly literature on Iraq, to the extent that they even thought about religion, they believed that the religious landscape in Iraq was self-policing. Thus, Iraqi society and the religious landscape were free from the influences of the regime ruling over them. The logical end of such assumptions was that the regime could be removed without causing too much trauma to Iraqi society. Such assumptions were mistaken. As this book has argued, a proper understanding of religion and politics in Iraq requires more than an examination of public manifestations of ideology and religious discourse. One also needs to understand the relationship between the religious landscape that produces such discourses and the ruling regime's authoritarian structures. Only then can one understand what those who wished to rule Iraq would face following 2003. This critical issue has been almost completely ignored by academics and policymakers. The results have been tragic. When the regime was removed, it left Iraq's religious landscape adrift with no means of curbing those who promoted increasingly radical interpretations of Islam. The result was a deadly cocktail of unhinged religious discourses and a population that had become accustomed to religion playing a significant role in their public lives.

Conclusion

*Saddam the Counter-Insurgent and
Other Reflections on Ruling Iraq*

This book has outlined the integration of religion into Saddam's ruling strategy and how that process affected the insurgencies that emerged in the country following his regime's demise. In concluding this book, it is worth reflecting in the opposite direction. What do the religious insurgencies that emerged in post-2003 Iraq tell us about how Saddam ruled and the potential for anyone to rule over a unified Iraq?

In some ways, the potential for religious insurgencies to undermine Iraqi unity existed long before 2003. Saddam and the Ba'thists clearly recognized this as a latent possibility. Their report from the Ba'th Party's Ninth Regional (Iraqi) Conference, held in 1982, mentioned that groups espousing political Islam had existed since the Arab renaissance (*nahda*) of the early 20th century. The report argued that since their inception, these groups had been a force for discord in Iraq. The Sunnis did not accept the Shi'is and vice versa. Furthermore, the report continued, these groups had often resorted to terrorism and violence, either in their ambition to take power or in confronting existing powers.[1] By 1982, the Iraqi Ba'thists had been confronting both Sunni and Shi'i Islamists for over a decade, and they would continue to do so until 2003. Thus, although Saddam appears to have possessed an ideological propensity to instrumentalize religion as part of his ruling strategy, his decision to do so also related to practical security concerns.

Interestingly, Saddam dealt with the threat of religious insurgencies in a manner that had a good deal of overlap with classic counter-insurgency doctrine developed by Western powers in the 20th and 21st centuries. Initially, connecting a regime like Ba'thist Iraq to Western counter-insurgency theory may seem counter-intuitive. The former was known for its brutality and its use of hard power to maintain control. The latter is supposed to rely on reducing civilian casualties, encouraging deployment, and winning hearts and minds. However, when one scratches below the surface, Saddam's ruling strategy and Western counter-insurgency strategies have a good deal in common, including a surprisingly similar intellectual heritage. The famous counter-insurgency field manual that General David Petraeus composed and applied in Iraq during the troop surge of 2007–08, begins with a nod to the 1964 book, *Counterinsurgency Warfare*, by the famous French counter-insurgency theorist David Galula.[2] But Galula's outlook was shaped by ideas and people whom Saddam appreciated and in some ways attempted to emulate. The introduction to Galula's book begins with an epitaph that quotes none other than Mao Zedong. Galula took from Mao the idea that insurgencies and counter-insurgencies are not as much about hard power as they are all-encompassing political projects. Thus, Galula concludes his study of counter-insurgency by stating "its essence can be summed up in a single sentence: Build (or rebuild) a political machine from the population upward."[3]

From the outside, Saddam's regime seemed to be based on hard power, but it actually relied on many of the same ideas Galula had. Saddam read Mao as a young man, and quoted him during closed door policy debates.[4] Throughout Saddam's presidency, Iraqi manuals on "Counterinsurgency" and "Guerrilla Warfare" drew heavily on Mao and quoted him directly.

These manuals often referenced Mao's famous assertion that insurgents were like fish in water.[5] In other words, insurgents did not exist in a vacuum. They were imbedded and could only function in a certain political, and in this case, a religious, environment. Defeating such insurgents required depriving them of a religio-political environment in which they could thrive. Doing so, to paraphrase Galula, required that the Ba'thists build a religio-political project from the population upward. Thus, the Ba'thists needed to co-opt and create Iraqi religious institutions and to shape the Iraqi religious landscape in a manner that stifled potential religious insurgencies.

Importantly, the regime conceptualized Islam in a manner that downplayed sectarian discourses and promoted interpretations of religion that emphasized patriotic Arab and Iraqi nationalisms. This interpretation of Islam was designed to foster unity and help to bind society together, with the regime acting as the essential linchpin. It also delegitimized Islamism as deviant and unpatriotic. The Ba'thists spent considerable time and resources enforcing this interpretation of Islam, and they had to fight constantly to ensure that religious discourse remained within what they considered to be acceptable limits.

As this book has highlighted, Iraqis very often veered into unacceptable interpretations of Islam. In such cases, the regime needed both the knowledge that such ideological breaches had occurred and the means to address them. Consequently, maintaining control over religious discourse required extensive bureaucratic and institutional capabilities, which took the regime decades to construct. The system was based on two pillars: first, the regime created a large cadre of religious leaders who could be trusted to act in a manner it found acceptable; second, intricate layers of security ensured that Iraqis remained within the regime's designated parameters of acceptable religious discourse. Only with this system in place were the Ba'thists able to instrumentalize religion vigorously at the same time as they suppressed interpretations of Islam that would either undermine the authority of their regime or that would lead to large-scale sectarian strife between Sunnis and Shi'is.

The American-led occupation force that replaced the Baʿthist re-gime in 2003 did not have anything near the institutional capabilities or intelligence resources that Saddam had possessed and that essential to Western counter-insurgency theory. Furthermore, the US military did not possess an "organizational culture" that was capable of quickly adapting to counter-insurgency missions.[6] When the United States did begin to adjust in 2007, it did so not only by implementing a troop surge, but also by attempting to recreate the institutional capacity and intelli-gence structures that were necessary for fighting religious insurgencies. The American forces allocated enormous amounts of resources to co-opt local Iraqi leaders. Craig Whiteside, who served as an American Army officer in Iraq and then wrote a PhD dissertation on Islamic terrorists in the country, has argued that a central component of American success during the surge was "recruiting high-quality local leaders to fill the roles of mayors, police chiefs, army commanders, and auxiliaries."[7] This was an important first step, and it certainly helped to stop the bloodletting temporarily. However, it only worked as long as American resources con-tinued to flow into these localities. It did not constitute the rebuilding of a complete political machine from the population up that Galula had counseled and that the Americans had set as their goal. A critical mass of Iraq's Sunni Arabs never felt that they had a political future in the new system, and many of Iraq's Shiʿis remained loyal to religiously motivated militias rather than the Iraqi state. In that sense, the American-led counter-insurgency in Iraq never succeeded in fostering a political proj-ect that could offer a viable alternative to the religious insurgents. For that reason it ultimately failed.

In 2014, the Islamic State emerged from the ashes of the surge to cap-ture and hold large parts of northern and western Iraq. It then moved toward the heavily Shiʿi areas of the country around Baghdad. The US-trained Iraqi Army was largely inept in the face of this onslaught. In some places it simply dissolved. Thus, Iraqi Shiʿis depended on sectarian Shiʿi militias for their defense. As of this writing in 2017, the country remains sharply divided between various sects.

If Iraq is to regain stability and remain a unified country, Iraqi leaders will need to build a political project from the population up. Saddam and the Ba'thists were able to do so, but at a great cost to human rights and basic decency. The central question for future Iraqi leaders will be whether or not they can carry out a similar project without resorting to such brutality. This question has yet to be answered; attempts to do so will undoubtedly shape Iraq's future.

NOTES

INTRODUCTION

1. Qur'an: 2:256.
2. Patricia Crone, "No Compulsion in Religion: Q. 2:256 in Medieval and Modern Interpretation," in M. A. Amir-Moessi, M. M. Bar-Asher, and S. Hopkins, eds., *Le Shi'ism Imamite Quarante ans après* (Turnhout, Belgium: Brepols, 2009), 131–178.
3. In addition to published sources, this book relies on extensive research using the Ba'thist Regime's documents formerly housed at the Conflict Records Research Center (CRRC) at the National Defense University in Washington, DC, as well as the Ba'th Regional Command Collection (BRCC) and the Northern Iraqi Data Set (NIDS), currently housed at the Hoover Institution at Stanford University.
4. See, for example, Amatzia Baram, *Saddam Husayn and Islam, 1968–2003: Ba'thi Iraqi from Secularism to Faith* (Baltimore, MD: Johns Hopkins University Press, 2014); and Michael Weiss and Hassan Hassan, *ISIS: Inside the Army of Terror* (New York: Regan Arts, 2015). For broader narratives about how rulers in the Muslim World turned to Islam to penetrate their societies, see Vali Reza Nasr, *Islamic Leviathan: Islam and the Making of State Power* (Oxford: Oxford University Press, 2001).
5. The term "instrumentalization" will be used in this book to describe the process by which the regime transformed Islam into a means to achieve its broader social and political goals. This is very similar to the idea of "functionalization" in Gregory Starrett, *Putting Islam to Work: Education, Politics, and Religious Transformation in Egypt* (Berkeley: University of California Press 1998), 10.
6. See, for example, Baram, *Saddam Husayn and Islam, 1968–2003*; as well as Weiss and Hassan, *ISIS*.
7. For the regime's strategy and plans on instituting Ba'thification, see "A Project Plan for Working toward Coordination between the Party and the Mass Organizations in the Field of the Ba'thification of Society," *BRCC*, 025-5-5 (0476-0497), no date but from 1988 or earlier. See also Aaron M. Faust, *The Ba'thification of Iraq: Saddam Hussein's Totalitarianism* (Austin: University of Texas Press, 2015). Helpfully, Faust provides a translation of the regime's plan for Ba'thifiaction in an appendix, pp. 193–201.

8. This book relies on Joel Migdal's definition of *control*. Migdal claims that "social control" can take three forms: compliance, participation, and legitimation. One can find examples of each of these in the regime's interaction with Iraqi religious leaders. Although often it is evident which type of control I intend, one can assume that at minimum I mean compliant. Joel Migdal, *State-Society Relations and State Capabilities in the Third World* (Princeton, NJ: Princeton University Press, 1988), 32–33.

9. The choice of the term "authoritarian" is not obvious here. Some would prefer to describe Saddam's Iraq as totalitarian. Semantic debates over what constitutes a totalitarian system as opposed to an authoritarian system have taken place since World War II. There is no agreement. I am agnostic about these debates and have thus decided to use the lowest common denominator—"authoritarian."

10. See, James D. Fearon and David D. Laitin. "Ethnicity, Insurgency, and Civil War." *The American Political Science Review* 97, no. 1 (2003), 75–90; and, Lars-Erik Cederman and Manuel Vogt "Dynamics and Logics of Civil War," *Journal of Conflict Resolution* 61, no. 9 (2017): 1992–2016.

11. Niccolò Machiavelli, *The Prince*, trans. Luigi Ricci (London: Grant RiChards, 1903), 70.

12. Gary K. Leak and Brandy A. Randall, "Clarification of the Link between Right-Wing Authoritarianism and Religiousness: The Role of Religious Maturity," *Journal for the Scientific Study of Religion* 34, no. 2 (June 1995): 245.

13. Quoted in Carl Friedrich and Zbigniew Brzezinski, *Totalitarian Dictatorship and Autocracy* (New York: Frederick A. Praeger, 1964), 249.

14. See David I. Kertzer, *The Pope and Mussolini: The Secret History of Pius XI and the Rise of Fascism in Europe* (New York: Random House, 2014).

15. Hannah Arendt, *The Origins of Totalitarianism* (New York: Harcourt, Brace and World, 1966), 346. The Nazi official that Arendt quotes is Martin Bormann, and the text is titled "Relationship of National Socialism and Christianity." A full translation of this text can be found in Appendix 15 of John S. Conway, *The Nazi Persecution of the Churches 1933–45* (London: Weidenfeld & Nicolson, 1968), 383–384.

16. Conway, *Nazi Persecution of the Churches*, 26.

17. Ibid., 26, 34.

18. Anthony Gill, *Rendering unto Caesar: The Catholic Church and the State in Latin America* (Chicago: University of Chicago Press, 1998); Richard Gott, *Hugo Chavez and the Bolivarian Revolution* (New York: Verso, 2000), 298.

19. Robert Kaplan, "The Vietnam Solution," *The Atlantic*, June 2012, 62. See also Neil L. Jamieson, *Understanding Vietnam* (Berkeley: University of California Press, 1993).

20. Starrett, *Putting Islam to Work*, 24.

21. "The Activities for Hostile Movements," *BRCC*, 030-5-5 (0029-0030), August 13, 1990.

22. Friedrich and Brzezinski, *Totalitarian Dictatorship and Autocracy*, 258–259.

23. Conway, *Nazi Persecution of the Churches*, 15.

24. Friedrich and Brzezinski, *Totalitarian Dictatorship and Autocracy*, 247–263.

25. Ibid., 257.

26. Merle Fainsod, *Smolensk under Soviet Rule* (New York: Vintage Books, 1963), 437.

27. Aleksandr Solzhenitsyn, *The Gulag Archipelago, 1918–1956: An Experiment in Literary Investigation, Volume One* (Boulder, CO: Westview Press, 1998), 347–348.

28. Fainsod, *Smolensk under Soviet Rule*, 434–437 (quote from p. 434).

29. Edward E. Roslof, *Red Priests: Renovationism, Russian Orthodoxy, and Revolution, 1905–1946* (Bloomington and Indianapolis: Indiana University Press, 2002). See also Glennys Young, *Power and the Sacred in Revolutionary Russia: Religious Activists in the Village* (University Park: Pennsylvania State University Press, 1997).

30. Friedrich and Brzezinski, *Totalitarian Dictatorship and Autocracy*, 252.

31. Vincent Goossaert and David A. Palmer, *The Religious Question in Modern China* (Chicago: University of Chicago Press, 2010), 142.

32. Ibid., 152–153.

33. Fainsod, *Smolensk under Soviet Rule*, 430.

34. See "The Guiding Principles of the 'German Christians,'" in Peter Matheson, ed., *The Third Reich and the Christian Churches: A Documentary Account of Christian Resistance and Complicity during the Nazi Era* (Grand Rapids, MI: W. B. Eerdmans Publishing Co., 1981), 4–6.

35. "Report on the Saddam University for Islamic Studies: Needs and Aspirations," *BRCC*, 3493_0001 (0025-0033), September 19, 1992.

36. See "The Ba'thist View of Religion," *BRCC*, 2225_0000 (0634-0638), May 1983.

37. Karen Elliot House, *On Saudi Arabia: Its People, Past, Religion, Fault Lines—and Future* (New York: Alfred A. Knopf, 2012), 149.

38. On the importance of opportunity to organize in rebellions against the ruling regime, see Fearon and Laitin; as well as, Cederman and Vogt.

CHAPTER 1

1. "Minutes of the Extraordinary Meeting of the State's High National Security Council," *BRCC (Ba'th Regional Command Collection)* 003-1-1 (0409-0414), March 12, 1979.

2. Con Coughlin, *Saddam: His Rise and Fall* (New York: Harper Collins Publishers, 2005), 155–163.

3. *Manual: Counterinsurgency Warfare*, CRRC [Conflict Records Research Center], SH-IZAR-D-000–296, October 1983.

4. Adeed Dawisha, *Iraq: A Political History from Independence to Occupation* (Princeton, NJ: Princeton University Press, 2009), 185.

5. For copies of Iraqi constitutions, see *Niqash: Briefings from Inside and Across Iraq*, "List of Iraq's Constitutions," http://www.niqash.org/articles/?id=2306; Robert Soeterik, "The Islamic Movement of Iraq (1958–1980)" (Occasional Paper no. 12, Middle East Research Associates, Amsterdam, December 1991), 18–19.

6. "Islamic Party Leader Concerned about Iraq Ulema," Rawalpindi, A-330, July 14, 1969, National Archives and Records Administration, RG 59, Central Files 1967–69, Box 2218. I would like to thank Brandon Friedman for this source.

7. Amatzia Baram, *Culture, History and Ideology in the Formation of Ba'thist Iraq, 1968–89* (New York: St. Martin's Press, 1991).

8. "Interview with Dr. Osama Tikriti," *Middle East Affairs Journal* 3, no. 1–2 (Winter/Spring 1997): 159.

9. One reason that some scholars of Iraq have considered Ba'thism to be anti-religious may be because they have mistakenly looked at this period as a baseline for Ba'thist ideology on religion instead of seeing it as the anomaly that it was.

10. "Minutes of the Extraordinary Meeting of the State's High National Security Council," *BRCC*, 003-1-1 (0409-0414), March 12, 1979.

11. Ibid., (0410-0414), March 12, 1979.

12. "The Minutes of an Extraordinary Meeting," *BRCC*, 003-1-1 (0371-0373), June 12, 1980.

13. The translator had this as "faith and heresy," but the word Saddam uses is "*ilhad*," which is better rendered as atheism. See page 5 of the Arabic text (both are cited in endnote 14, Chapter 1)..

14. Saddam Hussein, *Nazarah fi Din wal-Turath* (Baghdad: Dar al-Hurriyyah lil-Ṭiba'ah, July 1978). Translated and republished in Hussein, *On History, Heritage and Religion*, trans. Naji al-Hadithi (Baghdad: Translation and Foreign Language Publishing House, 1981), 21–37.

15. Ernest Dawn, "The Origins of Arab Nationalism," in Rashid Khalidi, Lisa Anderson, Muhammad Muslih, and Reeva S. Simon, eds., *The Origins of Arab Nationalism* (New York: Columbia University Press, 1991), 3–31.

16. This interpretation of the term *salafism* should not be confused with the salafism of Wahhabis and their like: See Bernard Haykel, "On the Nature of Salafi Thought and Action," in Roel Meijer, ed., *Global Salafism: Islam's New Religious Movement* (New York: Columbia University Press, 2009), 33–51.

17. On al-Banna, see Richard P. Mitchell, *The Society of the Muslim Brothers* (New York: Oxford University Press, 1993); and Brynjar Lia, *The Society of the Muslim Brothers in Egypt: The Rise of an Islamic Mass Movement, 1928–1942* (Reading, England: Ithaca Press, 1998).

18. For a good depiction of how this transformation took place, see Ahmed Tarabein, "'Abd al-Hamid al-Zahrawi: The Career and Thought of an Arab Nationalist," in Rashid Khalidi et al., eds., *The Origins of Arab Nationalism* (New York: Columbia University Press, 1991), 97–119.

19. For a range of views that Christian Arab nationalists held on Islam, see Spencer Lavan, "Four Christian Arab Nationalists: A Comparative Study," *The Muslim World* 57, no. 2 (1967): 114–125.

20. Qustantin Zuraiq, "Arab Nationalism and Religion," in Sylvia Haim, ed., *Arab Nationalism: An Anthology* (Berkeley: University of California Press, 1976), 169–170. Originally published in Beirut (1949).

21. Sylvia Haim, "Introduction," ibid., 59.

22. Michel Aflaq, "*Nazratuna li-l-Din*," in *Fi Sabil al-Ba'th* (Beirut: Dar al-Tali'a, 1963), 125. All of Aflaq's essays cited in this chapter are taken from this edition of *Fi Sabil al-Ba'th*.

23. Aflaq, "*Dhikra al-Rasul al-'Arab*," 55, 58.

24. See *BRCC*, 3156_0000 (0101-0111), March 19, 1995.

25. For example, see "Eighth Anniversary of the Death of the Founding Leader, May God Have Mercy on Him," *BRCC*, 028-5-1 (0497), June 2, 1997.

26. Aflaq, "*Dhikra al-Rasul al-'Arab*," 53–54.

27. Haim, *Arab Nationalism: An Anthology*, 64 (emphasis in original).
28. Aflaq, *"Dhikra al-Rasul al-'Arab,"* 60.
29. Ibid., 52.
30. Ibid., 54–55.
31. Aflaq, *"Nazratuna lil-Din,"* 128.
32. Aflaq, *"Qadiyyat al-Din fi al-Ba'th al-'Arab,"* 133–135.
33. Aaron M. Faust, *The Ba'thification of Iraq: Saddam Hussein's Totalitarianism* (Austin: University of Texas Press, 2015).
34. See, for example, "Study on Ba'th Party Principles and Iraqi and Islamic History," *CRRC*, SH-BATH-D-000-474, undated, but from late 1990s; and "Speech of The Leader President Saddam Hussein, May God Preserve Him, about the Ministry of Endowments and Religious Affairs, in the 11th meeting of the Parliament," *BRCC*, 2982_0000 (0603), March 3, 1996.
35. *Al-Taqrir al-Markazi lil-Mu'tamar al-Qutri al-Tasi', 1982* (Baghdad: Hizb al-Ba'th al-Arabi al-Ishtiraki, 1983), 265; "Celebration of the Birthday of the Honorable Prophet," *BRCC*, 063-2-4 (0043-0052), April 27, 2002.
36. "The Minutes of an Extraordinary Meeting," *BRCC*, 003-1-1 (0371-0373), June 12, 1980.
37. Ibid.
38. Ibid.
39. "Instructions," *BRCC*, 003-1-1 (0397-0405), March 22, 1980.
40. For a prominent example of public manifestations of the regime's policies, which could be misconstrued but become clear with access to the regime's internal records, see *Al-Taqrir al-Markazi lil-Mu'tamar al-Qutri al-Tasi'*, 263–304.
41. Saddam Hussein, *On History, Heritage and Religion*, 26–27.
42. Aflaq, *"Qadiyyat al-Din fi al-Ba'th al-'Arab,"* 133.
43. *Al-Taqrir al-Markazi li-l-Mu'tamar al-Qutri al-Tasi'*, 298–301.
44. See various documents titled "Instructions," *BRCC*, 003-1-1 (0375-0405), various dates in 1980.
45. "Report," *BRCC*, 046-3-6 (0619), September 9, 1984.

CHAPTER 2
1. "The Minutes of an Extraordinary Meeting," *BRCC*, 003-1-1 (0371-0373), June 12, 1980.
2. Ofra Bengio, "Iraq," in Colin Legum, Haim Shaked, and Daniel Dishon, eds., *Middle East Contemporary Survey, vol. 6, 1981-82* (New York: Holmes and Meier, 1984), 602.
3. "Reshuffle in the Iraqi Administration," *Iraqi News Agency*, June 28, 1982. BBC Summary of World Broadcasts.
4. Ofra Bengio, "Iraq," *Middle East Contemporary Survey, vol. 6, 1981-82* 602.
5. "Modification," *BRCC*, 23-4-7 (0171), February 17, 1985.
6. See *al-Jumhuriyya*, September 3, 1980.
7. Email correspondence by author with former Iraqi Major General Najim Jabouri, May 17, 2002.
8. See *al-Jumhuriyya*, September 22, 25, 27, 1980; April 6, 25, 1985.

9. "Report," *BRCC*, 046-3-6 (0620), September 9, 1984.

10. "The Scholars of Religion in Erbil and Their Role," *NIDS* [Northern Iraqi Data Set], 833734-833736, November 1982.

11. Achim Rohde, *State-Society Relations in Ba'thist Iraq: Facing Dictatorship* (New York: Routledge, 2010), 43.

12. See, for example, *al-Jumhuriyya*, April 1, 1983.

13. See various documents, *BRCC*, 015-4-5 (0001-0014), 1992.

14. "Intelligence Reports and Correspondence about the Situation in the Arabian Gulf (Persian Gulf) and the Foreign Military Presence in the Gulf," *CRRC* [Conflict Records Research Center], SH-GMID-D-000-526, December 1986.

15. Ofra Bengio, "Iraq," in Colin Legum, Haim Shaked, and Daniel Dishon, eds., *Middle East Contemporary Survey, vol. 5, 1980-81* (New York: Holmes and Meier, 1982), 584.

16. Ofra Bengio, "Iraq," in Itamar Rabinovich and Haim Shaked, eds., ibid., *vol. 10, 1986* (Boulder, CO: Westview Press, 1988), 379.

17. See the published documents of the conference: *Waqa'i' al-Mu'tamar al-Islami al-Sha'bi* (Baghdad: al-Najaf al-Ashraf, 1983).

18. See *Waqa'i' al-Mu'tamar al-Islami al-Sha'bi al-Thani* (Baghdad: The Iraqi Ministry of Endowments and Religious Affairs, 1986).

19. *Waqa'i' al-Mu'tamar al-Islami al-Sha'bi*, 1983, 4.

20. Liz Thurgood, "Iraq Executes Shi'a Leaders," *The Guardian*, June 28, 1983.

21. Ofra Bengio, "Iraq," *Middle East Contemporary Survey, vol. 5, 1980-81*, 590.

22. For his role, see *Waqa'i' al-Mu'tamar al-Islami al-Sha'bi*, 1983.

23. Ma'ruf, Bashshar 'Awwad, interview by author, Amman, Jordan, July 11, 2011. Much of this information is drawn from Ma'ruf's twenty-five page CV, which he graciously provided. For more on his role as the secretary general of the conference, see *Waqa'i' al-Mu'tamar al-Islami al-Sha'bi al-Thani*, 1986.

24. "Iraqi Leader's Address to Baghdad Islamic Conference on Iranian Arms, the War," *Voice of the Masses, Baghdad*, BBC Worldwide Monitoring, February 20, 1987.

25. Ibid.; Ofra Bengio, "Iraq," *Middle East Contemporary Survey, vol. 10, 1986*, 438.

26. See Subhi Muhammad Jamil, *Al-Shu'ubiyya wa-Dawruha al-Takhribi fi al-Fikr al-'Arab al-Islami* (Baghdad: The Popular Islamic Conference Organization, 1988); Faruq 'Umar Fawzi, *al-Khumayniyya wa-Silatuha bi-Harakat al-Ghuluww al-Farisiyya wa-bi-l-Irth al-Batini* (Baghdad: The Popular Islamic Conference Organization, 1988); Makki Khalil Hamud Zubaydi, *al-Haraka al-Batiniyya al-Muntalaqat wa-l-Asalib* (Baghdad: Popular Islamic Conference Organization, 1989).

27. The details of this phenomenon will be discussed in chapter 5.

28. For example, see *NIDS*, 808023, 1988.

29. "Untitled Report," *BRCC*, 2093_0003 (0498), March 1986.

30. Various correspondences titled "Sermon-Giver of [name withheld] Mosque," *BRCC*, 2093_0003 (0494-0497), April 1986.

31. Wendell Stevenson, *The Weight of a Mustard Seed* (London: Atlantic, 2009), 58–59; Makiya, *Republic of Fear*, 135.

32. See *NIDS*, 786904.

33. These harsher policies will be detailed further in chapter 4, which covers religious opposition movements.

34. *al-Jumhuriyya*, January 8, 1979.

35. *al-Jumhuriyya*, September 17, 20, 1980; as well as *al-Jumhuriyya*, January 8, 1979.

36. For an example of a file on one such Christian Ba'thist covering events from the 1970s and 1980s, see *BRCC*, 2522_0000, 1970s-80s.

37. "Actions of the Bishop," *BRCC*, 2522_0000 (0436-0437), February 19, 1983.

38. "Actions of the Bishop," *BRCC*, 2522_0000 (0431), February 25, 1983.

CHAPTER 3

1. Elisheva Machlis, *Shi'i Sectarianism in the Middle East: Modernisation and the Quest for Islamic Universalism* (London: I. B. Tauris, 2014); and Meir Litvak, *Shi'i Scholars of Nineteenth-Century Iraq: The 'Ulama' of Najaf and Karbala'* (Cambridge, England: Cambridge University Press, 2002).

2. Charles Tripp, *A History of Iraq* (Cambridge, England: Cambridge University Press, 2002), 202–204, 220–221; Eric Davis, *Memories of State: Politics, History, and Collective Identity in Modern Iraq* (Berkeley: University of California Press, 2005); Ofra Bengio, *Saddam's Word: Political Discourse in Iraq* (New York: Oxford University Press, 1998), 14; Patrick Cockburn, *Muqtada: Muqtada al-Sadr, the Shia Revival, and the Struggle for Iraq* (New York: Scribner, 2008), 65; Peter Sluglett and Marion Farouk-Sluglett, "Sunni and Shi'is Revisited: Sectarianism and Ethnicity in Authoritarian Iraq," in Derek Hopwood, Habib Ishow, and Thomas Koszinowski, eds., *Iraq: Power and Society* (Reading: Ithaca Press, 1993).

3. Fanar Haddad, *Sectarianism in Iraq: Antagonistic Visions of Unity* (London: Hurst & Company, 2011), 13; Aaron Faust, "The Ba'thification of Iraq: Saddam Hussein and the Ba'th Party's System of Control" (PhD diss., Boston University, 2012), 255; Dina Rizk Khoury, "The Security State and the Practice and Rhetoric of Sectarianism in Iraq," *International Journal of Contemporary Iraqi Studies* 4, no. 3 (2010); Joseph Sassoon, *Saddam Hussein's Ba'th Party: Inside an Authoritarian Regime* (New York: Cambridge University Press, 2012), 259–260.

4. Eric Davis discusses the regime's attempts to do the same thing in other spheres of Iraqi intellectual history. Davis, *Memories of State*, 2.

5. See chapter 5.

6. Faust, "The Ba'thification of Iraq: Saddam Hussein and the Ba'th Party's System," 255; Khoury, "The Security State"; Sassoon, *Saddam Hussein's Ba'th Party*, 259–260.

7. "Information," *BRCC*, 2383_0002 (0138-0139), September 26, 2002.

8. Ofra Bengio, "Iraq," in Colin Legum, Haim Shaked, and Daniel Dishon, eds., *Middle East Contemporary Survey, vol. 4, 1979-80* (New York: Holms and Meier, 1981), 515; Amatzia Baram, *Culture, History and Ideology*, 19.

9. Faust, "The Ba'thification of Iraq: Saddam Hussein and the Ba'th Party's System," 255; and Khoury, "The Security State."

10. Haddad, *Sectarianism in Iraq*, 58–59.

11. Sluglett and Farouk-Sluglett, "Sunni and Shi'is Revisited," 87.

12. Sassoon, *Saddam Hussein's Ba'th Party*, 3.

13. *BRCC*, 2868_0000 (0022-0042).

14. "Inventory," *BRCC*, 2135_0004 (0169-0175), September 18, 1988.

15. Khoury, "The Security State," 328.

16. See the *Shahadat Iraqiyya*, Seasons 1–4 (Iraq Memory Foundation 2005–2008).

17. See chapter 4.

18. Chibli Mallat, "Religious Militancy in Contemporary Iraq: Muhammad Baqer as-Sadr and the Sunni-Shia Paradigm," *Third World Quarterly* 10, no. 2 (April, 1988): 724.

19. "General Military Intelligence Directorate (GMID) Studies on the Foundation of the Da'wah Party and the Supreme Council of the Islamic Revolution Party," *CRRC*, SH-GMID-D-000-622, March–December 1995.

20. See, for example, "Report," *BRCC*, 046-3-6 (0621), September 9, 1984.

21. "The Occasion of the 10th of Muharram," *BRCC*, 23-4-7 (0566-0570), November 22, 1983.

22. "The Occasion of the Holy Month of Muharram," *BRCC*, 2135_0004 (0458-0464), August 18, 1987.

23. "The Plan for Distributing Duties on the Occasion of the Holy Month of Muharram for the Year 1987 for the Province of Najaf," *BRCC*, 2135_0004 (0465-0469).

24. "The Occasion of the Holy Month of Muharram," *BRCC*, 2135_0004 (0458-0464), August 18, 1987.

25. "The Occasion of the 10th of Muharram," *BRCC*, 23-4-7 (0566-0570), November 22, 1983.

26. Ibid.

27. Ibid.

28. In 1983, for example, the police were given a list of 163 authorized readers and told to prevent all others from doing so. See "The Occasion of the 10th of Muharram," *BRCC*, 23-4-7 (0574-0582), November 8, 1983.

29. "The Occasion of the Holy Month of Muharram," *BRCC*, 2135_0004 (0458), August 18, 1987.

30. Ibid.

31. "The Occasion of the 10th of Muharram," *BRCC*, 23-4-7 (0566-0570), November 22, 1983.

32. "The Occasion of the Holy Month of Muharram," *BRCC*, 2135_0004 (0458), August 18, 1987.

33. "The Occasion of the 10th of Muharram," *BRCC*, 23-4-7 (0566-0570), November 22, 1983.

34. Ibid.

35. "The Occasion of the Holy Month of Muharram," BRCC, 2135_0004 (0457), August 18, 1987.

36. In the margins next to this claim, there is a note asking for more info on this. In other documents in this file, regime officials sent out requests for information on this topic, and various reports came back in which they attempted to track these students down.

37. [Untitled Report], *BRCC*, 23-4-7 (0204-0206), February 14, 1985.

38. "Study," *BRCC*, 23-4-7 (0064-0072), February 23, 1985. For examples of these lists and reports on various scholars in Al-Khu'i's network, see *BRCC*, 23-4-7 (0223-233) and (0235-0249).

39. Liz Thurgood, "The Enemy Within—Kept at Bay by Ruthlessness," *The Guardian*, February 12, 1987.

40. See chapter 10.

41. "A Religious Study on *Marji'iyya* (source of emulation) at the *Hawza*," BRCC, 23-4-7 (0040-0041), undated, but probably from the early 1980s.

42. "Religious Schools," BRCC, 23-4-7 (0088-0090), March 9, 1988. See also "The *Hawza* and Religious Schools," BRCC, 23-4-7 (0109-0146); [Untitled Report], BRCC, 23-4-7 (0174-0210): both these reports exist in several different forms with different dates, but they are most likely from 1984 and 1985.

43. "A Religious Study on *Marji'iyya* (source of emulation) at the *Hawza*," BRCC, 23-4-7 (0052-0055), undated, but probably from the early 1980s.

44. Ibid.

45. Ofra Bengio, "Iraq," *Middle East Contemporary Survey, vol. 4, 1979-80*, 514.

46. [Untitled Report], BRCC, 23-4-7 (0174), February 14, 1985.

47. "A Religious Study on *Marji'iyya* (source of emulation) at the *Hawza*," BRCC, 23-4-7 (0020-0058), undated, but probably from the early 1980s.

48. Ibid.

49. [Untitled Report], BRCC, 23-4-7, (0193), February 14, 1985.

50. "Religious Schools," BRCC, 23-4-7 (0088-0090), March 9, 1988.

51. [Untitled Report Presented to Saddam], BRCC, 23-4-7 (0256-0257), August 28, 1984.

52. "A Religious Study on *Marji'iyya* (source of emulation) at the *Hawza*," BRCC, 23-4-7 (0051-0052), undated, but probably from the early 1980s.

53. Ibid.

54. "Report," BRCC, 046-3-6 (0622-0623), September 9, 1984.

55. *Al-Jumhuriyya*, May 20, 1983; *al-Jumhuriyya*, April 2, 1985.

56. See *al-Jumhuriyya*, April 5, 1985.

CHAPTER 4

1. Sami Shourush, "Islamist Fundamentalist Movements among the Kurds," in Faleh Abdul-Jabar, ed., *Ayatollahs, Sufis and Ideologues: State, Religion and Social Movements in Iraq* (London: Saqi, 2002).

2. The Muslim Brotherhood originated in Egypt. For a discussion of its origins, see Mitchell, *The Society of Muslim Brothers*. For the history of the Muslim Brotherhood in Iraq, see Rashid al-Khayyun, *100 'am min al-Islam al-Siyasi bi-l-'Iraq*, vol. 2-al-Sunna (Dubai: Al Mesbar Studies and Research Center, 2011); Basim al-Azami, "The Muslim Brotherhood: Genesis and Development," in Abdul-Jabar, ed., *Ayatollahs, Sufis and Ideologues: State, Religion and Social Movements in Iraq* (London: Saqi, 2002), 162–176; and Tarik Hamdi al-Azami, "The Emergence of the Contemporary Revival in Iraq (Sunni Component)," *Middle East Affairs Journal* 3, no. 1–2 (Winter/Spring 1997): 123–141.

3. Ibid.

4. Al-Khayyun, vol. 2-al-Sunna, 66–68.

5. "Interview with Dr. Osama Tikriti," *Middle East Affairs Journal* 3, no. 1–2 (Winter/Spring 1997): 159.

6. Al-Khayyun, vol. 2-al-Sunna, 110–111.

7. Reidar Visser, "Iraq" in Assaf Moghadam, ed., *Militancy and Political Violence in Shiism* (New York: Routledge, 2012), 97.

8. Toby Jones, "Saudi Arabia" in Assaf Moghadam, ed., *Militancy and Political Violence in Shiism* (New York: Routledge, 2012), 140.

9. Ofra Bengio, "Iraq," in Colin Legum, Haim Shaked, and Daniel Dishon, eds., *Middle East Contemporary Survey, vol. 7, 1982-3* (New York: Holms and Meier, 1985), 578–579.

10. See, for example, "A Study on How to Defeat the Iraqi Opposition Inside and Outside Iraq," *CRRC*, CRRC SH-IISX-D-000-360, 2001; "General Military Intelligence Directorate (GMID) Studies on the Foundation of the Da'wah Party and the Supreme Council of the Islamic Revolution Party," *CRRC*, SH-GMID-D-000-622, March–December 1995; and numerous reports from the 1980s titled "Activities of Hostile Movements," found in *BRCC*, 027-3-5.

11. "General Military Intelligence Directorate(GMID) Studies on the Foundation of the Da'wah Party and the Supreme Council of the Islamic Revolution Party," *CRRC*, SH-GMID-D-000-622, March–December 1995.

12. See, for example, "Activities of Hostile Parties and Movements," *BRCC*, 027-3-5 (0112), March 5, 1986.

13. See, for example, "Summary Political Report for the Directorate of *al-'Amn al-'Amm* for the month of December 1973," *BRCC*, 3378_0000 (0012), December 1973; and "Discovery of the Da'wa Party and Baha'i Organizations," *BRCC*, 3378_0000 (0269), March 13, 1974.

14. Some reports from the 1980s refer back to a November 1978 memo that orders all the Party Bureaus to create regular reports. See, for example, "Inventory of Political Movements," *BRCC*, 2814-0003 (0081), September 20, 1981.

15. Mehdi Kassem Lafteh Temimy, *Shahadat Iraqiyya*, Disk 5, Season 3 (Iraq Memory Foundation, Recorded April 11, 2007).

16. Ali Fadil Abbas al-Zubaydi, *Shahadat Iraqiyya*, Disk 3, Season 3 (Iraq Memory Foundation, Recorded May 26, 2007).

17. See, for example, Mallat, "Religious Militancy in Contemporary Iraq," 699–729.

18. "Differing Statistics," *BRCC*, 814-0003 (0043), March 9, 1983.

19. See, for example, "Inventory of Political Movements for the Office of the Bureau of the South," *BRCC*, 2814-0003 (0098), undated, but likely from 1980; and "Inventory of Political Movements for the Office of the Bureau of the South," *BRCC*, 2814-0003 (0089), undated, but likely from 1981.

20. "Inventory of Political Movements," *BRCC*, 2814-0003 (074-6), January 4, 1982; "Inventory of Political Movements for the Office of the Bureau of the South," *BRCC*, 2814-0003 (0089), undated, but likely from 1981.

21. Ofra Bengio, "Iraq," in Ami Ayalon and Haim Shaked, eds., *Middle East Contemporary Survey, vol. 12, 1988* (Boulder, CO: Westview Press, 1990), 519.

22. Ali Fadil Abbas al-Zubaydi, *Shahadat Iraqiyya*, Disk 3, Season 3 (Iraq Memory Foundation, Recorded May 26, 2007).

23. See Mallat, "Religious Militancy in Contemporary Iraq," 699–729; Hanna Batatu, "Iraq's Underground Shi'a Movements: Characteristics, Causes and Prospects," *Middle East Journal* 35, no. 4 (Autumn, 1981): 578–594; and Faleh A. Jabar, *The Shi'ite Movement in Iraq* (London: Saqi Books, 2003), among many others.

24. Khalaf Abdul-Samad Al Awad, *Shahadat Iraqiyya*, Disk 4, Season 3 (Iraq Memory Foundation, Recorded January 13, 2007).

25. For example, in northern Iraq, see Rida Abbas Amin Amin, *Shahadat Iraqiyya*, Disk 3, Season 3 (Iraq Memory Foundation, Recorded December 11, 2006). For an example from southern Iraq, see Aqil Yusef Naser, *Shahadat Iraqiyya*, Disk 2, Season 3 (Iraq Memory Foundation, Recorded July 20, 2007).

26. Dawud Salman Shehab, *Shahadat Iraqiyya*, Disk 1, Season 3 (Iraq Memory Foundation, Recorded January 12, 2007).

27. "The Reactionary Da'wa Party," *BRCC*, 003-1-1 (0089-0090), February 20, 1980.

28. See *Shahadat Iraqiyya*, Seasons 1–4 (Iraq Memory Foundation, 2005–2008).

29. [Untitled], *BRCC*, 2178_0001 (0072), August 27, 1995.

30. Jamal Hindar Jadir al-Idani, *Shahadat Iraqiyya*, Disk 3, Season 3 (Iraq Memory Foundation, Recorded April 5, 2007); Khalaf Abdul-Samad Al Awad, *Shahadat Iraqiyya*, Disk 4, Season 3 (Iraq Memory Foundation, Recorded January 13, 2007).

31. "Activities of Hostile Movements," *BRCC*, 027-3-5 (0252), June 24, 1985.

32. Ibid. (0173-0174), January 21, 1986.

33. "Interview with Dr. Osama Tikriti," 159.

34. Faust, "The Ba'thification of Iraq: Saddam Hussein and the Ba'th Party's System," 199.

35. See, for example, "Inventory of Political Movements," *BRCC*, 2814-0003 (0005), January 7, 1988.

36. [Untitled], *BRCC*, 2664_0001 (0130-0133), 1984.

37. "Survey of General Political Movements of the Country for the Year 1989," *BRCC*, 3778-0000 (0009), May 26, 1990.

38. Patrick Cockburn argues that the uprising was essentially over as early as the summer of 1980. Cockburn, *Multada*, 50. See also, Mallat, "Religious Militancy in Contemporary Iraq," 699–729

39. See, for example, "Inventory of Political Movements," *BRCC*, 2814-0003 (0035-0036), January 7, 1984; ibid. (0025-0027), December 15, 1984.

40. "Activities of Hostile Parties and Movements," *BRCC*, 027-3-5 (0109-0111), March 5, 1986; "Discovery of a Hostile Organization," *BRCC*, 2074_0002 (0272-0278), May 22, 1986; and [Various Reports], *BRCC*, 2135_0004 (0001-0131), various dates.

41. "Activities of Hostile Movements," *BRCC*, 027-3-5 (0063-0066), January 8, 1986.

42. "Iraqi Armed Forces General Command Study on Being Captured and on Prisoners of War," *CRRC*, SH-AFGC-D-000-694, May–August 1981.

43. Sassoon, *Saddam Hussein's Ba'th Party*, 268–274.

44. "Activities of Hostile Movements," *BRCC*, 027-3-5 (0166-0171), January 21, 1986.

45. "Inventory of Political Movements," *BRCC*, 2814-0003 (0018-0022), January 7, 1986. Of course, this could simply be a case of regime officials making excuses; but as noted previously, when there were actual increases in opposition numbers and activities, the reports said so.

46. "Inventory of Political Movements," *BRCC*, 2814-0003 (0012-0017), December 30 1986; "Inventory of Political Movements," *BRCC*, 2814-0003. (0002-0005), January 7, 1988.

47. "Activities of Hostile Movements," *BRCC*, 027-3-5 (0064), January 8, 1986.

48. "Inventory of Political Movements," *BRCC*, 2814-0003 (0002-0005), January 7, 1988; Also see "General Military Intelligence Directorate Studies on the Foundation

of the Da'wa Party and the Supreme Council of the Islamic Revolution," *CRRC*, SH-GMID-D-000-622, March–December 1995.

49. "Special Controls on dealing with Ba'thists who are from [Families] with Criminals from Elements of Hostile Parties," *BRCC*, 2135_0004 (0304), October 13, 1987.

50. Faust, "The Ba'thification of Iraq: Saddam Hussein and the Ba'th Party's System," 565–566.

51. Ofra Bengio, "Iraq," *Middle East Contemporary Survey, vol. 12, 1988*, 520.

52. "Operational Report," *BRCC*, 2135_0004 (0233-0239), August 10, 1988.

53. Amir Ali Yasin al-Tamimi, *Shahadat Iraqiyya*, Disk 2, Season 3 (Iraq Memory Foundation, Recorded April 12, 2007).

54. "Manual: Counterinsurgency Warfare," *CRRC*, SH-IZAR-D-000-296, October 1983.

55. "Religious Schools," *BRCC*, 23-4-7 (0088-0090), March 9, 1988.

56. See, for example, Abbas Kadhim's discussion at the Imam Khoie Foundation in the United Kingdom, October 12, 2012. http://www.youtube.com/watch?v=-SMtA2i9fKU

57. United Nations Economic and Social Council, Commission Report on Human Rights (1992), Report on the Situation of Human Rights in Iraq, Prepared by Mr. Max van der Stoel, Special Rapporteur on Human Rights, in Accordance with Commission 1991/74, February 18, 1992, E/CN.4/1992/31, 34.

58. "Report on the Occasion of 10 Muharram and the Visit of the Forty of 20 Safar," *BRCC*, 001-5-4 (0006-0009), October 1989.

59. "The Occasion of the 10th of Muharram," *BRCC*, 23-4-7 (0568-0569), November 22, 1983.

60. "Report on the Occasion of 10 Muharram and the Visit of the Forty of 20 Safar," *BRCC*, 001-5-4 (0006-0009), October 1989.

61. Faust, "The Ba'thification of Iraq: Saddam Hussein and the Ba'th Party's System," 188.

62. "The Activities for Hostile Movements," *BRCC*, 030-5-5 (0030-0031), August 13, 1990.

63. "Answer," *BRCC*, 2687-0001 (0441-0444), December 5, 1989.

CHAPTER 5

1. For example, see *BRCC*, 2225_0000, 1970s and 1980s.

2. See "The Ba'thist View of Religion," *BRCC*, 2225_0000 (0634-0638), May 1983.

3. "Modification," *BRCC*, 23-4-7 (0171), February 17, 1985.

4. See chapters 2 and 3 of this book as well as Liz Thurgood, "Iraq Executes Shi'a Leaders," *The Guardian*, June 28, 1983.

5. Abbas Kadhim, "The Hawza Under Siege: A Study in the Ba'th Party Archive" (Occasional Paper no. 1, Institute for Iraqi Studies at Boston University [IISBU], June 2013), 26–27.

6. See *Waqa'i' al-Mu'tamar al-Islami al-Sha'bi*, 1983.

7. See *Waqa'i' al-Mu'tamar al-Islami al-Sha'bi al-Thani*, 1986.

8. Samuel Helfont, "Saddam and the Islamists: The Ba'thist Regime's Instrumentalization of Religion in Foreign Affairs," *Middle East Journal* 68, no. 3

(Summer 2014); Hassan Abbas, "Pakistan," 166. It should also be noted that with the exception of Iraqis, Pakistanis made up the single largest delegation at the second Popular Islamic Conference. See *Waqa'i' al-Mu'tamar al-Islami al-Sha'bi al-Thani*, 1986.

9. Bashshar 'Awwad Ma'ruf, interview by Samuel Helfont, Amman, Jordan, July 11, 2011.

10. See, for example, Musa al-Musawi, "Wilayat al-Faqih," in *Makhatir al-Khumayniyya 'ala al-Umma wa-'Aqidatiha* (Baghdad: The Popular Islamic Conference Organization, 1988), 59–60.

11. Bashshar 'Awwad Ma'ruf, interview by Samuel Helfont, Amman, Jordan. July 11, 2011.

12. Muhammad Ibrahim Shaqra, *Shahadat Khumayni fi Ashab Rasul Allah* (Baghdad: The Popular Islamic Conference, circa 1988); *Makhatir al-Khumayniyya 'ala al-Umma wa-'Aqidatiha* (Baghdad: Popular Islamic Conference Organization, 1988). For similar coded critiques of Shi'ism by Bashshar 'Awwad Ma'ruf, see Bashshar 'Awwad Ma'ruf, *'Ali wa-l-Khulafa'* (Cairo: Maktabat al-Imam al-Bajari li-l-Nashr wa-l-Tawzi', 1988).

13. *Tatarruf al-Din* (Baghdad, College of Shari'a, the University of Baghdad, March 31, 1986), 7.

14. For example, see *Tatarruf al-Din*, 17–24.

15. Ibid., 58.

16. Ibid., 54–57.

17. Parentheses are in the original.

18. "Islamic College of the University," *BRCC*, 029-1-6 (0083-0085), June 30, 1988.

19. "Decision," *BRCC*, 046-3-6 (0613), September 9, 1984.

20. "Nominating Men of Religion," *BRCC*, 046-3-6 (0584), November 27, 1984; "Decision," *BRCC*, 046-3-6 (0614), September 23, 1984; ibid. (0594), November 10, 1984.

21. "Nomination," *BRCC*, 046-3-6 (0582), December 31, 1984,

22. "Nominating Men of Religion," *BRCC*, 046-3-6 (0590), November 15, 1984.

23. See, for example, "Comrades who wish to work as Men of Religion," *BRCC*, 046-3-6 (0603).

24. "Order of Multiple Ministries," *BRCC*, 23-4-7 (0017, 0156-0157), 1985–87.

25. "The Profession of Imam," *BRCC*, 23-4-7 (0162), June 29, 1985.

26. *al-Jumhuriyya*, July 9, 1986.

27. These parentheses are in the original Arabic document. Thus, the document defines "*hakimiyya*" as the "politicization of religion." *Hakimiyya* simply means sovereignty. The Egyptian Muslim Brother, Sayyid Qutb—following the work of the Pakistani intellectual, Abul Ala Mawdudi—popularized the term in Islamist discourse by claiming that God was the only sovereign. Therefore, any form of government other than theocracy inherently usurped God's sovereignty.

28. "Islamic College of the University," *BRCC*, 029-1-6 (0088-0089), June 30, 1988.

29. "Islamic College of the University," *BRCC*, 029-1-6. (0078-0086), August 6, 1988; and "Islamic College of the University," *BRCC*, 029-1-6 (0074-0077), August 11, 1988.

30. "Speech of The Leader President Saddam Hussein, May God Preserve Him, about the Ministry of Endowments and Religious Affairs, in the 11th meeting of the Parliament, given March 3rd, 1996," *BRCC*, 2982_0000 (0596).

31. See, for example, the forms *BRCC*, 2868_0000 (0022-0042).

32. For examples, see "Information Form for Advanced Students of High Studies and Masters Degrees," *BRCC*, 2868_0000 (0018-0020).

33. For an example of this type of form, see *BRCC*, 2868_0000 (0016-0020).

34. *BRCC*, 3246-0000 (0118-0126), 2002.

CHAPTER 6

1. Saddam Hussein, "Text of Saddam's Speech," Associated Press, August 10, 1990.

2. Saddam Hussein, "Call For Jihad, 5 Sep 1990," in Ofra Bengio, ed., *Saddam Speaks on the Gulf Crisis: A Collection of Documents* (Tel Aviv: Moshe Dayan Center for Middle Eastern and African Studies, Tel Aviv University, 1992), 136–143.

3. Conor Cruise O'Brien, "Saddam Comes Out Fighting As Champion of the Fanatics," *Times* (London), August 14, 1990, *BBC Monitoring*.

4. James Rupert, "Once-Secularist Saddam Discovers Benefits of Moslem Piety," *Washington Post*, October 5, 1990, *BBC Monitoring*.

5. Timothy Phelps, "Saddam's Holy War Wins Support from the Believers: Why Islamic Radicals are Ba0cking Secular Iraq," *The Guardian*, September 1, 1990, *BBC Monitoring*; Alan Cowell, "CONFRONTATION IN THE GULF; Islam's Influence Weighed Differently Since Crisis," *New York Times*, October 4, 1990, *BBC Monitoring*.

6. Jerry M. Long, *Saddam's War of Words: Politics, Religion, and the Iraqi invasion of Kuwait* (Austin: University of Texas Press, 2004), 53, 94–95, 97. For similar examples, see, Amatzia Baram, "From Militant Secularism to Islamism"; and James Piscatori, ed., *Islamic Fundamentalisms and the Gulf Crisis* (Chicago: American Academy of Arts and Sciences with the Fundamentalism Project, 1991).

7. "The Occasion of the Holy Month of Muharram," BRCC, 2135_0004 (0457), August 18, 1987.

8. For some reason, the English translation of this communique renders the Arabic *al-Islam* as "the Quran."

9. "Final Communique," *Twelfth Islamic Conference of Foreign Ministers*, Baghdad, Republic of Iraq, June 1–5, 1981. This document can be found in the archives of the Organization of the Islamic Conference, which has since changed its name to "Organization of Islamic Cooperation"; http://ww1.oic-oci.org/arabic/conf/fm/12/12-icfm-fc-ar.htm

10. The quotes in this section are taken from Baram, *Saddam Husayn and Islam*, 219–220.

11. Aflaq, "*Dhikra al-Rasul al-'Arab*," 53–54.

12. Ibid., 50–51.

13. Aflaq, "*Nazratuna lil-Din*," 128.

14. Ofra Bengio, "Iraq," *Middle East Contemporary Survey, vol. 12, 1988*, 519.

15. Long, *Saddam's War of Words*, 70–71.

16. Ofra Bengio, "Iraq," *Middle East Contemporary Survey, vol. 12, 1988*, 519; Ibrahim al-Marashi and Sammy Salama, *Iraq's Armed Forces: An Analytical History* (London: Routledge, 2008), 149–152.

17. *al-Jumhuriyya*, June 27, 28, 1990.

18. "Some of Saddam Hussein's Addresses and Meetings with Some Foreign Officials," *CRRC*, SH-PDWN-D-000-997, February–November 1990. (The speech was dated June 18, 1990.)

19. *al-Jumhuriyya*, June 29, 1990.

20. Long, *Saddam's War of Words*, 108.

21. Ibid., 123–125.

22. Ibid., 120.

23. Ibid., 125.

24. Ibid., 130–131.

25. Ibid., 122.

26. As chapter 7 will discuss, after the war, Shi'i areas of Iraq erupted in open rebellion.

27. "Miscellaneous Information Regarding the Iraqi Invasion of Kuwait and the American Operation to Liberate Kuwait," *CRRC*, SH-GMID-D-000-998, September–October 1990.

CHAPTER 7

1. In this instance, the term "salafi" is used to describe the strict literalists whom outsiders often call Wahhabis. They should not be confused with the Islamic modernists who are discussed in chapter 1.

2. David Commins, *The Wahhabi Mission and Saudi Arabia* (London: I. B. Tauris, 2006).

3. See Naveed Sheikh, *The New Politics of Islam: Pan-Islamic Foreign Policy in a World of States* (London: Routledge, 2002).

4. "Various Telegrams, Memos, and Intelligence Reports on the First Gulf War, 1990–1991." *CRCC*, SH-MISC-D-000-901, August–September 1990.

5. "The Activities for Hostile Movements," *BRCC*, 030-5-5 (0029-0030), August 13, 1990.

6. Faust, "The Ba'thification of Iraq: Saddam Hussein and the Ba'th Party's System," 180.

7. The regime used Wahhabi and Salafi synonymously.

8. "Untitled," *BRCC*, 3778-0000 (0008-0010), May 26, 1990. (It should be noted that although this report is dated May 1990, it covers the year 1989.)

9. "Wahhabi Movement," *BRCC*, 3265_0003 (0100-0102), August 21, 1990.

10. "Intellectual Integrity," *BRCC*, 3265_0003 (0089-0097), August–September, 1990.

11. "Wahhabi Movement," *BRCC*, 3265_0003 (0100-0102), August 21, 1990.

12. "Iraq Invites Muslims to Gather in Baghdad," *Toronto Star*, December 31, 1990, FBIS (Foreign Broadcast Information Service).

13. *Islamic Conferences Held in the Kingdom of Saudi Arabia during the Arab Gulf Incidents* (Saudi Arabia: Saudi Press Agency, 1993), 156–226; and "Iraq Invites Muslims to Gather in Baghdad," *Toronto Star*, December 31, 1990, FBIS.

14. *al-Jumhuriyya*, June 23, 1990.
15. The circumstances of his appointment and the dismissal of the previous president, Bashshar 'Awwad Ma'ruf, will be discussed later.
16. "Report on the Saddam University for Islamic Studies: Needs and Aspirations," *BRCC*, 3493_0001 (0024), September 19, 1992.
17. Ibid., 0025-0033,
18. "Saddam University for Islamic Studies," *BRCC*, 3493_0001 (0020-0021), October 17, 1992.
19. Amatzia Baram, "From Militant Secularism to Islamism," 16–17.
20. See "The Ba'thist View of Religion," *BRCC*, 2225_0000 (0634-0638), May 1983.
21. "Report on the Saddam University for Islamic Studies: Needs and Aspirations," *BRCC*, 3493_0001 (0025-0033), September 19, 1992.
22. Ibid.
23. Haddad, *Sectarianism in Iraq*, 65–84, 117–132.
24. Makiya, *Republic of Fear*, xxx–xxxi; Haddad, *Sectarianism in Iraq*, 13; Khoury, *Iraq in Wartime*, 135–136; Tripp, *A History of Iraq*, 264–271; Cockburn, *Muqtada*, 79.
25. These articles were titled "What happened in late 1990 and these months of 1991, and why did it happen." Some—though unfortunately not all—can be found in the Moshe Dayan Center's Arabic newspaper archive at Tel Aviv University. For a good overview of the articles, see Haddad, *Sectarianism in Iraq*, 120–127.
26. Ibid., 65–86.
27. Khoury, "The Security State," 332.
28. Bassam Yousif, "The Political Economy of Sectarianism in Iraq," *International Journal of Contemporary Iraqi Studies* 4, no. 3 (2010): 361. Soon after, Saddam appointed him to be prime minister.
29. Baram, *Saddam Husayn and Islam*, 225.
30. This slogan has become a centerpiece of Shi'i depictions of 1991.
31. Haddad, *Sectarianism in Iraq*, 120; Davis, *Memories of State*, 243.
32. For example, Davis, *Memories of State*, 242; Cockburn, *Muqtada*, 79.
33. Davis, *Memories of State*, 248; Haddad, *Sectarianism in Iraq*, 241; Khoury, *Iraq in Wartime*, 135–136.
34. See, Davis, *Memories of State*, 244, footnote 54.
35. "Meeting between Saddam Hussein and Council of Ministers," *CRRC*, SH-SHTP-A-000-714, mid-1990s (exact date unknown).
36. For a copy of the plan, see "Information," *BRCC*, 2984_0000 (0079-0080), January 28, 1992.
37. "Suggestion," *BRCC*, 2984_0000 (0067-0068), February 17, 1992.
38. Ma'ruf, Bashshar 'Awwad, interview with Samuel Helfont. Amman, Jordan, July 11, 2011.
39. Samuel Helfont interview with former Iraqi Major General Najim al-Jabouri, who had worked in intelligence during this period, May 11, 2012. (The year of this letter may be slightly off, as it was an estimate. However, it was clearly in the early 1990s and after the uprisings in the south.)
40. "Guidance," *BRCC*, 3134_0002 (0008), May 22, 1997.

41. "Decisions and Recommendations of the Voluntary Popular Religious Supervision Conference," *BRCC*, 3156_0000 (0402-0403), January 24–26, 1995.

42. "Decision of the Revolutionary Command Council to Release the Following Law: Law Number 6 of 1995," *BRCC*, 3134_0002 (0131), 1995.

43. See "Iraqi Intelligence Service (IIS) Restructuring its Hostile Activities Directorate—M/40 in 1997," *CRRC*, SH-IISX-D-000-681, September 1997.

44. The regime's reports use these terms interchangeably.

45. See *BRCC*, 3199_0002, 1992; *BRCC*, 2753_0000, 1995; and *BRCC*, 2249_0000, 1998.

46. "Speech of The Leader President Saddam Hussein, May God Preserve Him, about the Ministry of Endowments and Religious Affairs, in the 11th meeting of the Parliament, Given March 3rd, 1996," *BRCC*, 2982_0000 (0597), March 3, 1996.

47. "Reappointment," *BRCC*, 2753_0000 (0012), August 12, 1996.

48. "Form Requesting Information," *BRCC*, 3246_0000 (0079), undated.

49. Khoury, "The Security State," 354.

50. See Mohammad Yaseen Sabti, *Shahadat Iraqiyya*, Disk 4, Season 3 (Iraq Memory Foundation, Recorded April 27, 2007).

51. Ahmad Ali Khatib, *Al-Tarbiya al-Islamiyya lil-Saff al-Khamis al-Ibtida'i* (Iraq: Ministry of Education, 1997), 38–39.

52. See, for example, "Makarim Al-Qa'id Section Command Meeting Minutes," *CRRC*, SH-BATH-D-001-094, October 2002–March 2003.

CHAPTER 8

1. "Decisions and Recommendations of the Voluntary Popular Religious Supervision Conference," *BRCC*, 3156_0000 (0399-408), January 24–26, 1995.

2. "Conference," *BRCC*, 3156_0000 (0397), February 22, 1995.

3. Rohde, *State-Society Relations*, 13; Makiya, *Republic of Fear*, xv; Davis, *Memories of State*, 227; and Bernard Lewis, *Notes on a Century: Reflections of a Middle East Historian* (New York: Viking, 2012), 329–330.

4. Haddad, *Sectarianism in Iraq*, 109.

5. Ronen Zeidel, "On Servility and Survival: The Sunni Opposition to Saddam and the Origins of the Current Sunni Leadership in Iraq," in Amatzia Baram, Achim Rohde, and Ronen Zeidel, eds., *Iraq between Occupations: Perspectives from 1920 to the Present* (New York: Palgrave Macmillan, 2010), 163–165.

6. Baram, "From Militant Secularism to Islamism."

7. Faust, "The Ba'thification of Iraq: Saddam Hussein and the Ba'th Party's System," 109.

8. Al-Khayyun, Vol. 2-al-Sunna, 83.

9. See the comment section of al-Samarrai's obituary on alukah.net, July 21, 2013, http://www.alukah.net/culture/0/57161/

10. William McCants, *The Believer: How an Introvert with a Passion for Religion and Soccer Became Abu Bakr al-Baghdadi, Leader of the Islamic State* (Washington, DC: Brookings Institution, 2015).

11. William McCants, *The ISIS Apocalypse: The History, Strategy, and Doomsday Vision of the Islamic State* (New York: St. Martin's Press, 2015), 69.

12. See Joseph Sassoon, "Review of State-Society Relations in Ba'thist Iraq," *International Journal of Middle Eastern Studies* 43, no. 3 (August 2011): 561.

13. See, for example, the front-page of the leading daily *al-Jumhuriyya*, June 25, 1993.

14. Baram, "From Militant Secularism to Islamism."

15. Davis, *Memories of State*, 2.

16. "Islamic College of the University," *BRCC*, 029-1-6 (0088-0089), June 30, 1988.

17. Both occurred in June 1993. See *al-Jumhuriyya*, June 25, 1993; and Ofra Bengio, "Iraq," in Ami Ayalon, ed., *Middle East Contemporary Survey, vol. 17, 1993* (Boulder, CO: Westview Press, 1995), 392.

18. "Important and Special Suggestions on the Position of Men of Religion and those who have been endorsed by the Meeting of the Comrades of the Secretariat of the Leadership of the Branches included under the Tanzims of Provinces of the Central Region," *BRCC*, 3559_0001 (0163-4), undated, but probably from 1992.

19. "Lists of Names," *BRCC*, 3134_0002 (0112), October 1996; for other lists of students, see various files in *BRCC*, 2868_0000 (0001-0010), 1995.

20. This pertained to Iraqi, not foreign students.

21. "Report on the Saddam University for Islamic Studies: Needs and Aspirations," *BRCC*, 3493_0001 (0025-0033), September 19, 1992.

22. Davis, *Memories of State*, 180.

23. Migdal, *State-Society Relations*, 32–33.

24. "Nomination to be Designated in a Vacant Position," *BRCC*, 3246-0000 (0147), December 30, 2001.

25. See, for example, Ayad Sham'un Bulos Butros, *Shahadat Iraqiyya*, Disk 1, Season 3, (Iraq Memory Foundation, Recorded January 20, 2007).

26. The case is covered in documents titled "Reappointment" and "Statement of Opinion" in *BRCC*, 2753-0000 (0096-0134), 1995–1997.

27. "Imam and Sermon-Giver of the Mosque," *BRCC*, 3844_0000 (0261-0262), October 30, 2001. For the imam's version of the events, see Untitled Letter from Imam to the Minister of Endowments and Religious Affairs, *BRCC*, 3844_0000 (0274-0275), August 26, 2001.

CHAPTER 9

1. Untitled, *BRCC*, 2982_0000 (0850-0851), June 29, 1996.

2. For the details of these anti-sectarian policies, see chapter 7.

3. "Guidance," *BRCC*, 3134_0002 (0008), May 22, 1997.

4. "Report on the Situation of Human Rights in Iraq," United Nations Economic and Social Council, Commission Report on Human Rights (1992), 34.

5. Ofra Bengio, "Iraq," in Ami Ayalon, ed., *Middle East Contemporary Survey, vol. 16, 1992* (Boulder, CO: Westview Press, 1995), 476.

6. See, for example, "Designation of a Mosque Imam," and "Information," *BRCC*, 2753_0000 (0073-0089), August–October, 1997. Examples involving higher ranking Shi'i clerics will be discussed later.

7. See Central Intelligence Agency, "Special Intelligence Memorandum: Humanitarian Situation in the Marshes," Near Eastern and South Asian Analysis, August 20, 1993; available at the National Security Archives, The George Washington University,

http://www.gwu.edu/~nsarchiv/NSAEBB/NSAEBB167/11.pdf; and Untitled, *BRCC*, 2178_0001 (0547-8), July 19, 1995.

8. "Statement of Mr. Max Van Der Stoel, Special Rapporteur of the Commission on Human Rights on the Situation of Human Rights in Iraq," Fifty-fifth Session of the U.N. Commission on Human Rights, March 22—April 30, 1999. See Item 9, Question of the violation of human rights and fundamental freedoms in any part of the world, March 31, 1999.

9. Cockburn, *Muqtada*, 107.

10. Ibid., 95.

11. See files titled "Designation of a Mosque Imam," and "Information," *BRCC*, 2753_0000 (0073-0089), August–October, 1997.

12. "Issuing of a Fatwa," *BRCC*, 028-5-1 (0583-5), May 19, 1997. For more details, see later.

13. Fatwas from the four highest ranking Shi'i scholars in Najaf can be found in *BRCC*, 009-2-5 (0001-0007), September 2002.

14. Ofra Bengio, "Iraq," *Middle East Contemporary Survey, vol. 16, 1992*, 479–480. Two years later, the Ba'thists assassinated Taqi, along with his brother-in-law and six-year-old nephew. See Special Rapporteur for Iraq Expresses Concern over Killings of Shi'a Religious Leaders, United Nations Press Release, HR/98/45, July 2, 1998.

15. "Al-Sadr II Speaking about His Relation with the Iraqi State," date unknown. Translated by Abbas Kadhim and included as Appendix II in Kadhim, "The Hawza Under Siege: A Study in the Ba'th Party Archive," 64–66.

16. Ibid. The evidence that Kadhim musters from the archive only deals with the later years of al-Sadr's life and therefore does not refute the idea that he had maintained a better relationship with the regime earlier.

17. "Issuing of a Fatwa," *BRCC*, 028-5-1 (0583-5), May 19, 1997.

18. Quoted in Kadhim, "The Hawza Under Siege," 27.

19. For Sadr's interaction with regime officials, see "Issuing of a Fatwa," *BRCC*, 028-5-1 (0583-5), May 19, 1997.

20. Ibid.; and *BRCC*, 009-2-5 (0001-0007), September 2002.

21. Rashid al-Khayyun, *100 'am min al-Islam al-Siyasi bi-l-'Iraq*, Vol. 1-al-Shi'a, 185; and Baram, *Saddam Husayn and Islam*, 275–276.

22. "Friday Prayer," *BRCC*, 2348_0000 (0482-0483), April 4, 1999; and "Information," *BRCC*, 2348_0000 (0552), February 22, 1999.

23. See, for example, this exchange: "Information," *BRCC*, 2348_0000 (0450), May 8, 1999; "Information," *BRCC*, 2348_0000 (0451), May 18, 1999; as well as "Information," *BRCC*, 2348_0000(0338), June 28, 1999.

24. "Information," *BRCC*, 2348_0000 (0338), June 28, 1999.

25. Ibid. (0557), February 22, 1999.

26. Lisa Blaydes came to a similar conclusion after studying the regime's records. See Lisa Blaydes "Compliance and Resistance in Iraq under Saddam Hussein: Evidence from the Files of the Ba'th Party" (paper presented at the Annual Meeting of the Association for Analytic Learning on Islam and Muslim Societies, Rice University, April 2013), April 2, 2013.

27. For numerous reports on this topic spanning several years, see the *BRCC* files 3134_0002 and 3190-0003.
28. See Ayad Sham'un Bulos Butros, *Shahadat Iraqiyya*, Disk 1, Season 3 (Iraq Memory Foundation, Recorded January 20, 2007).
29. Ibid.
30. "Guidance," *BRCC*, 3134_0002 (0008), May 22, 1997.
31. "Plans to Recruit Iranians on Pilgrimage to Iraq," *CRRC*, SH-GMID-D-000-771, December 1990–August 1997.
32. Faust, "The Ba'thification of Iraq: Saddam Hussein and the Ba'th Party's System," 188.
33. For a detailed comparison between the regime's policies toward the Shi'is in the 1980s and 1990s, see Abbas Kadhim, "The Hawza Under Siege," 11. Kadhim argues that a comparison of regime documents on cases ranging from the early 1980s to the late 1990s demonstrates "similarities in the language, the assessment of the threat, and the response by the Ba'th Party" with regard to the Shi'is.
34. "A Study on the Phenomenon of Marching," *BRCC*, 3134_0002 (0089-0091), November 11, 1996.
35. "Practices," *BRCC*, 3190-0003 (0212-0214), March 29, 1997.
36. "A Study on the Phenomenon of Marching," *BRCC*, 3134_0002 (0089-0091), November 11, 1996.
37. Ibid.
38. See the 1995 report on Muharram; *BRCC*, 3134_0002 (0299), 1995.
39. Untitled, *BRCC*, 3134_0002 (0195-0196), 1990s.
40. See "Executing the Emergency Plan," *BRCC*, 3134_0002 (0375-0377), June 9, 1995; and Untitled, *BRCC*, 3134_0002 (0331), 1995.

CHAPTER 10

1. Kevin M. Woods et al., *Iraqi Perspectives Project: A View of Operation Iraqi Freedom from Saddam's Senior Leadership* (Washington, DC: United States Joint Forces Command, 2006), 26–27.
2. Ibid., 62.
3. For more on the Special Security Organization, see Sassoon, *Saddam Hussein's Ba'th Party*, 98–112.
4. "Information," *BRCC*, 2696_0002 (0755-0757), September 5, 1993.
5. "Information," *BRCC*, 2696_0002 (0759-0760), August 25, 1993.
6. "Information," *BRCC*, 063-2-4 (0060), October 15, 2002.
7. "Information," *BRCC*, 2696_0002 (0755-0757), September 5, 1993.
8. See "Methods of Defeating the Opposition Parties Inside and Outside Iraq," *CRRC*, SH-IISX-D-000-360, 2001, pp. 55–56.
9. See "Imams, preachers reportedly arrested for criticizing regime," *Voice of the Iraqi People*, November 21, 1994, *BBC World Monitor*; and "Opposition radio says preachers executed for anti-government sermons," *Voice of the Iraqi People*, November 28, 1994, *BBC World Monitor*.
10. Davis, *Memories of State*, 234.

11. Samuel Helfont interview with former Iraqi Major General Najim al-Jabouri, May 11, 2012.
12. "Statement of Mr. Max Van Der Stoel."
13. See files titled "Information," *BRCC*, 063-2-4 (0062-0068), October 14–December 10, 2000.
14. Untitled, *BRCC*, 2696_0002 (0721), January 2, 1994.
15. Untitled, *BRCC*, 2696_0002 (0766), August 28, 1993.
16. Samuel Helfont interview with former Iraqi Major General Najim al-Jabouri, May 11, 2012.
17. "Important and Special Suggestions on the Position of Men of Religion and Those Who Have Been Endorsed by the Meeting of the Comrades of the Secretariat of the Leadership of the Branches Included under the Tanzims of Provinces of the Central Region." *BRCC*, 3559_0001 (0163-4), undated, but probably from 1992.
18. See "Iraqi Intelligence Service (IIS) Restructuring its Hostile Activities Directorate— M/40 in 1997," *CRRC*, SH-IISX-D-000-681, September 1997.
19. "Information," *BRCC*, 2696_0002 (0755-0757), September 5, 1993.
20. For a full translation of this booklet, see [Name Withheld], "The Emergence of Al-Wahhabiyya Movement and Its Historic Roots," in Kevin Woods (Project Manager), *Iraqi Perspectives Project: Primary Source Materials for Saddam and Terrorism: Emerging Insights from Captured Iraqi Documents, Volume 5 (Redacted)* (Washington, DC: Institute for Defense Analysis, 2007), 161–218; the anecdote about Jewish origins of Saudis and Wahhabis can be found on pages 209–210.
21. "Information," *BRCC*, 2348_0000 (0567), February 17, 1999.
22. See, for example, "Hostile Publication," 2688_0002 (0009), *BRCC*, December 29, 1993.
23. See the regime's post-1991 assessments: "General Military Intelligence Directorate (GMID) Studies on the Foundation of the Da'wah Party and the Supreme Council of the Islamic Revolution Party," *CRRC*, SH-GMID-D-000-622, March–December 1995.
24. Untitled, *BRCC*, 2178_0001 (0635), July 15, 1995.
25. "Assessment," *BRCC*, 2753-0000 (0294), November 13, 1994.
26. "Assessment," *BRCC*, 2753-0000 (0005), December 28, 1995.
27. For numerous reports of this type, see *BRCC*, 2753-0000 (0178-677). They are all from 1995.
28. "Assessment," *BRCC*, 2753-0000 (0093), September 9, 1997.
29. For example, see the case of an Assistant Dean of Saddam College for Imams and Sermon-Givers who is assigned to work on one of the oversight committees: "Party Committees," *BRCC*, 3496_0001 (0056), October 19, 2000.
30. "Party Committees," *BRCC*, 3496_0001 (0009), April 30, 2002. It should be noted that the female referenced here was eventually dismissed due to "weakness."
31. "Party Committees," *BRCC*, 3496_0001 (0004), May 26, 2002.
32. "Party Committees," *BRCC*, 3496_0001 (0007), May 7, 2002.
33. See "Party Committees," *BRCC*, 3496_0001 (0064), September 17, 2000.
34. "Nominating an Imam," *BRCC*, 2753-0000 (0029), January 20, 1998.

35. "Transfer of a Mosque Sermon-Giver," *BRCC*, 2753-0000 (0036), October 15, 1997.

36. "Changing of a Mosque Imam," *BRCC*, 2527_0000 (0424), April 28, 2002.

37. "Imam and Sermon-Giver of the Mosque," *BRCC*, 3844_0000 (0261-0262), October 30, 2001. For the imam's version of the events, see Untitled Letter from Imam to the Minister of Endowments and Religious Affairs, *BRCC*, 3844_0000 (0274-0275), August 26, 2001. In a somewhat happy twist, a year later the imam petitioned the regime to be reinstated. See files titled "Return to the Profession of Sermon-Giver," *BRCC*, 3844_0000 (0247-0260), September 16–December 16, 2002.

38. "Activities that were taken by the Comrades Officials of the Tanzims about the Hostile Activities in Mosques," *BRCC*, 2696_0002 (0723-0724), early 1990s. Party branches also submitted monthly status reports to the Party Secretariat that included a category titled "the Religious Phenomenon." Items within this category were universally negative. In fact, some branches used the term "Deviants," in place of "Religious Phenomenon," suggesting both that they accepted Ba'thist interpretations of Islam and that any deviation from it was inherently problematic. See, for example, "The Security Stance for the Month of December 1998," *BRCC*, 037-3-4 (0093), December 1998.

39. It is possible that other inventories were also conducted, but I was only able to find these. For the 1992 inventory, see *BRCC*, 3199_0002, 1992; for 1995, see *BRCC*, 2753_0000, 1995; and for 1998, see *BRCC*, 2249-0000, 1998. In the following footnotes, these surveys will be referred to as "1992 Inventory," "1995 Inventory," and "1998 Inventory," respectively.

40. See Untitled, *BRCC*, 2753_0000 (0371), October 1, 1995; and "Assessment," *BRCC*, 2753_0000 (0374), September 2, 1995.

41. "Information," *BRCC*, 3199_0002 (0139), July 22, 1992.

42. "Inventory," *BRCC*, 3199_0002 (0017), July 30, 1992. The regime's view of Sufis was not as clear-cut as it was toward other groups. At times, the regime described some Sufi orders as completely non-political, and it therefore largely left them alone. However, the manner in which the regime saw specific Sufi orders was difficult to interpret from the outside. For example, Amatzia Baram portrays the Kasnazaniyya order as having close ties to the regime because the Ba'thists considered it to be non-political. Yet, the regime's internal records demonstrate that the Ba'thists felt the movement's principles contradicted those of the Party. Ultimately, the Ba'th Party assessed that it was a "political movement under the cover of a Sufi order ..." and the regime attempted to dissuade Iraqis from joining it. See "A study on the Religious Movements and the Men of Religion," *BRCC*, 3559_0001 (0064-0067) August 1, 1992.

43. Untitled, *BRCC*, 2982_0000 (0794), July 18, 1996.

44. Untitled, *BRCC*, 2249-0000 (0004), December 5, 1998.

45. See, for example, the reports from Karbala: 1998 Inventory, *BRCC*, 2249-0000 (0029).

46. Yet, even if we take this precaution into consideration, one can assume that these numbers at least represent the regime's perception, which is still very important. After all, the regime formed its policies based on these perceptions.

47. 1992 Inventory, *BRCC*, 3199_0002 (0169, 0190, 0282).

48. 1998 Inventory, *BRCC*, 2249_0000 (0023, 0036-0043); and 1992 Inventory, *BRCC*, 3199_0002 (0193).
49. Ibid. (0001).
50. 1992 Inventory, *BRCC*, 3199_0002 (0188, 0322-0326); and 1998 Inventory, *BRCC*, 2249_0000 (0061).
51. His current status was unclear: 1992 Inventory, *BRCC*, 3199_0002 (0193).
52. 1992 Inventory, *BRCC*, 3199_0002 (0309).
53. Ibid. (0168, 0454).
54. 1998 Inventory, *BRCC*, 2249_0000 (0133-0135).
55. 1992 Inventory, *BRCC*, 3199_0002 (0198).
56. Stevenson, *Weight of a Mustard Seed*, 193.
57. "Coordination," *BRCC*, 2348_0000 (0643), November 30, 1998.
58. Untitled, *BRCC*, 037-3-4 (0411), June 29, 1999.
59. "Reappointment," *BRCC*, 2753_0000 (0008), January 28, 1998.
60. In Arabic, the word the reports use is "*takfir.*"
61. "Reappointment," *BRCC*, 2753_0000 (0012), August 12, 1996.
62. Haddad, *Sectarianism in Iraq*, 108.
63. See chapter 11.
64. See Ofra Bengio, "Iraq," in Ami Ayalon and Bruce Maddy-Weitzman, eds., *Middle East Contemporary Survey, vol. 18, 1994* (Boulder, CO: Westview Press, 1996), 337.
65. David Blair, "Saddam has Koran written in his blood," *The Daily Telegraph*, December 14, 2002. http://www.telegraph.co.uk/news/worldnews/middleeast/iraq/1416155/Saddam-has-Koran-written-in-his-blood.html
66. John F. Burns, "Threats and Responses: The Iraqi Leader; Hussein's Obsession: An Empire of Mosques," *New York Times*, December 15, 2002. http://www.nytimes.com/2002/12/15/world/threats-and-responses-the-iraqi-leader-hussein-s-obsession-an-empire-of-mosques.html?pagewanted=all
67. Untitled, *BRCC*, 2982_0000 (0850-0851), June 29, 1996.
68. "Information," *BRCC*, 2348_0000 (0123), October 3, 1999.
69. For changing the name, see "Changing of the Name of the Mosque," *BRCC*, 2834_0001 (0593), May 6, 1997; for rebuilding, see "Statement of Opinion," *BRCC*, 3844_0000 (0671-0679), April–Oct 2002.
70. See, for example, files entitled "Statement of Opinion," *BRCC*, 3844_0000, (0205-0222), August–December, 2002.
71. "Building of a Mosque," *BRCC*, 2834_0001 (0576), May 12, 1997.
72. For example, see "Statement of Opinion," *BRCC*, 3844_0000 (0022), December 29, 2002.
73. "Building a Mosque," *BRCC*, 2834_0001 (0147), November 11, 1997.
74. "Statement of Opinion," *BRCC*, 3844_0000 (473), November 18, 2002.
75. "Building of an Alms House (*takiyah*)," *BRCC*, 2834_0001 (0028), December 11, 1997.
76. "Statement of Opinion," *BRCC*, 3844_0000 (0193), December 22, 2002.
77. See files entitled "Statement of Opinion," *BRCC*, 3844_0000 (0205-0222), August–December, 2002.
78. "Statement of Opinion," *BRCC*, 3844_0000 (0467), November 18, 2002.

79. Nora Boustany, "A Religious Revival, With Iraq's Blessing; Baghdad Finds Piety Good for Morale," *Washington Post*, April 5, 1998, *BBC World Monitor*.

80. See Hadad, *Sectarianism in Iraq*, 93; and Jo Abraham, "Baghdad Diary," *The Guardian*, March 3, 1997, *BBC World Monitor*.

81. I found no instances of a request to build a church being approved. However, it is possible that such examples do exist elsewhere in the archive, and public documents from the period suggest that new churches were built. See Baram, *Saddam Husayn and Islam*, 263.

82. "Building a Church," *BRCC*, 2834_0001 (0535), July 13, 1997.

83. "Building of a Mosque," *BRCC*, 2834_0001 (0576), May 12, 1997.

84. See, for example, "Statement of Opinion," *BRCC*, 3844_0000 (0417-0423), September 11, 2002; "Statement of Opinion," *BRCC*, 3844_0000 (049), November 15, 2002; and "Building a Church," *BRCC*, 2834_0001 (0535), July 13, 1997.

CHAPTER 11

1. Phillip Smucker, "Iraq Builds 'Mother of all Battles' Mosque in Praise of Saddam," *Sunday Telegraph* (London), July 29, 2001, *BBC World Monitor*.

2. "Holy Koran Radio to Start on 15th October," *INA News Agency, Baghdad*, September 24, 1997, *BBC World Monitor*.

3. Ofra Bengio, "Iraq," in Bruce Maddy-Weitzman ed., *Middle East Contemporary Survey, vol. 19, 1995*. (Boulder, CO: Westview Press, 1997), 334.

4. This differed from the schoolbooks from the 1970s that were published in a period when the regime had attempted to keep religion out of the public sphere. However, even secular Arab women sometimes wear the hijab in certain religious settings, and Ba'thists had suggested that doing so was appropriate well before the Faith Campaign. For example, in November 1984, Saddam's deputy headed a committee that suggested women wear a hijab when they attend religious schools. See "Untitled," *BRCC*, 23-4-7 (0194), February 14, 1985. See Baram, *Saddam Husayn and Islam*, 283.

5. See, for example, Michael Theodoulou, "Iraq Introduces Islamic Law," *Times*, June 6, 1994, *BBC World Monitor*.

6. "Ministerial Order," *CRRC*, SH-MISC-D-001-446, November 1994.

7. See "Saddam and Military Officials Discussing Reorganizing the Intelligence Service," *CRRC*, SH-SHTP-A-001-219, January 14, 2001, cited in Kevin M. Woods, David D. Palkki, and Mark E. Stout, eds., *The Saddam Tapes*, 84.

8. "Speech of The Leader President Saddam Hussein, May God Preserve Him, about the Ministry of Endowments and Religious Affairs, in the 11th meeting of the Parliament, given March 3rd, 1996," *BRCC*, 2982_0000 (0595-0628).

9. Abd al-Rahman al-Bazzaz, "Islam and Arab Nationalism," in Sylvia Haim, ed., *Arab Nationalism: An Anthology* (Berkeley: University of California Press, 1976), 176. Originally published in Baghdad, 1952.

10. Ibid., 177.

11. Ibid., 184.

12. See, for example, Sati' al-Husri, "Muslim Unity and Arab Unity," in Sylvia Haim, ed., *Arab Nationalism: An Anthology* (Berkeley: University of California Press,

1976), 147–149. Originally published as "Views and Addresses on Patriotism and Nationalism" in Cairo, 1944.

13. Aflaq, *"Dhikra al-Rasul al-'Arab,"* 55–56.

14. "Speech of The Leader President Saddam Hussein, May God Preserve Him, about the Ministry of Endowments and Religious Affairs, in the 11th meeting of the Parliament, given March 3rd, 1996," *BRCC*, 2982_0000 (620).

15. Ibid., (600).

16. Ibid., (601). It should be noted that Arab nationalists such as Gamal abd al-Nasser had a deep respect for Islam as well.

17. Sassoon, *Saddam Hussein's Ba'th Party*, 3.

18. For a chart that tracks the changes to these registers, see Khoury, *Iraq in Wartime*, 180.

19. See, for example, "Cultural Plan," *BRCC*, 2982_0000 (0377-0379), January 9, 1997.

20. It was a slight modification of a previous law to the same effect.

21. "Decision of the Revolutionary Command Council. Number 12, for the year 1997," *BRCC*, 028-5-1 (0207-0208), July 7, 1997. The law was signed by Saddam Hussein.

22. Sassoon, *Saddam Hussein's Ba'th Party*, 259–267.

23. Davis, *Memories of State*, 251–252; Baram, *Saddam Husayn and Islam*, 307.

24. Al-Bazzaz, "Islam and Arab Nationalism," 179.

25. Baram, *From Militant Secularism to Islamism*, 13.

26. "Iraq: In Brief; Saddam Husayn's Remarks to Judges," *Iraqi News Agency*, August 12, 1979, *BBC World Monitor*.

27. "The Minutes of an Extraordinary Meeting," *BRCC*, 003-1-1 (0371-0373), June 12, 1980.

28. "Activities that Were Taken by the Comrades Officials of the Tanzims about the Hostile Activities in Mosques," *BRCC*, 2696_0002 (0723-4), undated, from the 1990s.

29. "Courses for Studying the Qur'an," *BRCC*, 3190-0003 (0139-0140), July 21, 1997.

30. "Secessions for Learning the Holy Qur'an," *BRCC*, 2982_0000 (0575-0576), October 5, 1996.

31. "Information," *BRCC*, 2696_0002 (0732-0733), October 19, 1993.

32. As it had in the past, the regime refers to these Pan-Islamic movements as the forces of *shu'ubiyya*.

33. "Plan for Party Cultural Indoctrination on Religious Practices," *BRCC*, 3190-0003 (0105-0110), August 4, 1997.

34. Jason Burke, "Saddam Exploits Apocalyptic Islamic Vision," *The Scotsman*, January 4, 2000, *BBC World Monitor*.

35. See Helfont, "Saddam and the Islamists."

36. For example, see "Untitled Report," *BRCC* 2664_0001 (0330-0345), August 2, 1984.

37. "Speech of The Leader President Saddam Hussein, May God Preserve Him, about the Ministry of Endowments and Religious Affairs, in the 11th meeting of the Parliament, given March 3rd, 1996," *BRCC*, 2982_0000 (0595-0628).

38. Ibid., (616).

39. "Study on Ba'ath Party Principles and Iraqi and Islamic History," *CRRC*, SH-BATH-D-000-474, 1994–2002.

40. Rushdi Muhammad 'Alyan, Tahsin Kafi Taha al-Alusi, and Hazim Hamadi Khadir, *al-Tarbiyah al-Islamiyah lil-Saff al-Rabi' al-'Amm* (Baghdad: Wizarat al-Tarbiyah, 2001), 3.

41. Khatib, *Al-Tarbiya al-Islamiyya lil-Saff al-Khamis al-Ibtida'i*, 41.

42. 'Alyan, al-Alusi, and Khadir, *Al-Tarbiyah al-Islamiyah lil-Saff al-Rabi'*, 5.

43. Muhammad abd al-Wahhab abd al-Qadir and Rushdi Muhammad Alyan, *al-Tarbiyah al-Islamiyah lil-Saff al-Khamis al-I'dadi* (Baghdad: Wizarat al-Tarbiyah, 2001), 54–55.

44. I found at least twelve cases. See ibid. pp. 55, 68, 70, 71, 74, 76, 77, 79, 81, and 82.

45. Ibid., 33.

46. Khoury, *Iraq in Wartime*, 165.

47. Ibid., 109.

48. See Decree No. 59, June 4, 1994, http://fas.org/irp/world/iraq/docs/decree_059.htm; Decree No. 96, July 28, 1994, http://fas.org/irp/world/iraq/docs/decree_096.htm; and Decree No. 115, August 25, 1994, http://fas.org/irp/world/iraq/docs/decree_115.htm.

49. Baram, *Saddam Husayn and Islam*, 288.

50. "Speech of Mr. President, The Leader, May God Preserve Him, during His Chairing of the Minister's Council Meeting," *CRRC*, SH-SPPC-D-000-448, August 21, 1994.

51. Ibid.

52. Paul Lewis, "Iraq Bans Public Use Of Alcohol," *New York Times*, August 21, 1994, *BBC World Monitor*.

53. For a translation, see Haim, *Arab Nationalism: An Anthology*, 238.

54. Dawisha, *Iraq: A Political History*, 185. See Iraq's 1968 Constitution, "List of Iraqi Constitutions" on the website Niqash.org, Niqash: Briefings from inside and across Iraq. http://www.niqash.org/articles/?id=2306; Soeterik, "Islamic Movement of Iraq," 18–19.

55. He refers to himself in the third person.

56. *Waqa'i' al-Mu'tamar al-Islami al-Sha'bi, 1983.* 28–29. For English translation of this speech, see Saddam Hussein, *President Saddam Hussein Addresses Moslem Ulema*, trans. Naji al-Hadithi (Baghdad: Dar al-Ma'mun for Translation and Publishing, 1983), 15.

57. See Aflaq, "*Dhikra al-Rasul al-'Arab*," 55, 58.

58. This speech was included in an official training manual for Ba'thist cadres. "Study on Ba'th Party Principles and Iraqi and Islamic History," *CRRC*, SH-BATH-D-000-474, undated, but from late 1990s.

59. Haim, *Arab Nationalism: An Anthology*, 64 (emphasis in the original).

60. "Celebration of the Birthday of the Honorable Prophet," *BRCC*, 063-2-4 (0043-0052), April 27, 2002.

61. Quoted in Ofra Bengio and Uriel Dann, "Iraq," *Middle East Contemporary Survey, vol. 3, 1978-9*, 570–571.

62. "'Aziz on Embargo, US Effort against Regime," *Baghdad Iraq Television Network*, September 16, 1999, *BBC World Monitor*.

63. Syed Saleem Shahzad, "Commentary: A 'third force' awaits US in Iraq," *Asia Times*, March 1, 2003, http://www.atimes.com/atimes/Middle_East/EC01Ak04.html

64. "Information," *BRCC*, 3342_0003 (0235), April 23, 1993; and "Information," *BRCC*, 3342_0003 (0236), March 20, 1993.
65. "Guidance," *BRCC*, 011-1-2 (0050-0053), June 11, 2002.
66. Stevenson, *Weight of a Mustard Seed.*

CHAPTER 12

1. A compilation and analysis of these Senate reports can be found at the National Security Archives, http://nsarchive.gwu.edu/NSAEBB/NSAEBB254/
2. Michael R. Gordon and General Bernard E. Trainor, *Cobra II: The Inside Story of the Invasion and Occupation of Iraq* (New York: Random House, 2007), 318.
3. "Interview with COL (ret) Kevin Benson," The Operational Leadership Experience Project—Interview Collection, Combat Studies Institute, Fort Leavenworth, Kansas, March 13, 2013, p. 5. http://cgsc.contentdm.oclc.org/utils/getfile/collection/p4013coll13/id/3026/filename/3029.pdf
4. Bob Woodward, *Plan of Attack: The Definitive Account of the Decision to Invade Iraq* (New York: Simon and Schuster, 2004), 414.
5. For example, Baram refers to "the relative leniency of the regime during the faith campaign"; Baram, *Saddam Husayn and Islam*, 277.
6. Kadhim, "The Hawza Under Siege," 53–54.
7. In the following section, the names of Iraqi religious scholars and sometimes the sources on which I rely have been withheld to protect the identities of those involved.
8. "Our travels to [withheld]," *BRCC*, 2348_0000 (0384), June 3, 1999.
9. See "Issuing of a Fatwa," *BRCC*, 028-5-1 (0583-5), May 19, 1997; and four *fatwas* from senior clerics in *BRCC*, 009-2-5 (0001-0007), September 2002.
10. "Information," *BRCC*, 2348_0000 (0338), June 28, 1999. For details, see chapter 9.
11. Quoted in Kadhim, "The Hawza Under Siege," 27.
12. For example, see "Issuing of a Fatwa," *BRCC*, 028-5-1 (0583-5), May 19, 1997.
13. *Desert Crossing After Action Report*, June 28, 1999, 28. Available at the National Security Archives, The George Washington University, http://nsarchive.gwu.edu/NSAEBB/NSAEBB418/docs/1%20-%20Desert%20Crossing%20After%20Action%20Report_1999-06-28.pdf
14. Rohde, *State-Society Relations in Ba'thist Iraq*, 13; Davis, *Memories of State*, 227.
15. Baram, "From Militant Secularism to Islamism"; Zeidel, "On Servility and Survival," 163–165. For more details, see chapter 8.
16. Makiya, *Republic of Fear*, xv.
17. See Jordan Michael Smith, "Makiya Has No Regret about Pressing the War in Iraq: Ten Years Later, a Moral Architect of the Invasion Stands by His Words," *Boston Globe*, March 16, 2013, http://www.bostonglobe.com/ideas/2013/03/16/kanan-makiya-regret-about-pressing-war-iraq/k6ZsBxp4sXptfXrcRAocdO/story.html
18. Lewis, *Notes on a Century*, 329–330.
19. Michael R. Gordon and General Bernard E. Trainor, *The Endgame: The Inside Story of the Struggle for Iraq, from George W. Bush to Barack Obama* (New York: Random House, 2012), 7–8.
20. *Desert Crossing After Action Report*, June 28, 1999, 5.

21. Ibid., 17.
22. Gordon and Trainor, *Cobra II*, 318.
23. Cockburn, *Muqtada*, 115.
24. Ibid.
25. Gordon and Trainor, *Cobra II*, 366.
26. "Contingency instructions for Iraqi government personnel in case of regime defeat," *CRRC*, SH-PDWN-D-000-012, January 23, 2003; Gordon and Trainor, *Cobra II*, 311–333.
27.. "Contingency instructions for Iraqi government personnel in case of regime defeat," *CRRC*, SH-PDWN-D-000-012, January 23, 2003; and "A Ba'th Party file on Al-Diwaniyyah emergency and maneuver plans during the war," *CRRC*, SH-BATH-D-000-778, March 17, 2003. See section 11 of the file titled "Media."
28. "Contingency instructions for Iraqi government personnel in case of regime defeat," *CRRC*, SH-PDWN-D-000-012, January 23, 2003.
29. Ibid.
30. George Packer, *The Assassins' Gate: America in Iraq* (New York: Farrar, Straus and Giroux, 2005), 108.
31. Ibid., 109.
32. See chapter 9.
33. *BRCC*, 009-2-5 (0001-0007), September 2002.
34. Gordon and Trainor, *Endgame*, 69.
35. L. Paul Bremer, *My Year in Iraq: The Struggle to Build a Future of Hope* (New York: Simon and Schuster, 2006), 18.
36. Ibid., 38.
37. Neil Swidey, "Where did ISIS come from? The story starts here." *Boston Globe*, March 10, 2016, http://www.bostonglobe.com/magazine/2016/03/10/where-did-isis-come-from-the-story-starts-here/eOHwJQgnZPNj8SE91Vw5hK/story.html?event=event25.
38. *Desert Crossing After Action Report*, June 28, 1999, 28.
39. Rory Stewart, *The Prince of the Marshes: And Other Occupational Hazards of a Year in Iraq* (Orlando, FL: Harcourt, 2006), 6.
40. Gordon and Trainor, *Cobra II*, 77.
41. Woodward, *Plan of Attack*, 414.

CHAPTER 13

1. On the importance of the ability to organize as a cause in rebellions, see, Fearon and Laitin; as well as, Cederman and Vogt.
2. Stewart, *Prince of the Marshes*, 6.
3. Al-Khayyun, Vol. 1-al-Shi'a, 353.
4. Ibid.
5. Bremer, *My Year in Iraq*, 121.
6. *BRCC*, 009-2-5 (0001-0007), September 2002.
7. "Asharq Al-Awsat Interview: Sheikh Harith al-Dari," *Ashaq al-Awsat*, March 20, 2012, https://eng-archive.aawsat.com/theaawsat/features/asharq-al-awsat-interview-sheikh-harith-al-dari

8. "Information," *BRCC*, 2696_0002 (0732-0733), October 19, 1993.

9. Al-Khayyun, Vol. 2-al-Sunna, 177–207; and   Roel Meijer, "The Association of Muslim Scholars in Iraq," *Middle East Report* 237 (Winter 2005).

10. Ibid.

11. Joby Warrick, *Black Flags: The Rise of ISIS* (New York: Penguin Random House, 2015), 113.

12. Abu Musab al-Zarqawi, "Zarkawi's Cry," Febuary 12, 2004. This letter can be found in Haverford College's database of Jihadist materials, http://thesis.haverford.edu/dspace/bitstream/handle/10066/4795/ZAR20040214.pdf

13. "Who was the Real Abu Omar al-Baghdadi?," *Asharq al-Awsat*, April 20, 2010.

14. See Craig Whiteside, "If Only there were Real Baathists in the Islamic State, . . . " Conference of Defence Associations Institute, August, 27, 2015. https://www.cdainstitute.ca/en/blog/entry/if-only-there-were-real-baathists-in-the-islamic-state; and Michael Weiss and Hassan Hassan, "Mystery Man: Everything We Knew About This ISIS Mastermind Was Wrong," *The Daily Beast*, April 15, 2016. http://www.thedailybeast.com/articles/2016/04/15/everything-we-knew-about-this-isis-mastermind-was-wrong.html

15. "Behind the Revival of the Islamic State in Iraq, Interview with Naval War College Prof Craig Whiteside," Musings on Iraq, June 22, 2015, http://musingsoniraq.blogspot.com/2015/06/behind-revival-of-islamic-state-in-iraq.html

16. Aymenn Jawad Al-Tamimi, "Enemy of my enemy: Re-evaluating the Islamic State's Relationship with the Ba'athist JRTN," *IHS Jane's Terrorism and Insurgency Monitor*, June 2015, available at http://www.aymennjawad.org/16692/enemy-of-my-enemy-re-evaluating-the-islamic-state

17. Meijer, "Association of Muslim Scholars."

18. Abu Musab al-Zarqawi, "Zarkawi's Cry." Also   see   McCants, *The ISIS Apocalypse*, 10–11.

19. Martin Chulov, "Isis: The Inside Story," *The Guardian*, December 11, 2014, http://www.theguardian.com/world/2014/dec/11/-sp-isis-the-inside-story?CMP=share_btn_tw

20. Ibid.

21. Gordon and Trainor, *End Game*, 48–49.

CONCLUSION

1. *Al-Taqrir al-Markazi lil-Mu'tamar al-Qutri al-Tasi', 1982*, 267.

2. Galula's *Counterinsurgency Warfare: Theory and Practice*, is listed as the first of three works that the authors include in their "Acknowledgements" section. They also quote Galula in the epitaph for chapter 2. David Petraeus and James Amos, *Counterinsurgency, FM 3-24*, Department of the Army, 2006.

3. David Galula, *Counterinsurgency Warfare: Theory and Practice* (Westport, CT: Praeger Security International, 2006), 95.

4. "Saddam and High Ranking Officers Discussing Plans to Attack Kurdish 'Saboteurs' in Northern Iraq and the Possibility of Using Special Ammunition (Weapons)," *CRRC*, SH-SHTP-A-001-045, 1985; "Speech of The Leader President Saddam Hussein, May God Preserve Him, about the Ministry of Endowments and

Religious Affairs, in the 11th meeting of the Parliament, given March 3rd, 1996," *BRCC*, 2982_0000 (0612-0613).

5. "Manual: Counterinsurgency Warfare," *CRRC*, SH-IZAR-D-000-296, October 1983; "Memorandum about the War of Struggle or the Guerilla War," *CRRC*, SH-MISC-D-001-078, 2002.

6. John Nagl, *Learning to Eat Soup with a Knife: Counterinsurgency Lessons from Malay to Vietnam* (Chicago: University of Chicago Press, 2005).

7. Craig Whiteside, "War Interrupted, Part I: The Roots of Jihadist Resurgence in Iraq," *War on the Rocks*, November 5, 2014, http://warontherocks.com/2014/11/war-interrupted-part-i-the-roots-of-the-jihadist-resurgence-in-iraq/

BIBLIOGRAPHY

ARCHIVES

Archives of the Organization of Islamic Cooperation. Available online at https://www.oic-oci.org/

Ba'th Regional Command Collection, Hoover Institution at Stanford University, Stanford, CA.

Conflict Records Research Center, the National Defense University in Washington, DC.

Library of Congress, Near East Section Arabic Newspaper Archives in Washington, DC.

Moshe Dayan Center, Arabic Newspaper Archive, Tel Aviv University, Israel.

National Security Archives, George Washington University in Washington, DC. Available online at http://www2.gwu.edu/~nsarchiv/

Northern Iraqi Data Set, Hoover Institution at Stanford University.

The Operational Leadership Experience Project—Interview Collection, Combat Studies Institute, Fort Leavenworth, Kansas. Available online at http://cgsc.contentdm.oclc.org/cdm/landingpage/collection/p4013coll13

NEWSPAPERS AND PRESS

BBC Summary of World Broadcasts.

Foreign Broadcast Information Service (FBIS).

Al-Jumhuriyya (Iraq).

Al-Thawra (Iraq).

ASharq al-Awsat (Pan-Arab; Online at https://english.aawsat.com)

PUBLISHED SOURCES

Abbas, Hassan. "Pakistan." In *Militancy and Political Violence in Shiism*, edited by Assaf Moghadam, 155–180. New York: Routledge, 2012.

Abd al-Qadir, Muhammad abd al-Wahhab and Rushdi Muhammad 'Alyan. *al-Tarbiyah al-Islamiyah lil-Saff al-Khamis al-I'dadi*. Baghdad: Wizarat al-Tarbiyah, 2001.

Abu Jaber, Kamel. *The Arab Ba'th Socialist Party: History Ideology, and Organization*. Syracuse, NY: Syracuse University Press, 1966.

Aflaq, Michel. "*Dhikra al-Rasul al-'Arab.*" In *Fi Sabil al-Ba'th*. Beirut: Dar al-Tali'a, 1963.

Aflaq, Michel. "*Nazratuna li-l-Din.*" In *Fi Sabil al-Ba'th*. Beirut: Dar al-Tali'a, 1963.

Aflaq, Michel. "*Qadiyyat al-Din fi al-Ba'th al-'Arab.*" In *Fi Sabil al-Ba'th*. Beirut: Dar al-Tali'a, 1963.

Ahram, Ariel. "Iraq in the Social Sciences: Testing the Limits of Research." *Journal of the Middle East and Africa* 4, no. 3 (2013): 251–266.

Alvarez, Julia. *In the Time of Butterflies*. Chapel Hill, NC: Algonquin Books of Chapel Hill, 1994.

'Alyan, Rushdi Muhammad, Tahsin Kafi Taha al-Alusi, and Hazim Hamadi Khadir. *al-Tarbiyah al-Islamiyah lil-Saff al-Rabi' al-'Amm*. Baghdad: Wizarat al-Tarbiyah, 2001.

Arendt, Hannah. *The Origins of Totalitarianism*. New York: Harcourt, Brace and World, 1966.

Ayubi, Nazih N. *Over-Stating the Arab State: Politics and Society in the Middle East*. New York: I. B. Tauris, 1995.

Al-Azami, Basim. "The Muslim Brotherhood: Genesis and Development." In *Ayatollahs, Sufis and Ideologues: State, Religion and Social Movements in Iraq*, edited by Abdul-Jabar, 162–177. London: Saqi, 2002.

Al-Azami, Tarik Hamdi. "The Emergence of the Contemporary Revival in Iraq (Sunni Component)." *Middle East Affairs Journal* 3, no. 1–2 (Winter/Spring 1997): 123–141.

Baram, Amatzia. *Culture, History, and Ideology in the Formation of Ba'thist Iraq: 1968–89*. New York: St. Martin's Press, 1991.

Baram, Amatzia. "From Militant Secularism to Islamism: The Iraqi Ba'th Regime 1968–2003." Occasional paper, Washington, D.C.: Woodrow Wilson International Center for Scholars, October 2001.

Baram, Amatzia. *Saddam Husayn and Islam, 1968–2003: Ba'thi Iraqi from Secularism to Faith*. Baltimore, MD: Johns Hopkins University Press, 2014.

Batatu, Hanna. "Iraq's Underground Shi'a Movements: Characteristics, Causes and Prospects." *Middle East Journal* 35, no. 4 (Autumn 1981): 578–594.

Al-Bazzaz, Abd al-Rahman. "Islam and Arab Nationalism." In *Arab Nationalism: An Anthology*, edited by Sylvia Haim. Berkeley: University of California Press, 1976. 172–188 in 1962 ed.

Bengio, Ofra. "Iraq." In *Middle East Contemporary Survey, vol. 4, 1979–80*, edited by Colin Legum, Haim Shaked, and Daniel Dishon. New York: Holms and Meier, 1981.

Bengio, Ofra. "Iraq." In *Middle East Contemporary Surve, vol. 5, 1980–81*, edited by Colin Legum, Haim Shaked, and Daniel Dishon. New York: Holmes and Meier, 1982.

Bengio, Ofra. "Iraq." In *Middle East Contemporary Survey, vol. 6, 1981–82*, edited by Colin Legum, Haim Shaked, and Daniel Dishon. New York: Holmes and Meier, 1984.

Bengio, Ofra. "Iraq." In *Middle East Contemporary Survey, vol. 7, 1982–3*, edited by Colin Legum, Haim Shaked, and Daniel Dishon. New York: Holms and Meier, 1985.

Bengio, Ofra. "Iraq." In *Middle East Contemporary Survey, vol. 10, 1986*, edited by Itamar Rabinovich and Haim Shaked. Boulder, CO: Westview Press, 1988.

Bengio, Ofra. "Iraq." In *Middle East Contemporary Survey, vol. 12, 1988*, edited by Ami Ayalon and Haim Shaked. Boulder, CO: Westview Press, 1990.

Bengio, Ofra. "Iraq." In *Middle East Contemporary Survey, vol. 16, 1992*, edited by Ami Ayalon, 447–499. Boulder, CO: Westview Press, 1995.

Bengio, Ofra. "Iraq." In *Middle East Contemporary Survey, vol. 17, 1993*, edited by Ami Ayalon, 364–407. Boulder, CO: Westview Press, 1995.

Bengio, Ofra. "Iraq." In *Middle East Contemporary Survey, vol. 18, 1994*, edited by Ami Ayalon and Bruce Maddy-Weitzman, 320–367. Boulder, CO: Westview Press, 1996.

Bengio, Ofra. "Iraq." In *Middle East Contemporary Survey, vol. 19, 1995*, edited by Bruce Maddy-Weitzman, 310–349. Boulder, CO: Westview Press, 1997.

Bengio, Ofra. *Saddam's Word: Political Discourse in Iraq*. New York: Oxford University Press, 1998.

Bengio, Ofra and Uriel Dann. "Iraq." In *Middle East Contemporary Survey, vol. 3, 1978–9*, edited by Colin Legum, Haim Shaked, and Daniel Dishon. New York: Holms and Meier, 1980.

Benson, Kevin. Interview with COL (ret) Kevin Benson. *The Operational Leadership Experience Project—Interview Collection, Combat Studies Institute, Fort Leavenworth, Kansas*, March 13, 2013.

Blair, David. "Saddam has Koran Written in his Blood." *Daily Telegraph*, December 14, 2002.

Blaydes, Lisa. "Compliance and Resistance in Iraq under Saddam Hussein: Evidence from the Files of the Ba'th Party." Paper presented at the Annual Meeting of the Association for Analytic Learning on Islam and Muslim Societies, Rice University, April 2, 2013.

Bremer, L. Paul. *My Year in Iraq: The Struggle to Build a Future of Hope*. New York: Simon and Schuster, 2006.

Burns, John F. "Threats and Responses: The Iraqi Leader; Hussein's Obsession: An Empire of Mosques." *New York Times*, December 15, 2002.

Cederman, Lars-Erik and Manuel Vogt. "Dynamics and Logics of Civil War." *Journal of Conflict Resolution* 61, no. 9 (2017), 1992–2016.

Chulov, Martin. "Isis: The Inside Story." *Guardian*, December 11, 2014.

Cockburn, Patrick. *Muqtada: Muqtada al-Sadr, the Shia Revival, and the Struggle for Iraq*. New York: Scribner, 2008.

Commins, David. *The Wahhabi Mission and Saudi Arabia*. London: I. B. Tauris, 2006.

Conway, John S. *The Nazi Persecution of the Churches 1933–45*. London: Weidenfeld & Nicolson, 1968.

Corboz, Elvire. "Negotiating Loyalty across the Shi'i World: The Transnational Authority of the al-Hakim and al-Khu'i Families." PhD diss., Faculty of Oriental Studies, University of Oxford, 2009.

Coughlin, Con. *Saddam: His Rise and Fall*. New York: Harper Collins Publishers, 2005.

Crone, Patricia. "No Compulsion in Religion: Q. 2:256 in Medieval and Modern Interpretation." In *Le Shi'ism Imamite Quarante ans après*, edited by M. A. Amir-Moessi, M. M. Bar-Asher, and S. Hopkins, 131–178. Turnhout, Belgium: Brepols, 2009.

Davis, Eric. *Memories of State: Politics, History, and Collective Identity in Modern Iraq*. Berkeley: University of California Press, 2005.

Dawisha, Adeed. "'Identity' and Political Survival in Saddam's Iraq." *Middle East Journal* 53, no. 4 (Autumn 1999): 553–567.

Dawisha, Adeed. *Iraq: A Political History from Independence to Occupation.* Princeton, NJ: Princeton University Press, 2009.

Dawn, Ernest. "The Origins of Arab Nationalism." In *The Origins of Arab Nationalism,* edited by Rashid Khalidi, Lisa Anderson, Muhammad Muslih, and Reeva S. Simon, 3–30. New York: Columbia University Press, 1991.

Fainsod, Merle. *Smolensk under Soviet Rule.* New York: Vintage Books, 1963.

Faust, Aaron M., "The Ba'thification of Iraq: Saddam Hussein and the Ba'th Party's System of Control." Phd diss., Boston University, 2012.

Faust, Aaron M. *The Ba'thification of Iraq: Saddam Hussein's Totalitarianism.* Austin: University of Texas Press, 2015.

Fawzi, Faruq 'Umar. al-*Khumayniyya wa-Silatuha bi-Harakat al-Ghuluww al-Farisiyya wa-bi-l-Irth al-Batini.* Baghdad: The Popular Islamic Conference Organization, 1988.

Fearon, James D. and David D. Laitin. "Ethnicity, Insurgency, and Civil War." *The American Political Science Review* 97, no. 1 (2003): 75–90.

Friedrich, Carl and Zbigniew Brzezinski. *Totalitarian Dictatorship and Autocracy.* New York: Frederick A. Praeger, 1964.

Galula, David. *Counterinsurgency Warfare: Theory and Practice.* Westport, CT: Praeger Security International, 2006.

Goossaert, Vincent and David A. Palmer. *The Religious Question in Modern China.* Chicago: University of Chicago Press, 2010.

Gordon, Michael R. and General Bernard E. Trainor. *Cobra II: The Inside Story of the Invasion and Occupation of Iraq.* New York: Random House, 2007.

Gordon, Michael R. and General Bernard E. Trainor. *The Endgame: The Inside Story of the Struggle for Iraq, from George W. Bush to Barack Obama.* New York: Random House, 2012.

"The Guiding Principles of the 'German Christians.'" In *The Third Reich and the Christian Churches: A Documentary Account of Christian Resistance and Complicity during the Nazi Era,* edited by Peter Matheson. Grand Rapids, MI: W. B. Eerdmans, 1981.

Haddad, Fanar. *Sectarianism in Iraq: Antagonistic Visions of Unity.* London: Hurst & Company, 2011.

Haim, Sylvia, ed. *Arab Nationalism: An Anthology.* Berkeley: University of California Press, 1976.

Haim, Sylvia. "Introduction." In *Arab Nationalism: An Anthology,* edited by Sylvia Haim. Berkeley: University of California Press, 1976. 3–74 in 1962 ed.

Haykel, Bernard. "On the Nature of Salafi Thought and Action." In *Global Salafism: Islam's New Religious Movement,* edited by Roel Meijer, 33–57. New York: Columbia University Press, 2009.

Helfont, Samuel. "Saddam and the Islamists: The Ba'thist Regime's Instrumentalization of Religion in Foreign Affairs." *Middle East Journal* 68, no. 3 (Summer 2014): 352–366.

The Holy Qur'an.

House, Karen Elliot. *On Saudi Arabia: Its People, Past, Religion, Fault Lines—and Future.* New York: Alfred A. Knopf, 2012.

Al-Husri, Sati'. "Muslim Unity and Arab Unity." In *Arab Nationalism: An Anthology,* edited by Sylvia Haim. Berkeley: University of California Press, 1976. 147–154 in 1962 ed.

Hussein, Saddam. "Call For Jihad, 5 Sep 1990." In *Saddam Speaks on the Gulf Crisis: A Collection of Documents*, edited by Ofra Bengio. Tel Aviv: Moshe Dayan Center for Middle Eastern and African Studies, Tel Aviv University, 1992.

Hussein, Saddam. *On History, Heritage and Religion*, translated by Naji al-Hadithi. Baghdad: Translation and Foreign Language Publishing House, 1981.

Hussein, Saddam. *Nazarah fi Din wal-Turath*. Baghdad: Dar al-Hurriyyah lil-Ṭibaʻah, July 1978.

Hussein, Saddam. *President Saddam Hussein Addresses Moslem Ulema*, translated by Naji al-Hadithi. Baghdad: Dar al-Maʼmun for Translation and Publishing, 1983.

Hussein, Saddam. "Text of Saddam's Speech." *Associated Press*, August 10, 1990.

Interim Constitution [of Iraq]. September 21, 1968.

Interim Constitution of the Iraqi Republic. July 16, 1970.

"Interview with Dr. Osama Tikriti." *Middle East Affairs Journal* 3, no. 1–2 (Winter/Spring 1997), 159.

Islamic Conferences Held in the Kingdom of Saudi Arabia during the Arab Gulf Incidents. Saudi Arabia: Saudi Press Agency, 1993.

Jabar, Faleh A. *The Shi ite Movement in Iraq*. London: Saqi Books, 2003.

Jamieson, Neil L. *Understanding Vietnam*. Berkeley: University of California Press, 1993.

Joffe, Lawrence. "Obituary: Ayatollah Mohammad Baqir al-Hakim." *Guardian*, August 29, 2003.

Jones, Toby. "Saudi Arabia." In *Militancy and Political Violence in Shiism*, edited by Assaf Moghadam, 135–154. New York: Routledge, 2012.

Kadhim, Abbas. "The Hawza Under Siege: A Study in the Baʻth Party Archive." Occasional Paper no. 1, Institute for Iraqi Studies at Boston University (IISBU), June 2013.

Kaplan, Robert. "The Vietnam Solution." *Atlantic*, June 2012.

Kertzer, David I. *The Pope and Mussolini: The Secret History of Pius XI and the Rise of Fascism in Europe*. New York: Random House, 2014.

Khatib, Ahmad Ali. *Al-Tarbiya al-Islamiyya lil-Saff al-Khamis al-Ibtidaʼi*. Iraq Wizarat al-Tarbiyah, 1997.

Khatib, Ahmad Ali. *100 ʻam min al-Islam al-Siyasi bi-l-ʼIraq 2- al-Sunna*. Dubai, United Arab Emirates: Al Mesbar Studies and Research Center, 2011.

Al-Khayyun, Rashid. *100 ʻam min al-Islam al-Siyasi bi-l-ʼIraq 1- al-Shiʻa*. Dubai, United Arab Emirates: Al Mesbar Studies and Research Center, 2011.

Khoury, Dina Rizk. *Iraq in Wartime: Soldiering, Martyrdom and Remembrance*. New York: Cambridge University Press, 2013.

Khoury, Dina Rizk. "The Security State and the Practice and Rhetoric of Sectarianism in Iraq." *International Journal of Contemporary Iraqi Studies* 4, no. 3 (2010): 325–338.

Kuran, Timur. "The Vulnerability of the Arab State: Reflections on the Ayubi Thesis." *Independent Review* 3, no.1 (Summer 1998): 111–123.

Lavan, Spencer. "Four Christian Arab Nationalists: A Comparative Study." *Muslim World* 57, no. 2 (1967): 114–125.

Leak, Gary K. and Brandy A. Randall. "Clarification of the Link between Right-Wing Authoritarianism and Religiousness: The Role of Religious Maturity." *Journal for the Scientific Study of Religion* 34, no. 2 (June 1995): 245–252.

Lewis, Bernard. *Notes on a Century: Reflections of a Middle East Historian.* New York: Viking, 2012.

Lia, Brynjar. *The Society of the Muslim Brothers in Egypt: The Rise of an Islamic Mass Movement, 1928–1942.* Reading, England: Ithaca Press, 1998.

Litvak, Meir. *Shi'i Scholars of Nineteenth-Century Iraq: The 'Ulama' of Najaf and Karbala'.* Cambridge, England: Cambridge University Press, 2002.

Long, Jerry M. *Saddam's War of Words: Politics, Religion, and the Iraqi Invasion of Kuwait.* Austin: University of Texas Press, 2004.

Machlis, Elisheva. *Shi'i Sectarianism in the Middle East: Modernisation and the Quest for Islamic Universalism.* London: I. B. Tauris, 2014.

Makhatir al-Khumayniyya 'ala al-Umma wa-'Aqidatiha. Baghdad: Popular Islamic Conference Organization, 1988.

Makiya, Kanan. *Republic of Fear: The Politics of Modern Iraq.* Berkeley: University of California Press, 1998.

Mallat, Chibli. "Religious Militancy in Contemporary Iraq: Muhammad Baqer as-Sadr and the Sunni-Shia Paradigm." *Third World Quarterly* 10, no. 2 (April 1988): 699–729.

Al-Marashi, Ibrahim and Sammy Salama. *Iraq's Armed Forces: An Analytical History.* London: Routledge, 2008.

Ma'ruf, Bashshar 'Awwad. *'Ali wa-l-Khulafa'.* Cairo: Maktabat al-Imam al-Bajari li-l-Nashr wa-l-Tawzi', 1988.

McCants, William. *The Believer: How an Introvert with a Passion for Religion and Soccer Became Abu Bakr al-Baghdadi, Leader of the Islamic State.* Washington, DC: Brookings Institution, 2015.

McCants, William. *The ISIS Apocalypse: The History, Strategy, and Doomsday Vision of the Islamic State.* New York: St. Martin's Press, 2015.

Meijer, Roel. "The Association of Muslim Scholars in Iraq." *Middle East Report* 237 (Winter 2005): 12–19.

Menashri, David. "Ayatollah Khomeini and Velayat-e-Faqih." In *Militancy and Political Violence in Shiism,* edited by Assaf Moghadam, 49–70. New York: Routledge, 2012.

Migdal, Joel. *State-Society Relations and State Capabilities in the Third World.* Princeton, NJ: Princeton University Press, 1988.

Milgram, Stanley. *Obedience to Authority: An Experimental View.* New York: Harper Perennial, 1974.

Mitchell, Richard P. *The Society of the Muslim Brothers.* New York: Oxford University Press, 1993.

Al-Musawi, Musa. "*Wilayat al-Faqih.*" In *Makhatir al-Khumayniyya 'ala al-Umma wa-'Aqidatiha.* Baghdad: The Popular Islamic Conference Organization, 1988.

Nagl, John. *Learning to Eat Soup with a Knife: Counterinsurgency Lessons from Malay to Vietnam.* Chicago: University of Chicago Press, 2005.

Nasr, Vali Reza. *Islamic Leviathan: Islam and the Making of State Power.* Oxford: Oxford University Press, 2001.

Packer, George. *The Assassins' Gate: America in Iraq.* New York: Farrar, Straus and Giroux, 2005.

Petraeus, David and James Amos. *Counterinsurgency, FM 3-24.* Washington, DC: Department of the Army, 2006.

Piscatori, James, ed. *Islamic Fundamentalisms and the Gulf Crisis*. Chicago: American Academy of Arts and Sciences with the Fundamentalism Project, 1991.

Reid, Donald Malcolm. "Postage Stamps: A Window on Saddam Hussein's Iraq." *Middle East Journal* 47, no. 1 (Winter 1993): 77–89.

"Report on the Situation of Human Rights in Iraq, Prepared by Mr Max van der Stoel, Special Rapporteur on Human Rights, in Accordance with Commission 1991/74." United Nations Economic and Social Council, Commission Report on Human Rights (1992), February 18, 1992.

Rohde, Achim. *State-Society Relations in Ba'thist Iraq: Facing Dictatorship*. New York: Routledge, 2010.

Roslof, Edward E. *Red Priests: Renovationism, Russian Orthodoxy, and Revolution, 1905–1946*. Bloomington: Indiana University Press, 2002.

Sassoon, Joseph. "Review of State-Society Relations in Ba'thist Iraq." *International Journal of Middle Eastern Studies* 43, no. 3 (August 2011): 561–563.

Sassoon, Joseph. *Saddam Hussein's Ba'th Party: Inside an Authoritarian Regime*. New York: Cambridge University Press, 2012.

Shahadat Iraqiyya, Seasons 1–4. Iraq Memory Foundation, 2005–2008.

Shahzad, Syed Saleem. "A 'Third Force' Awaits US in Iraq." *Asia Times*, March 1, 2003.

Shaqra, Muhammad Ibrahim. *Shahadat Khumayni fi Ashab Rasul Allah*. Baghdad: The Popular Islamic Conference, circa 1988.

Sheikh, Naveed. *The New Politics of Islam: Pan-Islamic Foreign Policy in a World of States*. London: Routledge, 2002.

Shourush, Sami. "Islamist Fundamentalist Movements among the Kurds." In *Ayatollahs, Sufis and Ideologues: State, Religion and Social Movements in Iraq*, edited by Faleh Abdul-Jabar, 177–182. London: Saqi, 2002.

Al-Shu'ubiyya wa-Dawruha al-Takhribi fi al-Fikr al-'Arabi al-Islami. Baghdad: The Popular Islamic Conference Organization, 1988.

Sluglett, Peter and Marion Farouk-Sluglett. "Sunni and Shi'is Revisited: Sectarianism and Ethnicity in Authoritarian Iraq." In *Iraq: Power and Society*, edited by Derek Hopwood, Habib Ishow, and Thomas Koszinowski. Reading, UK: Ithaca Press, 1993.

Smith, Jordan Michael. "Makiya Has No Regret about Pressing the War in Iraq: Ten Years Later, a Moral Architect of the Invasion Stands by His Words." *Boston Globe*, March 16, 2013.

Soeterik, Robert. "The Islamic Movement of Iraq (1958–1980)." Occasional Paper no. 12, Middle East Research Associates, Amsterdam, December 1991.

Solzhenitsyn, Aleksandr. *The Gulag Archipelago, 1918–1956: An Experiment in Literary Investigation, Volume One*. Boulder, CO: Westview Press, 1998.

Special Rapporteur for Iraq Expresses Concern over Killings of Shi'a Religious Leaders. United Nations Press Release. HR/98/45, July 2, 1998.

Starrett, Gregory. *Putting Islam to Work: Education, Politics, and Religious Transformation in Egypt*. Berkeley: University of California Press 1998.

"Statement of Mr. Max Van Der Stoel, Special Rapporteur of the Commission on Human Rights on the Situation of Human Rights in Iraq." Fifty-fifth Session of the U.N. Commission on Human Rights. March 22–April 30, 1999.

Stevenson, Wendell. *The Weight of a Mustard Seed*. London: Atlantic, 2009.

Stewart, Rory. *The Prince of the Marshes: And Other Occupational Hazards of a Year in Iraq.* Orlando, FL: Harcourt, 2006.

Swidey, Neil. "Where Did ISIS Come From? The Story Starts Here." *Boston Globe,* March 10, 2016.

Al-Tamimi, Aymenn Jawad. "Enemy of My Enemy: Re-evaluating the Islamic State's Relationship with the Ba'athist JRTN." *IHS Jane's Terrorism and Insurgency Monitor,* June 2015.

Al-Taqrir al-Markazi lil-Mu'tamar al-Qutri al-Tasi', 1982. Baghdad: Hizb al-Ba'th al-Arabi al-Ishtiraki, 1983.

Tarabein, Ahmed. "'Abd al-Hamid al-Zahrawi: The Career and Thought of an Arab Nationalist." In *The Origins of Arab Nationalism,* edited by Rashid Khalidi et al, 97–119. New York: Columbia University Press, 1991.

Tatarruf al-Din. Baghdad: College of Shari'a, the University of Baghdad, March 31, 1986.

Thurgood, Liz. "The Enemy Within—Kept at Bay by Ruthlessness." *Guardian,* February 12, 1987.

Thurgood, Liz. "Iraq Executes Shi'a Leaders." *Guardian,* June 28, 1983.

Tripp, Charles. *A History of Iraq.* Cambridge, England: Cambridge University Press, 2002.

Visser, Reidar. "Iraq." In *Militancy and Political Violence in Shiism,* edited by Assaf Moghadam, 95–111. New York: Routledge, 2012.

Waqa'i' al-Mu'tamar al-Islami al-Sha'bi. Baghdad: al-Najaf al-Ashraf, 1983.

Waqa'i' al-Mu'tamar al-Islami al-Sha'bi al-Thani. Baghdad: The Iraqi Ministry of Endowments and Religious Affairs, 1986.

Warrick, Joby. *Black Flags: The Rise of ISIS.* New York: Penguin Random House, 2015.

Weiss, Michael and Hassan Hassan. "Everything We Knew About This ISIS Mastermind Was Wrong." *Daily Beast,* April 15, 2016.

Weiss, Michael and Hassan Hassan. *ISIS: Inside the Army of Terror.* New York: Regan Arts, 2015.

Whiteside, Craig. "If Only There were Real Baathists in the Islamic State. . . ." *Conference of Defence Associations Institute,* August 27, 2015.

Whiteside, Craig. "War Interrupted, Part I: The Roots of Jihadist Resurgence in Iraq." *War on the Rocks,* November 5, 2014.

Woods, Kevin M. et al. *Iraqi Perspectives Project: A View of Operation Iraqi Freedom from Saddam's Senior Leadership.* Washington, DC: United States Joint Forces Command, 2006.

Woods, Kevin M., David D. Palkki, and Mark E. Stout, eds. *The Saddam Tapes: The Inner Workings of a Tyrant's Regime 1978–2003.* New York: Cambridge University Press, 2011.

Woodward, Bob. *Plan of Attack: The Definitive Account of the Decision to Invade Iraq.* New York: Simon and Schuster, 2004.

Young, Glennys. *Power and the Sacred in Revolutionary Russia: Religious Activists in the Village.* University Park: Pennsylvania State University Press, 1997.

Yousif, Bassam. "The Political Economy of Sectarianism in Iraq." *International Journal of Contemporary Iraqi Studies* 4, no. 3 (2010): 357–367.

Zaman, Muhammad Qasim. *The Ulama in Contemporary Islam: Custodians of Change.* Princeton, NJ: Princeton University Press, 2007.

Zeidel, Ronen. "On Servility and Survival: The Sunni Opposition to Saddam and the Origins of the Current Sunni Leadership in Iraq." In *Iraq between Occupations: Perspectives from 1920 to the Present*, edited by Amatzia Baram, Achim Rohde, and Ronen Zeidel, 159–172. New York: Palgrave Macmillan, 2010.

Zubaydi, Makki Khalil Hamud. *al-Haraka al-Batiniyya al-Muntalaqat wa-l-Asalib.* Baghdad: Popular Islamic Conference Organization, 1989.

Zuraiq, Qustantin. "Arab Nationalism and Religion." In *Arab Nationalism: An Anthology*, edited by Sylvia Haim. Berkeley: University of California Press, 1976. 167–171 in 1962 ed.

Printed in the USA/Agawam, MA
November 30, 2018

690311.011